# Edinburgh's Hidden Walks

## by Stephen Millar

# Edinburgh's Hidden Walks

Written by Stephen Millar
Photography by Stephen Millar and Chris Dorney
Edited by Vicky Wilson
Book design by Lesley Gilmour and Susi Koch
Illustrations by Lesley Gilmour and Hannah Kershman

First edition published by Metro Publications 2017
Second revised edition 2021

Metro® is a registered trade mark of Associated Newspapers Limited. The METRO mark is under licence from Associated Newspapers Limited.

Printed and bound in Turkey. This book is produced using paper from registered sustainable and managed sources.

© 2021 Stephen Millar
British Library Cataloguing in Publication Data. A catalogue record for this book is available from the British Library.

ISBN 978-1-902910-69-7

For the kids

# Acknowledgements

I would like to thank Tony Whyte for reading through my original drafts and providing helpful feedback. Chris Dorney also did a great job in providing additional photographs.

Thanks also to those readers who have emailed me with suggestions and corrections. The city changes over the years, so it is always useful to receive updates from those following in my footsteps.

A big thank you to Andrew, Susi and Lesley at Metro, who have supported my London and Edinburgh walking guides over the years. In aggregate the books now cover many hundreds of miles which requires a great deal of time to update and keep relevant. I also thank my editor, Vicky Wilson, for all her diligence and attention to detail.

This book is also dedicated to John 'Hoppy' Hopkins (1937-2015) who provided great encouragement to me while I was working on my London books.

**Note: Larger maps of each walk are available to download and print. Just visit our website www.metropublications.com**

# Contents

# Introduction

Moving to Edinburgh in 2013 after 20 years of living in London was a challenge. After producing three volumes of *London's Hidden Walks*, I had got to know that city well, and here I was, an outsider, starting again. I remember on one of my first walks I stopped in a café in Dean Village. I told the chatty owner I was on my way to explore Leith and his face fell, warning me that Leithers would not welcome an outsider wandering their streets with notebook and camera. An hour later I ventured into Leith for the first time, slightly nervous. I soon realised his view of the area was fixed in c.1980 and he had probably not been there for years. For me it was the start of a steep learning curve.

Through my subsequent tramping around the city, I discovered where Walter Scott and Arthur Conan Doyle lived as children, and where Robert Burns kissed his Nancy for the last time. I walked in the footsteps of Spud, Renton, Sick Boy and John Lennon, and stood perplexed at the grave of an American Civil War hero covered in fresh flowers and tiny Confederate flags. I learnt about the old breweries for which Edinburgh was once famous, and visited streets were pirates were hung, horse races held, and where the ill-fated Darien Expedition set out.

I visited the place where JK Rowling learnt to teach children before writing for them, just around the corner from a Freemasons' Lodge that once welcomed Robert Burns as a hero. I became slightly obsessed with the Scottish Enlightenment, trying to trace a walking route that would do justice to a period of history that saw Edinburgh become one of the most influential cities in the world. I found out where Nirvana played and Northern Soulers danced the night away, and visited the grand residences that long-dead slave owners once called home.

I hope, with this book in hand, that you might learn something of the people and events that have shaped this city. In my experience, walking is the best way to make such discoveries. Remember to look up, and perhaps choose the walk that at first glance seems least appealing – it is often the less familiar areas that turn out to be the most rewarding.

Edinburgh is blessed with what might appear to be an embarrassment of riches, particularly in terms of its architectural history. In the first edition I mentioned tensions between the council, developers and many citizens. Several fascinating buildings seem to be under threat of being demolished or turned into hotels. No one wants the city to become a museum to past glories, but to keep evolving it needs people to live here. It cannot become an Airbnb wasteland or Disneyfied. After the book came out, there was an epic battle between developers and locals over plans to demolish a row of buildings on Leith Walk. This led to an amazing grassroots public campaign called *Save Leith Walk*. This demonstrated once again that, sadly, it often comes down to ordinary people banding together to fight unwelcome developments that will in the long run protect our city for future generations. I can only hope that those shaping its future show as much foresight and wisdom as their Enlightenment predecessors, who did so much to create and preserve this wondrous city.

Since the first edition of this book came out, I have spotted walkers in different parts of the city, and it is always a pleasure to see them. I try and say hello when I can so don't be surprised if you see a stranger edging up beside you...

Happy walking!

**Stephen Millar**

As ever, if you have any feedback, let me know at stephenwmillar@hotmail.com.

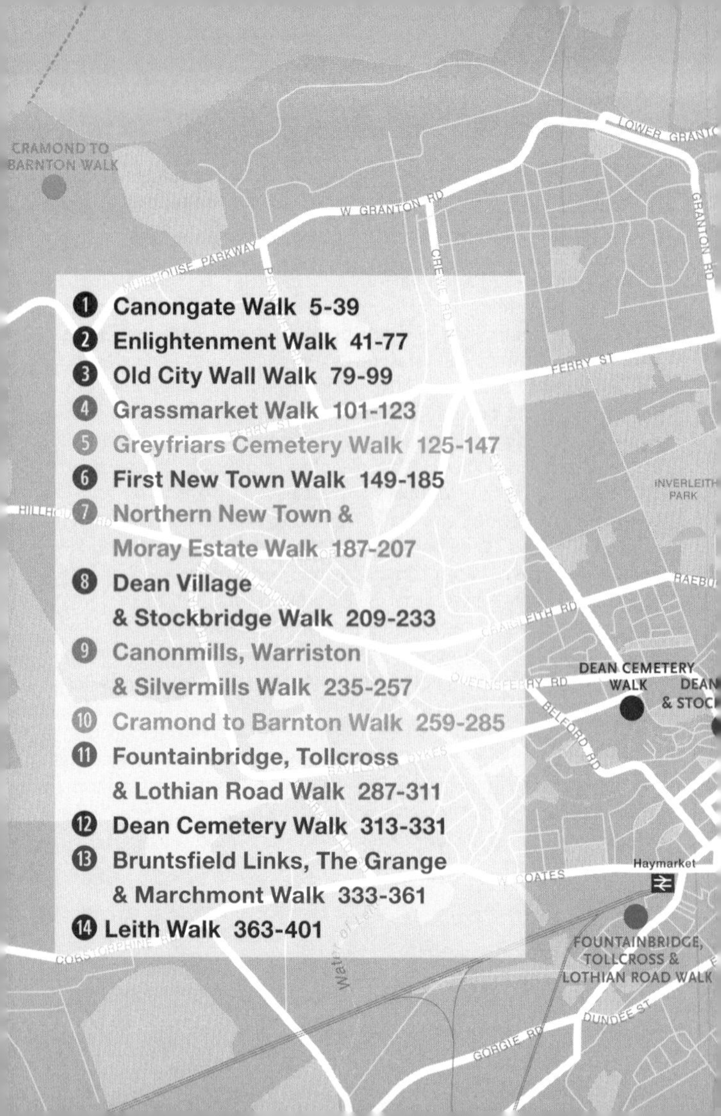
CRAMOND TO BARNTON WALK
LOWER GRANTON
W GRANTON RD
GRANTON RD
MUIRHOUSE PARKWAY
CREWE RD N
FERRY ST
INVERLEITH PARK
RAEBU
DEAN CEMETERY WALK
DEAN & STOC
QUEENSFERRY RD
BELFORD RD
Haymarket
W COATES
CORSTORPHINE
FOUNTAINBRIDGE, TOLLCROSS & LOTHIAN ROAD WALK
DUNDEE ST
GORGIE RD

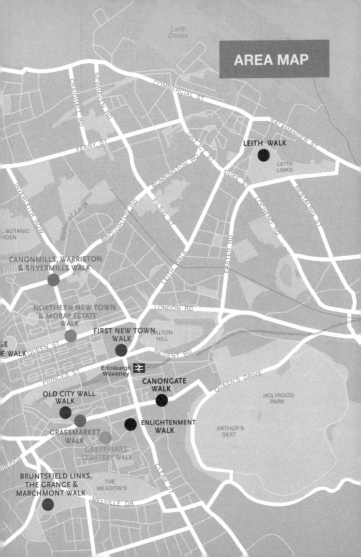

# AREA MAP

Old Playhouse Close, see p.13

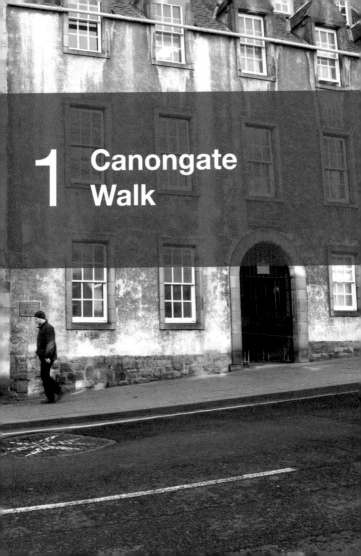

# 1 Canongate Walk

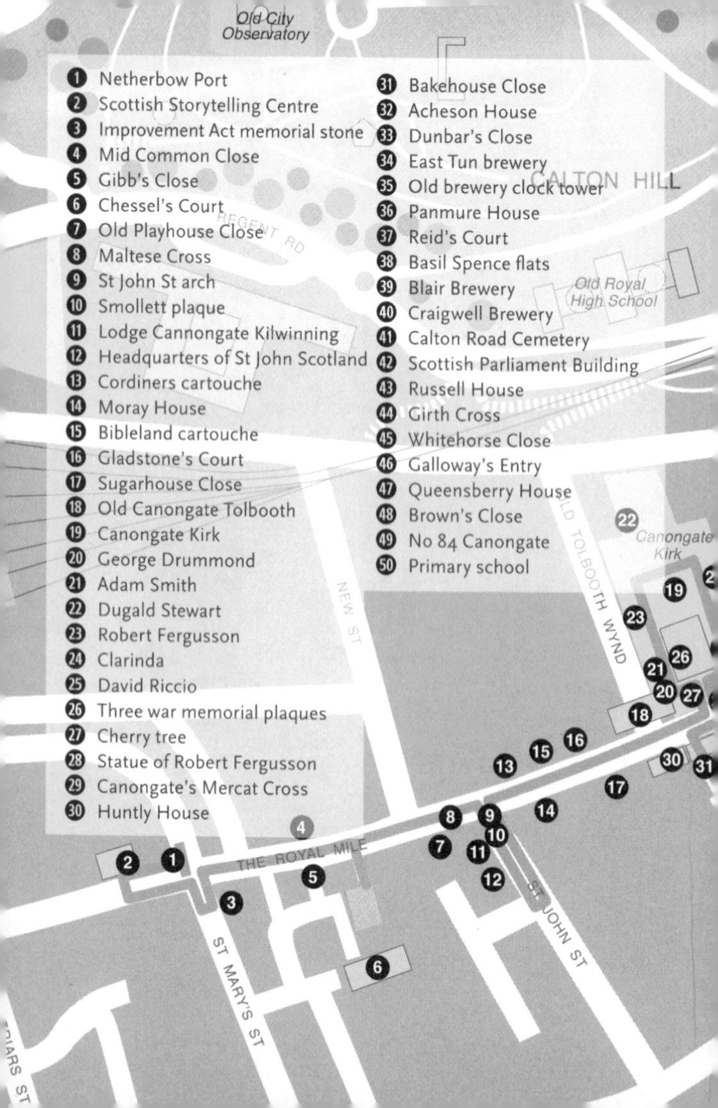

Old City
Observatory

CALTON HILL

Old Royal
High School

Old Royal
High School

Canongate
Kirk

1. Netherbow Port
2. Scottish Storytelling Centre
3. Improvement Act memorial stone
4. Mid Common Close
5. Gibb's Close
6. Chessel's Court
7. Old Playhouse Close
8. Maltese Cross
9. St John St arch
10. Smollett plaque
11. Lodge Cannongate Kilwinning
12. Headquarters of St John Scotland
13. Cordiners cartouche
14. Moray House
15. Bibleland cartouche
16. Gladstone's Court
17. Sugarhouse Close
18. Old Canongate Tolbooth
19. Canongate Kirk
20. George Drummond
21. Adam Smith
22. Dugald Stewart
23. Robert Fergusson
24. Clarinda
25. David Riccio
26. Three war memorial plaques
27. Cherry tree
28. Statue of Robert Fergusson
29. Canongate's Mercat Cross
30. Huntly House

31. Bakehouse Close
32. Acheson House
33. Dunbar's Close
34. East Tun brewery
35. Old brewery clock tower
36. Panmure House
37. Reid's Court
38. Basil Spence flats
39. Blair Brewery
40. Craigwell Brewery
41. Calton Road Cemetery
42. Scottish Parliament Building
43. Russell House
44. Girth Cross
45. Whitehorse Close
46. Galloway's Entry
47. Queensberry House
48. Brown's Close
49. No 84 Canongate
50. Primary school

REGENT RD

NEW ST

OLD TOLBOOTH WYND

THE ROYAL MILE

ST MARY'S ST

ST JOHN ST

FRIARS ST

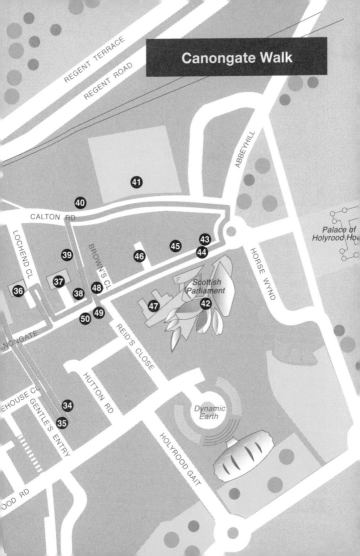

Canongate Walk

# Canongate Walk

Start: Jeffrey Street / The Royal Mile
Finish: Reid's Close
Distance: 1.3 miles

This walk begins on the Royal Mile at the junction of St Mary's Street and Jeffrey Street. It explores the Canongate area, which remained largely independent from Edinburgh from the 12th century until 1856 when it formally became part of the city itself. Before then Canongate was an autonomous administrative district known as a 'burgh', and along the walk you will see evidence of this historic status.

From here, look down on the pavement – opposite the World's End public house. You will see some brass studs which follow the outline of the ❶ **Netherbow Port** – one of half a dozen fortified gates in the city wall that were used to control entry in and out of Edinburgh, as well as helping to defend the city from attack. For several centuries the Netherbow Port was a major landmark in Edinburgh, and hundreds of people would have passed through the gatehouse every day. Up above, the heads of executed prisoners were displayed on spikes.

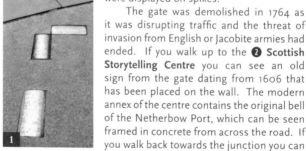

The gate was demolished in 1764 as it was disrupting traffic and the threat of invasion from English or Jacobite armies had ended. If you walk up to the ❷ **Scottish Storytelling Centre** you can see an old sign from the gate dating from 1606 that has been placed on the wall. The modern annex of the centre contains the original bell of the Netherbow Port, which can be seen framed in concrete from across the road. If you walk back towards the junction you can also see on the left-hand side a carving on the wall showing what the Netherbow Port looked like.

The Netherbow Port

The World's End pub on the corner is so named because for many years this was literally the end of the world for many poorer residents of Edinburgh who could not afford to pay tolls to go in and out of the Netherbow Port. As a result, many would have stayed within the confines of the city walls and rarely, if at all, have left Edinburgh.

On the night of 15 October 1977, two teenagers named Christine Eadie and Helen Scott were last seen alive in the pub. They began talking to two strangers – Angus Sinclair and his brother-in-law Gordon Hamilton. Tragically, they accepted a lift home from the men, and that night were both raped and murdered. In 2007, Sinclair was prosecuted for the crimes but the case against him collapsed in court. Under Scotland's 'double jeopardy' law he could not be prosecuted again for the same offence; however, the notoriety of the murders helped lead to a change in the law itself. In 2014, Sinclair was finally convicted of the murders, the first time such a conviction had been secured since the 'double jeopardy' law had changed. Sadly Hamilton escaped justice, having died several years before.

Walk down St Mary's Street to see a ❸ **memorial stone** on the building on the left. This recalls that this building was the first to be constructed as a result of the Improvement Act of 1867. This legislation came about because the town council wanted

to clear away a number of slums, many of which contained old buildings that had become structurally unsafe. The Improvement Act gave the council the power to pull down structures deemed to represent a risk, and replace them with new ones such as the one standing here. Many slums were swept away during this period, and a number of roads expanded or laid out for the first time.

The memorial refers to Lord Provost William Chambers (1800-83). With his brother Robert, Chambers founded the firm of W & R Chambers, which became a global force in publishing, best known for the Chambers Encyclopaedia. William also became a highly influential figure in Edinburgh's political and social circles.

St Mary's Street was originally called St Mary's Wynd. The Wynd was doubled in size during 1868-9 as part of the work carried out after the Improvement Act was passed, and also re-named. The redevelopment was the work of David Cousin and John Lessels. Cousin (1809-78) also designed a number of new privately owned burial grounds in Edinburgh during the mid-19th century, including Dean, Warriston and Rosebank cemeteries.

St Mary's Wynd was the site of a medieval Cistercian convent and hospital dedicated to the Virgin Mary. Its history is obscure; however, it may have been founded in around 1438 and most likely closed during the Scottish Reformation in the late 16th century. It has also been suggested that it continued for a while longer as a refuge for the poor run by the town council.

Retrace your steps and walk down Canongate. The street is named after the Augustinian canons of Holyrood Abbey, the ruins of which lie beside Holyrood Palace at the bottom of the Royal Mile. In 1128, King David I granted the abbey a charter for a 'burgh' between the abbey and Edinburgh, and Canongate was part of this district.

During the Scottish Reformation the abbey was closed, and Canongate came under the control of private landowners. With the Scottish monarchy often in residence at Holyrood Palace nearby, many nobles and foreign delegations acquired houses on Canongate to be near to the royal court.

In 1603, James VI of Scotland moved to London following the death of Elizabeth I, to be crowned James I of England. From this point onwards, Canongate gradually became less attractive to the Scottish nobility. However, in 1770 there were still two dukes, 16 earls, seven barons, seven judges and 13 baronets with houses in Canongate.

Many members of Edinburgh's prosperous middle class also lived here, but the social balance began to change fairly rapidly after the creation of the New Town from the 1770s. Those who could afford it began to move to the New Town, and Canongate gradually became less fashionable.

By the early 19th century, Canongate was becoming increasingly industrialised. As a result, many of the people living in the area were now working class, employed in the iron foundries, breweries, gas works and other industrial concerns that began to dominate the area. This only encouraged the better off to move away.

Continue down Canongate. On the left, look out for the sign for ❹ **Mid Common Close** and above it an odd little statue. This is known as Morocco Land and the statue is said to depict a 'Moor'. According to legend, this was once the home of Andrew Gray (or Grey), who was to be executed for his part in a riot. However, he escaped and fled abroad to Morocco. In 1645, Edinburgh was suffering from a terrible plague when a Moorish raiding ship appeared off Leith. The pirates demanded a ransom from the city, and the Lord Provost handed over his daughter – who was suffering from the plague – as a hostage. The leader of the Moors turned out to be Andrew Gray who, in the intervening years, had become rich working for the Emperor of Morocco. He cured the Provost's daughter of her illness and ended up marrying her, settling here in Canongate. As he had sworn during his exile never to return to Edinburgh, he stayed in Canongate and never crossed into the city itself.

On the south side, opposite the statue, is ❺ **Gibb's Close**. This is associated with the infamous West Port Murders of 1828 carried out by William Burke and William Hare. Both men had arrived in Edinburgh from Ireland to work as labourers on the Union Canal, but realised they could make more money killing people and selling the corpses to the anatomist Dr Robert Knox. Knox needed a constant supply of corpses to teach the students of his anatomy classes.

It was in Gibb's Close that Burke and Hare murdered Mary Paterson, who may have been a prostitute. Her corpse was swiftly taken in a tea chest to Dr Knox. Burke and Hare are believed to have killed 16 victims, but only Burke was convicted for the crimes. He was executed in 1829 while Hare was able to leave Edinburgh, having testified against his accomplice.

Continue along on the south side. Shortly on the right is ❻ **Chessel's Court**. The south side contains fine mansion flats dating from 1748. Designed to attract wealthier residents, they were built by Archibald Chessel, a merchant and wright.

The Court is associated with another infamous character in Edinburgh's history – Deacon Brodie (1741-88). William Brodie was a well-respected member of Edinburgh society, serving as deacon of a trades guild and also on the town council. By profession he was a cabinet maker and he mixed with many prominent people in Edinburgh during this period, including the portrait painter Sir Henry Raeburn and the poet Robert Burns.

However, Brodie also led a secret life as a thief and burglar, which was uncovered after he led a botched raid on the Excise Office in Chessel's Court. One of his accomplices informed the authorities about Brodie's involvement, and Brodie fled abroad. He was later captured, and after a sensational trial was hanged on the Royal Mile in front of a crowd of 40,000 people. The author Robert Louis Stevenson (1850-94) wrote a play about Brodie, and was almost certainly thinking of Brodie's strange life of deception when he wrote *The Strange Case of Dr Jekyll and Mr Hyde* (1886).

Continue along Canongate. On the right is ❼ **Old Playhouse Close**, named after a theatre founded here in 1747 by John Ryan of Covent Garden. This was during a period when the church authorities of Edinburgh tried to prevent any theatrical productions from taking place as they were believed to undermine public morality.

A fight broke out here in 1749 when English army officers asked the orchestra to play a tune named 'Culloden' – a provocative request given the English defeat of a Scottish army at Culloden just a few years before. The orchestra responded instead by playing a Jacobite tune which resulted in a fight between the English officers and members of the audience who intervened to protect the musicians.

In 1756, a play entitled *Douglas*, written by a church minister named John Home (1722-1808), was performed here. The church authorities were unable to stop the performance, but did force Home to leave the church. A patriotic audience member famously shouted out at the end of the performance, 'Whaur's your Willie Shakespeare noo?'. Sadly Home never did develop into a playwright of Shakespeare's reputation.

The famous philosopher David Hume (1711-76) – a notorious atheist who wanted to support his friend Home – acted out some scenes from *Douglas* during rehearsals. Hume used to live near here (approximately where New Street is today).

Just past Old Playhouse Close, look out for a sign with a ❽ **Maltese Cross** painted on the street. This commemorates the Cross of St John that once stood here, marking the boundary line between Edinburgh and Canongate.

The Order of the Knights of Saint John originated in Jerusalem in the late 11th century during the period of the Crusades. Like the famous Knights Templar, the Knights of Saint John were a powerful religious and military organisation whose original purpose was to provide medical care to pilgrims. In their heyday, the Knights of Saint John controlled vast landholdings in several countries, and they are believed to have owned property in Canongate in medieval times.

The Order was forced from Jerusalem in the 13th century, and was based in Malta until Napoleon captured the island at the end of the 18th century. The Order's cross became associated with Malta, hence it is described as a Maltese Cross. The current Scottish headquarters of the Order will be seen shortly.

In 1633, Charles I visited Edinburgh and was greeted at the Cross of St John by the Lord Provost, who was then knighted on this spot by the King.

Continue down Canongate and on the right walk under a large ❾ **arch** with a sign for St John Street. This is named for the Knights of Saint John, who owned property here.

As you pass under the arch, look back to see a ❿ **plaque** up above. This records that the Scottish writer and poet Tobias Smollett (1721-71) stayed here with his sister in 1766.

Smollett is best known for novels such as *The Expedition of Humphry Clinker* and his style is said to have influenced Charles Dickens. Described by George Orwell as 'Scotland's best novelist', he is one of a select band of Scottish writers whose faces are depicted on the Scott Monument on Princes Street.

Just past the arch on the right (No 23) is a historic Masonic lodge named ⓫ **Lodge Canongate Kilwinning**. The origins of the lodge date back to 1677, and a chapel was built here in the 1730s. The lodge is believed to contain the oldest purpose-built Masonic meeting room in the world. Scotland's great poet Robert Burns (1759-96) was affiliated with the lodge here from 1787, and was named its Poet Laureate. The lodge claims it was influential in encouraging Burns to live in Edinburgh and pursue his career as a poet.

Just past the lodge at No 21 is the ⓬ **headquarters of St John Scotland**. This was founded in 1947 as a revival of the original Order of Saint John. Today it is a charity that supports the coastguard and mountain rescue services, as well as the St John Eye Hospital in Jerusalem – appropriately given that the original Order of Saint John was founded there to help the sick.

In the mid-19th century the Edinburgh and Leith Brewery was situated to the west of St John Street. It was just one of about a dozen breweries based in and around Canongate. However, by the late 20th century they had all closed. You will learn a little more about Canongate's breweries as you continue on the walk.

Return to Canongate and continue downhill. Very shortly on the left, by No 197, look out for a **⓭ cartouche** of a crown and knife on the exterior wall. This early 18th-century tenement was known as Shoemakers' Land and was where the Hall of the Incorporation of Cordiners (or Shoemakers) once stood. The Incorporation was a trade guild and the sign depicts the paring knife used to cut leather and the crown of St Crispin – patron saint of the Cordiners. The Cordiners' name is derived from the Spanish city of Córdoba, which was the source of the best leather at the time.

Next on the right-hand side is **⓮ Moray House**, described in an architectural guide as 'the finest aristocratic mansion to survive in this degree of completeness in the Old Town'. It was built in the early 17th century for Mary, Countess of Home, and named for her daughter Margaret, Countess of Moray, who took over the property in the 1640s. Her descendants continued to own the property until 1845.

Oliver Cromwell stayed here twice – in 1648 and 1650 – and Charles I and Charles II also visited the house.

In 1650, a wedding party at the house celebrated the marriage of the Marquis of Argyll's son to the daughter of Lord Moray. They stood on the balcony you can still see today – just as Argyll's arch-enemy the Marquis of Montrose was being led up Canongate on a cart on his way to his execution. Montrose was being executed because of his support for Charles I and (then in exile) Charles II.

The wedding guests jeered at the condemned man, but Montrose won the sympathy of the crowd through the bravery he showed in response to such insults. Ironically, Argyll himself was led past the house on the way to his own execution in 1661, having fallen foul of Charles II because of his previous association with Oliver Cromwell. Argyll's head was displayed on the same spike, high up on the tollbooth by St Giles' Cathedral, that Montrose's head had been placed upon 11 years earlier.

The Acts of Union of 1707 created a political union between England and Scotland. They were ratified by the signatures of members of the Scottish Parliament, some of whom signed the ratification while hiding out in the summer house of Moray House. They were fearful of the angry mob running around Edinburgh trying to prevent the politicians from agreeing to end Scotland's independence. The summer house still exists but is not generally open to visitors.

Today Moray House is part of the University and used for teacher training. JK Rowling completed her teacher training course here in 1996 – the same year as she received a publishing deal for her first Harry Potter book. Roy Williamson and Ronnie Browne studied to be teachers here too, having first met at Edinburgh College of Art in 1955. They would go on to form The Corries, Scotland's most successful folk band. Williamson wrote *Flower of Scotland*, the nation's unofficial anthem that is sung before international rugby matches.

Almost opposite the entrance to Moray House is another **⑮ cartouche** above the door of a building known as Bibleland. This building is also associated with the Cordiners, and dates from 1677. The cartouche features a paring knife, and an open bible with an excerpt from Psalm 133.

As a separate burgh, Canongate had eight trade incorporations of its own that developed differently to their counterparts in Edinburgh. The Hammermen (or metalworkers) were the first to be established in 1540, followed by the Cordiners in 1554.

This building was restored by the architectural practice of Robert Hurd (1905-63) in the mid-20th century as part of a larger regeneration project carried out in Canongate during the 1950s and 60s. As mentioned earlier, by the early 19th century Canongate had become increasingly industrialised and was no longer fashionable.

As Canongate's industries began to decline during the 20th century, many of its residents became victims of the downturn and a large number of older buildings became run down and dilapidated. In the 1930s, it was reported that it was common to find a family of six or seven people living in a single room, and around 25 people sharing a single lavatory and water tap – 159 people lived in just one house on St John Street!

Faced with these social and housing issues, from the mid-20th century the council embarked on a regeneration project using architects such as Robert Hurd. Hurd worked on several restorations in the area, particularly during the 1950s. He is buried in Canongate Kirk (seen shortly).

The atmosphere of Canongate during the darker days of the industrial age was captured by the French author Jules Verne (1828-1905), who visited Edinburgh in 1859. In his book *Backwards to Britain* he described how, 'The area that leads to the royal palace is one of utter misery... in the middle of that abject populace, in the foul, disease-ridden atmosphere, on the muddy pavement and down

those dark, dank horrid lanes or closes which lead to revolting slums, slithering down stepless ramps towards the ravines on either side of the Canongate, one is gripped by the terrible poetry of old Scotland!' The days when aristocrats had large houses in Canongate had clearly long since passed by the time of Verne's visit.

Continue on the north side to ⑯ **Gladstone's Court**. It is named for William Gladstone MP (1809-98), who served as Prime Minister in the 19th century and who had extensive Scottish connections through his family. This was once the site of the Magdalene Asylum, which was founded by a philanthropic society in the early 19th century to look after 'young girls or fallen women who have deviated from the path of virtue and peace'. When the young women came to the Asylum their heads were shaved, and they were required to wear a uniform. The Asylum later moved out to Dalry.

In the late 19th century the area just to the north of Gladstone's Court was dominated by the vast Edinburgh Gas Works, with its huge 330-foot high chimney, and also the Canongate Iron Foundry. This former industrial site is still undergoing redevelopment.

As you continue down Canongate, look out for **17** **Sugarhouse Close** on the south side. It is named after the sugar refining that took place here from around 1750 until the 1820s. In those days sugar was brought from slave plantations in the West Indies to Leith docks, and then refined in one of a half-dozen sugar-refining factories – or 'sugarhouses' – in the city. The Edinburgh Sugar House Company was based here.

The north side is dominated by the tall tower of the ⓲ **Old Canongate Tolbooth**. The Tolbooth dates from 1591 (the clock is from 1884), and is where public dues or tolls were paid. It also served as Canongate's prison, and was where the local council would meet. As the main civic building in Canongate, it symbolised the burgh's independence from Edinburgh. Looking up, you can see the Canongate coat of arms, consisting of a stag's head and cross.

The arms recall the legend of the foundation of Holyrood Abbey. King David I was hunting when he was attacked by a white stag (or hart). He tried to grab the antlers but found himself holding a cross instead, and the animal ran away. In a dream he had a vision of St Andrew instructing him to found an abbey on the spot where he was saved. Holyrood abbey was founded by the king a year later, in 1128, and it exerted a huge influence on this part of Edinburgh until c.1559 when it closed during the Scottish Reformation. Canongate's arms have been officially obsolete since the abolishment of the burgh of Canongate in 1856.

Today this is the home of The People's Story – an excellent small museum that focuses on the social history of Edinburgh and its residents (see page 39). On the exterior of the Tolbooth, look for the memorial listing the many residents of Canongate who died fighting during WWI. In the early 20th century, Canongate, still heavily industrialised, had a much higher population density than it does today.

18

From here visit the **19** **Canongate Kirk** next door. For many years the parishioners of Canongate met in the old Holyrood Abbey. However, this kirk was built after James II of England decided to use the abbey as a chapel for the Order of the Thistle. Construction of the kirk began in the late 1680s and it opened in 1691. James was deposed during the Glorious Revolution of 1688, so the kirk is a rare example of a place of worship from his three-year reign. The very top of the kirk contains a gilded stag's head and cross – another reminder of the arms of the burgh of Canongate.

19

A number of prominent figures from the era of the Scottish Enlightenment are buried here, including **20** **George Drummond** (1688-1766), six times Lord Provost, whose efforts helped lead to the creation of the New Town; the philosopher and founder of modern economic theory **21** **Adam Smith** (1723-90); the philosopher **22** **Dugald Stewart** (1753-1828); and the poet **23** **Robert Fergusson** (1750-74).

A statue of Fergusson stands outside the kirk; Robert Burns was responsible for the

21

19 Canongate Kirk

gravestone (and epitaph) after he arrived in Edinburgh to find his literary hero had been buried in an unmarked grave. Fergusson died aged only 24, shortly after being committed to Edinburgh's notorious asylum known as Bedlam. His best work was written over just a two-year period, and was very influential on Burns' own poetry.

On the east side there is a memorial with the single word ㉔ '**Clarinda**'. When Burns moved to Edinburgh he struck up a secret relationship with Mrs Agnes Maclehose (1758-1841). As she was married, the couple corresponded using pen names, she going by 'Clarinda' with Burns as 'Sylvander'. A number of his songs and poems were dedicated to her, including one of his most famous – *Ae Fond Kiss*.

Burns wrote of Agnes, 'I am at this moment ready to hang myself for a young Edinr. Widow, who has wit and beauty more murderously fatal than the assassinating stiletto of the Sicilian banditti, or the poisoned arrow of the savage African'. However, Burns did not endear himself to Agnes after he began an affair with her maid, who then gave birth to a boy (named Robert Burns Clow).

*Ae Fond Kiss* was written after the final meeting between Burns and Agnes (at the White Hart Inn in Grassmarket), just before she left for the West Indies to attempt a reconciliation with her estranged husband. She later returned after finding that her husband had started a new family with his mistress, one of his many slaves.

Also at the east side, by the wall of the kirk, is the grave of **㉕ David Riccio** (1533-66), the Italian musician and secretary to Mary, Queen of Scots. He was viciously murdered in front of Mary – who was seven months pregnant at the time (with the future James VI) – by a group of nobles including Lord Darnley, her husband. Riccio (also known as Rizzio) was stabbed 56 times. Darnley himself was later murdered in Edinburgh, and Mary was believed to have been involved in the plot against him. Henry IV of France later suggested that James VI may have been 'David the fiddler's son' rather than Darnley's.

On the west wall of the kirk are **㉖ three plaques** that recall Canongate's historic links with the brewing industry. They commemorate those workers in the Younger's Brewery business who died in the two world wars.

*View of Old Royal High School from Canongate Kirk*

The first brewery established by William Younger in 1749 was in Leith. Another member of the Younger family founded a brewery by Holyrood Abbey in 1778, and a second one was acquired nearby a few years later. Younger's later merged with its arch-rival McEwan's in 1931, before merging again to become part of Scottish & Newcastle. These plaques were moved here after the old breweries were demolished to make way for the Scottish Parliament Building.

Near Fergusson's grave on the west side is the burial place of David Mitchelson, who emigrated from Scotland to Boston, Massachusetts. In 1770, a group of English soldiers shot dead some residents of Boston – an incident that became known as the 'Boston Massacre'. Mitchelson was called upon as a witness at the trial and was cross-examined by the soldiers' defence lawyer John Adams (1735-1826).

John Adams would later play an important role in the foundation of the United States of America and served as its second President. Adams' papers contain fascinating minutes of the trial of 1770. They record the actual dialogue that took place in court as Adams, the future President, cross-examined Michelson, a humble seal-engraver who had emigrated from Scotland. Michelson later returned to Edinburgh.

In 1841, Charles Dickens wandered through the kirkyard, the light fading. He saw a headstone with the name 'Ebenezer Lennox Scroggie – meal man', a reference to Scroggie's profession as a corn merchant. Dickens misread this as 'mean man', and the name helped to inspire his famous character Ebenezer Scrooge in *A Christmas Carol*.

In the late 18th century the Canongate poorhouse stood just to the north-west of the kirkyard and south of Calton Road. It remained here until the late 19th century, when the site was converted for use as the Epidemic (or Fever) Hospital.

As you leave the kirk, look out for the **㉗ cherry tree** just by the entrance (there is a plaque at ground level). It was planted by Queen Elizabeth II in 1952, shortly after she succeeded to the throne. Zara Phillips, daughter of Princess Anne and granddaughter of the Queen, married the former England rugby player Mike Tindall at the kirk on 30 July 2011.

The statue of the poet **㉘ Robert Fergusson** outside the kirk was unveiled in 2004. It was sculpted by David Annand, whose work was chosen by the people of Edinburgh out of three possible statues.

Just inside the railings on the east side you can see **29** **Canongate's Mercat Cross**. From the 12th century this stood in the centre of Canongate. It is where public proclamations were made, and represented the right of the burgh of Canongate to hold its own market. The Cross was moved away from its historic location in 1737 and arrived at this spot in 1953.

Opposite the kirk is the Museum of Edinburgh, which traces the history of the capital from prehistoric times to the present day (see page 39). You may wish to visit it now.

It is based in the 16th-century **30** **Huntly House** – known as the 'Speaking House' because of the Latin inscriptions on the exterior. There are five mottos, four from the 16th century and one which was added when the building was last restored in 1932. This building was originally three small 16th-century houses that were later joined together and extended. The name derives from the Duchess of Gordon, who married the Marquis of Huntly and lived here in the mid-18th century.

To the right of the museum is a substantial 16th-century arch that leads into the picturesque **❸❶ Bakehouse Close**. This is named after a bakehouse that was located here in the 19th century and run by the Incorporation of Bakers of Canongate. The buildings in the Close date largely from the 16th and 17th centuries.

If you walk down the Close on the left-hand side you will find **❸❷ Acheson House**. This was built in 1633 for Sir Archibald Acheson, who served as Secretary of State for Scotland under Charles I. It later became a brothel known as the Cock and Trumpet (said to be named after the Acheson coat of arms, but you can draw your own conclusions!). The Edinburgh World Heritage organisation is based here, and if the door is open you can look into the courtyard – worth a visit just to see a fascinating selection of historic stonework. Above the door is the Acheson coat of arms inscribed with the date 1633.

Return to Canongate. If you walk past the entrance to the museum you can also get an alternative view of Acheson House on the east side.

Continue along Canongate, and almost immediately after the Mercat Cross walk down **❸❸ Dunbar's Close**. This contains Dunbar's Close Garden – a hidden gem set out in the style of the 17th century. Many of the grand houses on Canongate during that period would have had gardens like this to the rear. Those gardens were gradually built over in the 18th and 19th centuries as the area become industrialised.

33  *Dunbar's Close Garden*

An oyster cellar run by Mrs Love was situated near here in the 18th century, which was visited by Robert Burns. He was fascinated by the fashionable ladies who would sneak into the cellar wearing masks before consuming oysters and porter beer. This tranquil spot is a good place for a break if you have brought some refreshments.

Return to Canongate and continue walking eastwards. On the south side is Crichton's Close, which is home to the Scottish Poetry Library – a good place to find works by Burns and Fergusson if this walk has whetted your appetite. Walk past the Poetry Library (see p.39) and on the left look out for the BBC sign. BBC Scotland is located inside the former ❸❹ **East Tun brewery building**, which was part of the Scottish & Newcastle complex that once dominated this area. Just opposite East Tun is the ❸❺ **old brewery clock tower**, originally the brewery's yeast house and now home to a branch of Pizza Express. This was formerly the site of the Holyrood Brewery with the Abbey Brewery lying just to the east (where the Scottish Parliament is now centred).

Retrace your steps back to Canongate. Shortly on the left, walk under the sign for Lochend Close. As you pass under the arch you will see directly ahead ❸❻ **Panmure House**. This dates from the 17th century, and is most notable for being the last and only surviving home of economist Adam Smith. Panmure House was originally the town house of the Jacobite Earl of Panmure.

Return to Canongate. Next on the north side is **37 Reid's Court**, which contains an early 18th-century villa now serving as the Canongate Manse (a manse is the home of a minister of the church). Reid's Court was home to Lord Advocate Sir John Nisbet and the Earls of Aberdeen during the 17th century. The Court is named after a later resident called Andrew Reid, a wealthy brewer and magistrate who lived here in around 1770.

The **38 modern flats** beside Reid's Court were designed by Basil Spence & Partners and completed by 1969. They are another example of the regeneration projects undertaken by the council in Canongate in the mid-20th century. The Scottish architect Sir Basil Spence (1907-76) was one of Britain's most prominent architects in the second half of the 20th century, responsible for a number of buildings in Edinburgh (see Brunstfield Walk, p.336). He is best known for his design for Coventry Cathedral.

Walk through the archway under the flats immediately after Reid's Court and continue down Campbell's Close. Bear right and continue northwards.

On the left is the former **39 Blair Brewery**, now converted into flats. Continue on to reach Calton Road and on the other side is the former **40 Craigwell Brewery**, again converted into residential flats. This brewery was built on the site of Craig's well, the original water supply for Holyrood. If you had walked this same route in the 1890s, to the east of Campbell's Close you would also have seen the Balmoral Brewery, and to the west a large gasometer. This whole area, being heavily industrialised, would have contrasted very sharply with the elegant neo-classical monuments visible up above on Calton Hill.

The dozen or so breweries that operated in Canongate from the 18th century were initially attracted by the good water supply and, compared to the separate burgh of Edinburgh, low taxes on beer production. In the 1880s, the number of breweries in Edinburgh as a whole peaked at around 40. As late as 1945 there were still 17 breweries in the city, employing around 4,500 people. However, falling exports, stricter licensing rules and increasing automation contributed to a long-term decline. Mergers took place that reduced the number of breweries even further and made it easier to transfer production to other cities. By the 1990s the brewery industry in and around Canongate had ceased.

You are now on Calton Road. Continue along it, passing the ❹ **Calton Road Cemetery** on your left. After a few minutes you reach Holyrood, the location of the Royal Palace and ruins of the abbey. You may wish to extend the walk by visiting the palace, and other attractions at this point.

On the other side of the road you will see a sign for Watergate. This was a medieval gate that controlled traffic in and out of the area, and allowed the burgh's custom charges to be collected. Its stone arch was blown down in 1822 and a wooden replacement lasted for around another 30 years.

Just to the north-east of here stood a real tennis court that was used by the Scottish monarchs, including Mary, Queen of Scots. The tennis court building doubled as a private theatre. There has been speculation that William Shakespeare was part of a group of English actors who came to Holyrood Palace to perform for James VI in around 1600. Plays continued to be performed at the tennis court theatre until well into the late 17th century.

Follow the map to start heading back up Canongate. On the south side is the ❹ **Scottish Parliament Building**. It stands on the site of the Scottish & Newcastle Brewery, itself originally the Younger's Brewery. It was

43

opened in 2004 by Queen Elizabeth II and was designed by the Spanish architect Enric Miralles. The cost was over £400 million – more than ten times the original estimate. Miralles died of a brain tumour in 2000 at the age of 45, before the building was completed.

On the north side, by a gift shop, look out for ❸ **Russell House**. This dates from c.1690 and has been restored.

44

Just in front of Russell House, before the roundabout, is a circle marked out on the road surface. This indicates the site of the ❹ **Girth Cross**, which stood here for many centuries. The Cross helped to mark the limit of the sanctuary of Holyrood Abbey. Those fleeing the civic authorities could claim a right of sanctuary within the boundary, and even after the Reformation, when the abbey was closed, certain rights of sanctuary continued to exist. This was mostly to the benefit of debtors escaping their creditors. The most famous debtor living here was the Comte d'Artois, brother of Louis XVI and XVIII of France, who stayed here between 1796 and 1803. He later became Charles X of France, and returned here after being deposed during the July Revolution of 1830. Maps of the mid-19th century still traced the boundary line of the sanctuary. In 1880 the law changed so debtors could no longer be imprisoned and the need for sanctuary therefore ended.

45

Public proclamations and executions also took place at the Girth Cross. In 1600, a famous beauty named Lady Warriston was beheaded here for plotting to murder her bullying husband.

Continue up the hill. On the right is ⑮ **Whitehorse Close**, which you should enter. This is the location of an important 17th-century coaching inn named the White Horse. The Close served as a major arrival and departure point for those travelling between Edinburgh and London. This is probably where Dr Johnson arrived before he went to James Boyd's Inn (see p.95).

The original inn building was substantially rebuilt during the 19th and 20th centuries, but the Close looks pretty much as it would have done in Johnson's time. In 1745, Bonnie Prince Charlie's officers stayed at the inn while the Prince stayed at Holyrood Palace. Charles Edward Stuart was the grandson of James II of England who – as mentioned earlier – was deposed in 1688. William Dick (1793-1866), founder of the Royal School of Veterinary Studies in 1823, was born here. Today the school is part of the University of Edinburgh. The Close itself is said to be named after a horse owned by Mary, Queen of Scots.

Next on the right-hand side is **46** **Galloway's Entry**, where Whitefoord House is located. This dates from 1769 and was designed by Robert Mylne (1733-1811) for Sir John Whitefoord. Whitefoord is remembered today as being an important patron of Robert Burns. Mylne came from a well-known family of Scottish architects who designed many buildings in Edinburgh and Leith (see also Walks 5 and 14, p.125 and Leith walks p.363).

Whitefoord House was a minor work by Mylne, who is today best known for his design of Blackfriars Bridge in London and numerous canals around Britain. For a while he was regarded as being the equal of the great architect Robert Adam; however, he ultimately never achieved the same level of recognition.

The house stands on the site of a late-medieval palace owned by the Earls of Winton and used by a number of foreign ambassadors to the Scottish court. In 1565, Lord Darnley stayed here the night before his marriage to Mary, Queen of Scots. Mary may also have sought refuge here after the brutal murder of her servant David Riccio by Darnley and his fellow conspirators (see above).

In the 19th century the house fell into disrepair and was used as a factory. Since 1910, it has been occupied by the Scottish Veterans

organisation and it is not open to the public. The organisation was set up after its founders were shocked to find veterans of the Boer War sleeping rough on the streets of Edinburgh.

In 1926, Lady Haig's Poppy Factory was based here, and residents made poppies for sale in Scotland in order to raise money for other veterans. Lady Haig was the wife of Field Marshal Douglas Haig (1861-1928), the famous WWI army commander. Poppy production later moved to Panmure Close (near to Panmure House).

47 Queensberry House

On the south side is the vast **47 Queensberry House**, which dates from 1681. It now forms part of the Scottish Parliament complex. The building was once the home of James Douglas, the Second Duke of Queensberry (1662-1711). In 1706-7 the Duke played a critical role in mustering support for the political union with England. As the Queen's Lord High Commissioner, he also formally closed the Scottish Parliament when it met for the very last time in 1707.

The Duke is thought to have been provided with £20,000 by London to help buy the vote of members of the Scottish Parliament, and retained around £12,000 of this sum for his own 'expenses'. As mentioned earlier, the Edinburgh mob forced members of the Scottish Parliament to shelter in Moray House while they ratified the political union with England. The mob also threatened to burn Queensberry House and the Duke fled to London as his life was in danger.

On the day the Treaty was ratified, legend has it that the Duke's insane and violent son escaped from his room in Queensberry House and was later found eating the flesh of a servant boy whom he had caught and roasted over the fire. The fireplace where the incident took place features in Ian Rankin's Inspector Rebus novel *Set in Darkness* (2000), and the house is reputedly haunted by the ghost of the murdered servant boy.

Continue up Canongate and on the right is **48 Brown's Close**. This was once known as Golfer's Land after a shoemaker named John Paterson built a tenement here in the 17th century. Paterson was able to fund the construction after he was selected to partner the Duke of York (later James VII) in a match against two English noblemen on the golf course at Leith Links. Paterson and the Duke won the game, and Paterson was allowed to keep the substantial winnings from the victory. He later sold the land to a gardener or merchant called Brown, hence the current name.

Just up on the south side look out for **49 No 84**, which has a date of 1619 above the door (this is a modern replica of the original façade). It stands next to an imposing **50 primary school** that dates from the late 1880s and is a good example of Victorian design. The Education Act of 1872 revolutionised schooling in Scotland, providing board schools for all children between the ages of five and 13. As a result, a huge number of publicly funded schools such as this one were built, and this school represents a turning point in Canongate's history, when many children living in its slums first began to have a chance of receiving a decent education.

It stands on the site of Milton House, which was designed by John Adam and built in 1755. Adam (1721-92) was the eldest son of the prominent Scottish architect William Adam. John and his brothers Robert and James created a family style of neo-classical architecture that was hugely influential not only in 18th-century Britain but in other countries such as the United States. The school was originally called the Milton House Public School.

On the right is Clarinda's tearooms – named after Burns' great love. This is the end of the walk. ●

## VISIT...

**Scottish Storytelling Centre**
43-45 High St, EH1 1SR
*www.scottishstorytellingcentre.
co.uk*

**The People's Story**
The Royal Mile,
163 Canongate, EH8 8BN
*www.edinburghmuseums.org.uk*

**Museum of Edinburgh**
142 Canongate, EH8 8DD
*www.edinburghmuseums.org.uk*

**Palace of Holyrood**
Canongate, EH8 8DX
*www.rct.uk/visit/palace-of-
holyroodhouse*

**Scottish Poetry Library**
5 Crichton's Cl, Canongate,
EH8 8DT
*www.scottishpoetrylibrary.org.uk*

## EAT, DRINK...

**Café at the Palace**
Palace of Holyrood, Canongate,
EH8 8DX
Tel: 0131 652 3685

**Ondine**
2 George IV Bridge, EH1 1AD
*www.ondinerestaurant.co.uk*

View from Dugald Stewart Monument towards North Bridge

# 2 Enlightenment Walk

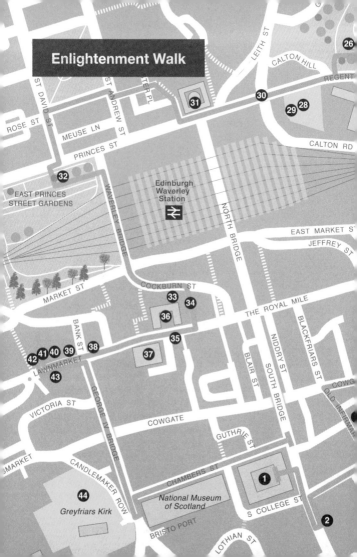

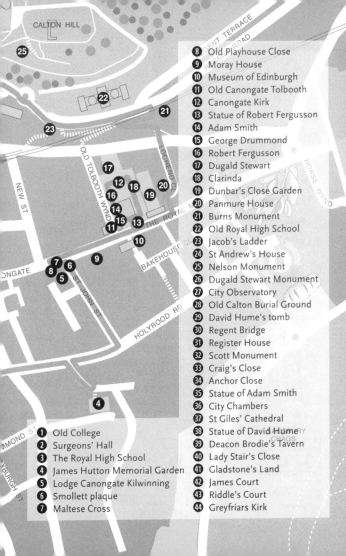

CALTON HILL

8 Old Playhouse Close
9 Moray House
10 Museum of Edinburgh
11 Old Canongate Tolbooth
12 Canongate Kirk
13 Statue of Robert Fergusson
14 Adam Smith
15 George Drummond
16 Robert Fergusson
17 Dugald Stewart
18 Clarinda
19 Dunbar's Close Garden
20 Panmure House
21 Burns Monument
22 Old Royal High School
23 Jacob's Ladder
24 St Andrew's House
25 Nelson Monument
26 Dugald Stewart Monument
27 City Observatory
28 Old Calton Burial Ground
29 David Hume's tomb
30 Regent Bridge
31 Register House
32 Scott Monument
33 Craig's Close
34 Anchor Close
35 Statue of Adam Smith
36 City Chambers
37 St Giles' Cathedral
38 Statue of David Hume
39 Deacon Brodie's Tavern
40 Lady Stair's Close
41 Gladstone's Land
42 James Court
43 Riddle's Court
44 Greyfriars Kirk

1 Old College
2 Surgeons' Hall
3 The Royal High School
4 James Hutton Memorial Garden
5 Lodge Canongate Kilwinning
6 Smollett plaque
7 Maltese Cross

# Enlightenment Walk
Start: Old College, South Bridge
Finish: South Bridge
Distance: 3.4 miles

**1** *Old College*

This walk begins at ❶ **Old College** – the historic heart of the University of Edinburgh.

The Scottish Enlightenment is an expression used to describe a broad-based intellectual movement that flourished during the 18th and early 19th centuries. The movement covered a wide range of fields, including philosophy, history, science, poetry and medicine. It also had no central organisation or single unified philosophy, thus making it difficult to define exactly what kind of intellectual movement it was.

It is perhaps best to see the Enlightenment as a period of increased tolerance that allowed talented individuals the relative freedom to progress their intellectual interests regardless of the eventual conclusions that might arise. This period of tolerance coincided with the development of mass communication in the form of cheaper books and periodicals. This allowed the ideas generated by the core group of intellectuals to be disseminated widely, satisfying a growing demand for knowledge among an increasingly literate population.

The controversial Scottish philosopher and historian David Hume (1711-76) personified this new age (see p.66). He became notorious for his atheist beliefs and was despised by the church authorities. While this caused him difficulties in his career, it did not prevent him from being able to publish his ideas or from mixing freely with whoever he wanted. In contrast to earlier centuries, the church no longer had the clout to have a troublesome character like Hume imprisoned or burnt at the stake – too many people in influential positions were interested in what he had to say (whether they admitted to it publicly or not).

The relatively progressive ethos of the University helped to provide the framework for this loosely linked intellectual movement to develop, and many of the prominent people mentioned on this walk were educated there or taught their ideas to its student body.

Walk around the courtyard of Old College. The University's official foundation date is 1582, though a law college existed before then. The foundation was largely thanks to the efforts of the town council, not to a particular patron or religious institution. This influenced how the University developed, and by the 18th century it was regarded as being more intellectually progressive and less stuffy than Oxford or Cambridge.

It was also much cheaper to attend, and so attracted a wider cross-section of society. In the 18th century Scotland is thought to have had the most literate population in the world, much of this attributable to the emphasis placed on the teaching of reading and writing in the church schools of the post-Reformation period. The Schools Act of 1696 also required schools to be set up in every parish.

Students at the University often began their studies in their early teens, and could attend lectures given by some of the greatest minds of the age. The spirit of the Enlightenment was therefore passed from gifted individuals to a far wider audience.

For many decades the University was spread throughout a number of buildings. However, in 1789 subscriptions were sought to create a new consolidated home. Old College was designed by the most famous architect of the Enlightenment age, Robert Adam (1728-92). He died before it was completed, but the project was later taken on by the equally gifted William Henry Playfair (1790-1857). Old College (or New College as it was originally known) was largely complete by 1830.

While the intellectual spirit of the Enlightenment era was evident in a number of European countries during the 18th century, the advances taking place in Scotland drew particular attention at the time. The French philosopher Voltaire (1694-1778) wrote 'We look to Scotland for all our ideas of civilisation', while Benjamin Franklin (1706-90) was of the view that 'the University of Edinburgh possessed a set of truly great men, Professors of Several Branches of Knowledge, as have ever appeared in any age or country'.

Robert Adam was the son of the noted architect William Adam (1689-1748), and studied at the University. His neo-classical style was influenced by spending his early years studying architecture on the Continent, and he developed (with his brothers John and James) a distinctive 'Adam' family style of architecture.

This was influential not just in Britain but was also credited with shaping the style of the early municipal buildings in America. Robert went on to hold the prestigious post of Architect of the King's Works and his surviving work in Edinburgh includes Register House and the City Chambers (both seen later) as well as parts of Charlotte Square in the New Town.

An important scientist of the Enlightenment period associated with the University was the chemist Joseph Black (1728-99). He studied medicine at Glasgow University and in 1752 transferred to Edinburgh University. He went on to become a great teacher of chemistry and produced original research into specific and latent heat – this directly helped the development of the steam engine. Black also identified 'fixed air', better known as carbon dioxide, and was able to demonstrate that a balloon filled with hydrogen would rise, leading to the first hot air balloon flights a few years later. In recent years excavations in the quadrangle of Old College uncovered chemical apparatus believed to have been used by Black.

Black was a close friend of James Watt (1736-1819), who, helped by Black's research, did so much to improve the steam engine and thus lay the foundation of the Industrial Revolution. Black was also close friends with other figures encountered along this walk including James Hutton and Adam Smith. This was typical of Edinburgh in the 18th century – the population was still fairly small (around 50,000

people in 1751) so those within the more educated classes probably knew most of the other people in an extended circle. This allowed ideas to spread rapidly, and for many the pursuit of intellectual progress was as much a part of their social life as it was of their working day.

The building on the south-west corner of the courtyard is today used by law students as a lecture theatre. However, this was once part of the medical school and was where dissections of corpses took place during anatomy classes. It was here that the corpse of the infamous serial killer William Burke was dissected, after his execution, by Alexander Monro, Professor of Anatomy, in 1829. Burke's body was carried into the University through a secret underground tunnel which still exists today (reached through a trap door in one of the offices). Burke and his accomplice William Hare killed 16 people over a 12-month period, the cadavers being sold to Dr Robert Knox in order that he could teach dissection to students during private anatomy classes.

From Old College, walk up Nicolson Street. Shortly on the left is ❷ Surgeons' Hall. This is the headquarters of the Royal College of Surgeons of Edinburgh, which moved here in the 1830s. The building was also designed by William Henry Playfair. The College can trace its history back to the 16th century, when the Guild of Barbers carried out most surgical procedures. It has a fascinating museum showing how surgical procedures have changed over the centuries (see p.77).

During the Enlightenment era Edinburgh became a world-leading centre for medical teaching and research, and at one point about half of the students at the University were studying medicine. The University's Medical School was founded in 1726, though medicine had been taught in Edinburgh since the 16th century.

Hands-on experience, particularly at the anatomy school, was encouraged. This was in sharp contrast to the more theoretical approach to teaching medicine found in England. As a result, the doctors and surgeons produced by Edinburgh were in high demand, particularly throughout the British Empire. Graduates from Edinburgh also founded prestigious medical schools in other countries, including Harvard, Yale and Sydney medical schools.

Retrace your steps and walk down Drummond Street and then head left down the steps of Old Infirmary Lane. At the bottom on your right is the building that was home to the Royal High School between 1777 and 1829. ❸ **The Royal High School**, founded in the 12th century, was then the most prestigious in Edinburgh, attended by important Enlightenment figures including Robert Adam, geologist James Hutton (1726-97), encyclopaedist William Smellie (1740-95), philosopher Dugald Stewart (1753-1828), poet Robert Fergusson (1750-74). On the column to the left of the entrance door are the initials 'W.S.', believed to belong to the young Sir Walter Scott.

The Royal Infirmary voluntary hospital was also based nearby. Its origins go back to 1729, and in the 1740s it moved into a new building on this site designed by William Adam (father of Robert Adam). The hospital provided medical students with a practical training of a kind unrivalled anywhere else in the world at that time.

The Royal Infirmary later acquired the building vacated by the Royal High School, and eventually moved away to Lauriston Place in the late 19th century (see p.341). It is today located in Little France in Edinburgh and is the oldest hospital in Scotland.

Continue down to the Cowgate and follow the map across the junction. Bear right up Viewcraig Gardens (passing an NCP car park on the right). Shortly on the right, look out for a staircase and a sign for the **❹ James Hutton Memorial Garden**. Walk up to see the small garden, which contains a memorial plaque. James Hutton (1726-97) may not be a household name, but he was

one of the most influential figures of the Enlightenment era. He was born in Edinburgh, and attended the University aged just 14.

Hutton made a good living from a business making smelling salts from coal soot and in his spare time studied the many volcanic rock formations around Edinburgh, including nearby Salisbury Crags (visible from the garden).

He realised it must have taken an enormous period of time to form these rock formations. This was a radical theory in an age when most people (using the chronology of the Bible) believed the Earth was only around 6,000 years old. His *Theory of the Earth* was presented to the Royal Society of Edinburgh in 1785 and published three years later. It was a key moment in scientific history and earned Hutton the informal title of the 'Father of Modern Geology'. Hutton built a house at 3 St John's Hill, very near to this site, and lived there with his three sisters from 1770 until his death. He was also close friends with Adam Smith and Joseph Black, founding a society with them named the Oyster Club. Visitors to the Oyster Club included Benjamin Franklin and James Watt.

The Oyster Club, together with the Select Society and the Poker Club, were just a few of the many dozens of so-called 'convivial societies' that flourished in Edinburgh during the 18th century. They were essentially groups of like-minded people (usually men) who drank and dined together in taverns or private homes. The societies allowed members to discuss ideas, news and ambitions informally. Given that the clubs contained some of the finest minds of the Enlightenment, there is no doubt that many great ideas came about because of the challenge and debate that took place over

copious amounts of alcohol and food. These less formal avenues for discussion were also important because they allowed members to escape to some extent the official standards of behaviour governing the more educated classes of Edinburgh, which were still very conservative in nature and influenced by the church authorities.

Retrace your steps and follow the map up St John Street. A Masonic centre known as ❺ **Lodge Canongate Kilwinning** is located at 23 St John Street. It is believed to contain the oldest purpose-built Masonic meeting room in the world. In the 18th century many well-known men of the Enlightenment movement were members here, the most famous being the poet Robert Burns. The amount of socialising that took place during this period at societies and Masonic meetings is hard to fathom in the modern age. The lawyer and conservationist Lord Cockburn estimated that he had only spent on average one night a month at home with his wife over a 30-year period. The rest was largely spent dining and socialising at one of the many societies or clubs of which he was a member.

As you pass under the archway, look back to see a ❻ **plaque** up above. This records that the Scottish writer and poet Tobias Smollett (1721-71) stayed here with his sister in 1766 (see p.14).

Turn left to walk up Canongate, looking out for the ❼ **Maltese Cross** painted on the street. This commemorates the Cross of St John that once marked the boundary between Edinburgh and Canongate (see p.14).

On the left is **❽ Old Playhouse Close**, which dates from the 16th century. This was the site of the Canongate Theatre founded in 1747 by John Ryan of Covent Garden in London. It continued to operate until the 1780s. This was the first public playhouse to be built after the Reformation in Scotland; however, the theatre was under continual attack from the church authorities, who felt it was undermining public morality. In 1756, a controversial play entitled *Douglas* was put on at the playhouse. Its author, the Reverend

John Home (1722-1808), was a leading Scottish dramatist of the Enlightenment period. The philosopher David Hume, already mistrusted by the church authorities because of his suspected atheism, supported his friend Home's production of the play and even took part in dress rehearsals. However, the church exacted revenge by forcing John Home to retire as a minister.

Turn around and continue to walk back down Canongate, passing **❾ Moray House** on your right. This was built in around 1620 for the Countess of Home and named for her daughter, the Countess of Moray. In 1707 members of the Scottish Parliament hid in the summer house at the rear of Moray House to sign a document that ratified the political union between Scotland and England. They were fearful of an angry mob roaming the streets of Edinburgh who wanted to block the union and keep Scotland independent.

This political union ushered in a period of relative peace and prosperity for Scotland, which allowed the Enlightenment movement to flourish. In previous centuries the town council had built city fortifications to keep invading armies out of Edinburgh. However, as the 18th century progressed, the town council not only pulled down the old walls

Old Tolbooth Wynd

but also began to erect new civic buildings, most famously a New Town to the north. This increasingly ambitious, optimistic spirit was shared by many of Edinburgh's citizens.

Another past resident of Moray House was Lord Kames (1696-1782). In 1755, the New House, or south wing, was built. Private tenants occupied the top floor, Lord Kames being the first. Kames was one of the best-known men in Edinburgh during the Enlightenment period. A distinguished lawyer and judge, he also managed to find time to produce works on philosophy, history and agrarian reform. He was also a major patron of Adam Smith and helped found the Philosophical Society of Edinburgh (later becoming the Royal Society of Edinburgh).

Today Moray House is the oldest building within the University of Edinburgh, and is used for teacher training. JK Rowling completed her teacher training course here in 1996 – the same year as she received an offer to have the first Harry Potter book published.

Shortly on your right is the ❿ **Museum of Edinburgh** and opposite, housed in the ⓫ **old Canongate Tolbooth**, is The People's Story museum (see p.77). Each a wealth of information about Edinburgh and its history. The Museum of Edinburgh also contains some of the original designs for the New Town, which is seen later on.

Next to the Tolbooth is ⑫ **Canongate Kirk**. Canongate was a separate burgh outside Edinburgh until it was incorporated into the city in 1856. The kirk was completed by 1691 and is the burial place of four notable figures of the Enlightenment period – the philosopher and economist Adam Smith, philosopher Dugald Stewart, poet Robert Fergusson and Lord Provost George Drummond. A bronze statue of ⑬ **Fergusson** by David Annand stands outside the kirk gate.

Walk around to the south-west side of the kirkyard to see the burial place of the philosopher and political economist ⑭ **Adam Smith** (1723-90). Smith was born in Kirkcaldy and aged just 14 began to study moral philosophy at Glasgow University before moving to Oxford. He found intellectual life there very stifling and was punished for reading the works of David Hume.

He later delivered lectures at Edinburgh University and became a professor at Glasgow University. Smith is best known for *The Wealth of Nations* (1776) – regarded as the founding work of modern economic theory and still influential to this day. Smith was close friends with other key figures living in Edinburgh such as David Hume, Joseph Black and James Hutton. He also corresponded regularly with influential men such as Benjamin Franklin. In *The Wealth of Nations* Smith advocated an economic system based on individual self-interest that would achieve the greatest good for all. While his book was regarded as a bible of capitalism, Smith was not uncritical of unrestrained free enterprise.

View of Old Royal High School from Canongate Kirk

In 1778, Smith became commissioner for customs and lived in Panmure House (seen shortly). He became a founding member of the Royal Society of Edinburgh in 1783 – a key institution of the Enlightenment dedicated to 'the advancement of learning and useful knowledge'. Other founding members included Joseph Black, James Hutton and Benjamin Franklin.

On the wall adjacent to Smith is a plaque indicating the burial place of **⓯ George Drummond** (1688-1766). He served six times as Lord Provost between 1725 and 1764, and he more than anyone convinced the town council to build both the New Town (from the late 1760s) and a number of public institutions that would bring Edinburgh into the modern age.

Walk along the west side (roughly in line with the rear of the kirk) to visit the grave of **⓰ Robert Fergusson**, generally regarded as the finest Scots poet of the Enlightenment behind Robert Burns. Writing in the Scots dialect, he produced most of his work over just two years. After suffering a head injury, he was confined to the city asylum and died there aged only 24.

Fergusson was buried here in an unmarked grave, but years later, on his first day in Edinburgh, Robert Burns hurried to this spot to pay homage. He also paid for a memorial headstone that was erected in 1787 and contributed the epitaph on the stone. Burns described Fergusson as 'my elder brother in misfortune, by far my elder brother in the muse'. In the 19th century the author Robert Louis Stevenson planned to renovate the headstone but died before this could be achieved. Fergusson was a member of a well-known society named the Cape Club; the site of the tavern the club met in will be seen later.

Walk to the north-west corner of the kirkyard to see the imposing but now eroded tomb of the philosopher and mathematician **⑰ Dugald Stewart** (1753-1828). He attended the Royal High School and lectured at the University, holding the prestigious chair of moral philosophy for 25 years.

Stewart's popularity among his students is credited with helping to spread the ideas of the Scottish Enlightenment internationally, particularly to America. He also gave a series of lectures on Adam Smith in 1798 that helped the economist's work to become widely known for the first time. Stewart also promoted the early career of Robert Burns, using his influence to ensure that the poet got a favourable review of his first book of poems (known as the *Kilmarnock edition*) from an important Edinburgh magazine. The publisher of the magazine, William Creech, later published Burns' next major work of poetry – known as the *Edinburgh edition*. Stewart lived near to here in Canongate, and students frequently lodged at his house. One student was the young Henry John Temple, later Prime Minister Lord Palmerston.

On the east side of the kirkyard is the burial place of Agnes Maclehose – or **⑱ 'Clarinda'** – a married woman whom Robert Burns fell in love with during his time in Edinburgh. In their love letters, Burns adopted the name 'Sylvander' and Agnes 'Clarinda'. Their romance inspired Burns' famous song *Ae Fond Kiss* (1791), and ended sadly when Agnes left Scotland for

the West Indies to attempt an unsuccessful reconciliation with her slave-owning husband.

When finished at the kirk, continue along Canongate and take the next left at Dunbar's Close to visit **⑲ Dunbar's Close Garden**, one of the most tranquil hidden spots in central Edinburgh. It is laid out in the style of the 17th century, and is a good stopping place if you have brought food with you.

Continue along Canongate to some modern shops at Lochend Close and walk through the archway to reach **⑳ Panmure House**. Built in 1691, it housed Adam Smith for the last 12 years of his life and is his only surviving home in Scotland. He came here after being appointed as the commissioner of customs in Scotland. He died in the north wing of the house on 17 July 1790.

Though astonishing to us now, on his death bed Smith expressed regrets that he had achieved so little in his life. This seems to have been a common concern among his contemporaries. Many juggled demanding careers alongside their intellectual pursuits, and yet still seem to have felt they were under-achievers. This suggests that one characteristic of the Scottish Enlightenment was the drive among many of its key figures to succeed and leave a legacy.

Follow the map down Lochend Close, crossing the road and then walking up the flight of steps on the other side.

As you walk up the hill, the path comes to a junction. Turn right and directly ahead is the **㉑ Burns Monument** by Thomas Hamilton (1784-1858) whose construction began in 1831. You might imagine the desire to commemorate Scotland's greatest poet came from Edinburgh residents, but the plan was in fact proposed by a Mr John Forbes Mitchell who lived in Bombay, while the organising committee was formed in London.

22 Old Royal High School

The best feature of the monument – a statute of Burns by the prominent sculptor John Flaxman – has long since been moved to avoid the pollution emitted by a gas works that once stood down below in Canongate. You can see the statute today in the Scottish National Portrait Gallery on Queen Street. It is no coincidence that the figure of Burns once looked over the final burial place of his great love – 'Clarinda' – seen earlier in Canongate kirkyard.

The structure that remains was designed by the architect Thomas Hamilton, who was also responsible for another Burns monument at Alloway and for the Royal High School (seen shortly). Hamilton based the design on the Choragic Monument of Lysicrates in Athens, at a time when the Greek Revival was in full swing. You can still see the original – dating from the 4th century BC – in Athens.

From here follow the map westwards, and on the north side of the road you will see the **22 Old Royal High School** building. Regarded as the finest neo-classical structure in the city, it was erected for the Royal High School between 1826 and 1829. As with the Burns Monument, it was designed in a Greek Revival style by Thomas Hamilton, and contributed to his reputation as one of the finest architects of his era. During the 20th century the Royal High

School moved away to Barnton, and this building has been largely empty for nearly 50 years. So many prominent figures of the Enlightenment attended the school that it has had, arguably, a greater influence on Scotland than any other school in the country.

In the early 1990s, the former school building was considered for the site of the new Scottish Parliament. A new building was constructed instead, and in recent years this site has stood defiantly empty while a bad-natured debate rages over its future use as a luxury hotel or music school. This is just one example of a series of controversies about the redevelopment of historic sites in the city that are said to be threatening Edinburgh's much valued World Heritage Site status. A number of prominent residents of Edinburgh, including the novelist Alexander McCall Smith, have been vocal in the campaign to preserve the former school building for a more appropriate use.

*View of Canongate Kirk*

Continue on, with magnificent views across Canongate, particularly of the kirk, against the backdrop of Arthur's Seat and Salisbury Crags.

On your left you pass the entrance to ㉓ **Jacob's Ladder**, a steep staircase carved from the volcanic rock of Calton hill.

Soon you reach on the left the monolithic, art-deco styled ㉔ **St Andrew's House**, headquarters of the Scottish Government. It dates from 1939 and was once the largest metal-framed building in Europe. The site contains the graves of ten

25

murderers who were executed after being held prisoner in Calton Jail which once stood here. The novelist Jules Verne, during his visit to Edinburgh in 1859, described the jail as being like a small medieval town, and Lord Cockburn thought this a strange site for its location – considering it 'bad taste to give so glorious an eminence to a prison'. The jail operated here from 1817 until the 1920s, before being demolished. Some remains of old cells exist inside, and the door of the 'Death Cell' – the place where prisoners were held just before their execution – can be seen today in the Beehive Inn in the Grassmarket (see p.122).

Opposite St Andrew's House is Calton Hill, and you can walk up the steps to see some of the city's most prominent monuments. The striking **25 Nelson Monument** was completed in 1815, and celebrates Admiral Horatio Nelson. The tower contains a time ball once used as a signal for ships down at Leith and in the Firth of Forth – it is still dropped at 1pm daily.

As you go up the steps, you soon see the **26 Dugald Stewart Monument**. This celebrates the famous professor of moral philosophy, whose tomb you may have seen earlier at Canongate Kirk. The structure probably looks familiar – like the Burns Monument, it was based on the Choragic Monument of Lysicrates in Athens. The Royal Society of Edinburgh – one of the few Enlightenment-era institutions that still thrives today in the city – commissioned the monument. It was designed by William Henry Playfair and completed in 1831.

Just behind the Dugald Stewart Monument is the **㉗ City Observatory**. The original design was by the architect James Craig (1739-95) – whose plan for the New Town of Edinburgh was adopted by the town council in 1767. This made him for a short while one of the best-known architects of the Scottish Enlightenment. The original plan comprised an observatory and house for the astronomer but only the house and wall were completed before funds ran out. The observatory was later built by Playfair, based (loosely) on the Temple of the Winds in Athens. Today Observatory House is all that remains of Craig's design.

You may wish to visit other monuments on Calton Hill at this point if you have time. Otherwise retrace your steps and follow the map to reach **㉘ Old Calton Burial Ground**. This opened in 1718 and many prominent figures of the Enlightenment period were buried here, most notably David Hume, the scientist John Playfair (who helped publicise the work of James Hutton), and the publisher William Blackwood (responsible for the influential *Blackwood's Edinburgh Magazine*).

Observatory House

**㉙ David Hume's tomb** was designed by Robert Adam. After Hume died, his friends kept a vigil by the burial site for eight days, fearing that their friend's atheist beliefs might cause hostile members of the pubic to desecrate his grave.

The Political Martyrs' Monument, a prominent obelisk, commemorates members of The Friends of the People – a movement that sought the liberalisation of the voting system and political reform. A number of members of The Friends were sentenced to deportation in 1793 after being convicted of sedition, and the harsh treatment of the men shocked many people. During the Enlightenment period, the mood of the public gradually swung in favour of political reform, no doubt helped by the events of the French and American Revolutions, and radical theories espoused by thinkers such as Thomas Paine, author of the influential *Rights of Man* (1791).

The Great Reform Act of 1832 was the first great shake-up of Britain's antiquated voting system, and the Monument was commissioned in 1844 by the Friends of Parliamentary Reform in England and Scotland. It is yet another construction designed by Thomas Hamilton, who is buried in this cemetery.

Follow the map along Waterloo Place, laid out in the year in which that memorable battle was fought.

*View from Dugald Stewart Monument towards North Bridge, Old Calton Burial Ground and David Hume's tomb*

You will soon cross **30** **Regent Bridge**, built in a Greek Revival style. Designed by Archibald Elliot (1761-1823) under the direction of the prominent engineer Robert Stevenson (1772-1850), the great arch below is ornamented by two open arches, supported by elegant Corinthian columns. Regent Bridge was opened on 18 August 1819 during the visit of Prince Leopold of Saxe Coburg, an event recalled today by an inscription.

The bridge is a reminder of a man who might have become a major figure in our history books. Leopold was a German prince who fought for the Russians against Napoleon, and later married Princess Charlotte, the only child of the Prince Regent (later George IV). Charlotte died in 1817, causing much public misery (largely because many people despised her father). If Charlotte had lived, Victoria would not have become queen, and Leopold would have played an important role in British history. Leopold remained very popular with the public – explaining why his visit to Edinburgh warranted the inscription on the bridge. He become the first King of the Belgians and was also instrumental in arranging the marriage of Victoria, his niece, to his nephew, Prince Albert.

At the junction on the right is **31** **Register House** (see also p.154). It was designed by Robert Adam and though work on it began in 1774, money problems meant it was not finished until the 1820s. Its purpose was to house the Public Records of Scotland and it continues this function today (although the role is shared with other sites).

The development of new civic buildings like Register House and (from the late 1760s) of the original New Town, is covered in more detail in another walk (see walk 6). However, buildings such as this – bold, functional and ambitious – embody the spirit of the Enlightenment in a physical form.

Follow the map to reach St Andrew Square, the eastern edge of the original New Town. Continue along the south side to reach the junction with South St David Street.

On this corner once stood the home of the philosopher **David Hume**. With the passage of time, he vies with Adam Smith for the title of being the greatest thinker produced during the Scottish Enlightenment period. He began his studies at Edinburgh University when he was only 12 years old and within a few years had already begun to prepare what became his most significant work – *A Treatise of Human Nature* (completed when he was only 26). In it, Hume tackles a number of complex matters, such as the origin and meaning of thoughts.

*A Treatise of Human Nature* was not initially well received and during his own lifetime Hume was best known as a historian, his *History of England* becoming a standard text. He was a rationalist and an empiricist, believing proof was needed to establish a truth.

Hume was generally regarded as an atheist, a stance that made him deeply unpopular with the church authorities in particular. They charged him with heresy and ensured that he was passed over for academic posts at the University. For many years he made his living from a variety of jobs. These included acting as tutor to a nobleman, serving as secretary to the British Embassy in Paris (where he became a friend of Voltaire), and in his later years serving as keeper of the Advocates' Library in Edinburgh.

When Hume came to live here, the New Town was still a huge building site and this was one of the earliest streets to be laid out. Hume was very proud of his new house, writing in a letter: 'Our New Town... exceeds anything you have seen in any part of the world'.

He was a sociable man, hosting many dinners at the house with regular guests including Adam Smith, James Hutton and historian William Robertson (1721-93), (see p.143). Sadly Hume's original house was demolished in the 1950s, though it is thought the remains of his once famous wine cellar may still exist.

In October 1771, Benjamin Franklin arrived in Edinburgh and stayed with Hume for several weeks. He later wrote a tongue-in-cheek account of his arrival at the house of the city's most notorious atheist: 'Thro' Storms and Floods I arrived here on Saturday night, late, and was lodg'd miserably at an Inn; But that excellent Christian David Hume, agreeable to the Precepts of the Gospel, has received the Stranger and I now live with him at this House in the new Town most happily.'

Walk down St David Street towards the 200-foot high ❸❷ **Scott Monument**, which was completed in 1844. You can walk up the 287 steps inside the Monument – see p.77 for details.

Sir Walter Scott (1771-1832) was brought up in the Old Town and then, like Hume, moved to the New Town. He was educated at the Royal High School and then at Edinburgh University. As a teenager he was taught by eminent men such as Dugald Stewart. He followed his father into the legal profession and for many years combined this with an increasingly stellar literary career that began with poetry but progressed to historical novels principally set in Scotland.

Described as the inventor of the historical novel, he became famous throughout Europe and America during his own lifetime and is credited with shaping how Scotland was seen throughout the world. Scott's most famous works are *Waverley*, a stirring tale of the Jacobite Rebellion; *Rob Roy*, about the Highland bandit; and *The Heart of Midlothian*. He also wrote books about themes from English history, most notably *Ivanhoe* and *Quentin Durward*.

Though respected today, Scott's books are no longer widely read. The huge size of the Monument is therefore an insight into how much he was once revered and into how literary tastes can change. Another legacy is in New York's Greenwich Village, where Art Street was renamed Waverly Place (sic) after Scott's most famous book in 1833.

The latter part of Scott's life was not easy. At the height of his fame, he faced bankruptcy after the collapse of a publishing and printing business he had a financial stake in. He was forced to sell his house in the New Town (on North Castle Street), and proceeded to work himself into an early grave in order to pay back creditors. Sadly, in recent years a small number of people have committed suicide by jumping from the top of the Monument.

You will now start to leave the New Town. Walk south, crossing Waverley Bridge, to reach Cockburn Street, named for Lord Henry Cockburn (1779-1854). Cockburn was an influential Edinburgh lawyer, writer and conservationist and one of the first people to try to prevent the demolition of the city's historic buildings. The Cockburn Association, which was founded in 1875, seeks to continue Lord Cockburn's efforts to protect Edinburgh's cultural and architectural heritage.

David Hume once walked a similar route to the one you are walking now. However, in his day the Nor' (or North) Loch, which had dominated the area north of Edinburgh Castle since medieval times, had only recently been drained. The land was still very boggy and Hume got caught in the thick mud. Fearing for his life, he called out to some old women nearby to save him. However, when they recognised him, they required the atheist to recite the Lord's Prayer before they would help him. Hume, ever the pragmatist, duly complied and was saved.

As you go up Cockburn Street, look out on the left and right for the narrow entrances into ㉝ **Craig's Close**. The Isle of Man Arms once stood on Craig's Close and this is where the Cape Club, mentioned earlier as having the poet Robert Fergusson as a member, held its meetings. Fergusson's most famous poem – *Auld Reekie* – is dedicated to his friends at the club, known as the Knights of the

Cape. Other members of the club included the famous portrait painter Henry Raeburn and Deacon Brodie (more on him shortly).

During the 19th century nearly all the great convivial societies of the Enlightenment age closed down (the Cape Club disbanded in 1841). However, the Cape was re-founded in the 1960s and still continues to this day as the Cape Society. Other institutions such as the Royal Society also continue, having their origins in the informal meetings of early members.

Craig's Close used to run up to the Royal Mile but the upper section was built over in the 1930s. On the north side of Cockburn Street you can see lettering in the pavement identifying the northern part of Craig's Close (now truncated) and there is also a plaque remembering Fergusson.

Just ahead on the right you pass ❸ **Anchor Close**; walk up this narrow thoroughfare to reach the Royal Mile. It was in Anchor Close that members of an exclusive drinking club named the Crochallan Fencibles met in a tavern owned by Daniel Douglas.

The club was founded by William Smellie (1740-95), the first editor of the *Encyclopaedia Britannica*, and members included Adam Smith and Robert Burns.

Smellie was a close friend of the poet and introduced him to the club. The two of them spent many a drunken evening here singing songs and reading out poems. It was in the tavern that Burns delivered his *Address to a Haggis* for the first time, now heard at many a Burns Supper.

35

36

36

Smellie was educated at the Royal High School and became a master printer. From his printing works located very near to here he produced the so-called *Edinburgh edition* of Burns' poems published by William Creech (there is more about Creech shortly).

At the top you reach the Royal Mile. Turn right, with St Giles' Cathedral visible up ahead on the left. Walk towards St Giles and just before you reach it look for the statue of **35 Adam Smith** (see p.55 for more info).

Facing the cathedral on the north side are the grand **36 City Chambers**, known as the Royal Exchange when opened in 1760 by Lord Provost George Drummond. The building was designed by John and Robert Adam and was intended to serve as a meeting place for the city's merchants. However, they never really took to the venue (preferring to huddle around the Mercat Cross), and it was later taken over by the town council.

By the entrance to City Chambers look out for hand-prints in the pavement belonging to a number of famous modern-day Scots and Edinburgh residents including the authors JK Rowling and Ian Rankin and the sportsman Sir Chris Hoy.

Walk up the Royal Mile, and immediately on the right is the location of Mary King's Close. Now a popular tourist attraction, the old Close was buried underground when the Royal Exchange was constructed, and many myths grew up around it, including that plague victims had been walled up inside The old tenements once stood seven storeys high on each side. The Close was re-opened to the public in 2003, and you can take a tour down below street level to see what remains – said to be haunted. It is fairly eerie, and crime novelist Ian Rankin features the Close in his book *Mortal Causes* (1994), with a corpse being discovered down below at the beginning of the story.

Continue uphill, passing **37** **St Giles' Cathedral** on the left. It was founded in the 12th century and much of the structure you see today dates from the late 14th century. It is not really a cathedral as it has not served as the seat of a bishop for hundreds of years; however, the title has stuck. The Mercat Cross stands near the cathedral and for centuries this was where public proclamations were read out and merchants met to discuss business. It was really the heart of the Old Town and during the Enlightenment period an Englishman visiting Edinburgh remarked (to William Smellie) that he could stand here and 'in a few minutes take 50 men of genius by the hand'. During this golden age of the Enlightenment, Edinburgh's population was no bigger than Dunfermline's today, a fact that helps explain why all the great figures of the period knew each other.

37  St Giles' Cathedral and Mercat Cross

The middle of the Royal Mile by the cathedral was once dominated by the Luckenbooths. This ramshackle group of buildings, which stood here from the 15th century until being demolished in the early 19th century, were home to a number of booksellers and other businesses.

One was a shop run by the poet and wigmaker Allan Ramsay (1686-1758). In 1752 he established a 'circulating library' – the first lending library in Scotland. Its popularity reflected an almost insatiable demand for reading among sections of Edinburgh's highly literate population. Ramsay tried to set up a theatre in Edinburgh but the church authorities forced him to close the venture down.

Later the publisher William Creech (1745-1815) took over Ramsay's shop. Today Creech is best known for publishing the works of his friend Robert Burns. He was even the subject of a Burns poem, *Willie's Awa!*. The shop became known as 'Creech's Land' and attracted many literary figures and hangers-on. Creech also served at one time as Lord Provost of Edinburgh.

As you continue along, you pass a grand statue of the philosopher ❸❽ **David Hume**.

Cross the road to stop outside ❸❾ **Deacon Brodie's Tavern**. When Robert Burns arrived in Edinburgh on 28 November 1786, he stayed in Baxter's Close, near where the pub is now located. He had a tiny room situated below a brothel, and one of the first things he did after arriving was to pay his respects at the grave of the poet Robert Fergusson in Canongate Kirk.

Known as the 'Ploughman Poet' because of his early life working on his family farm, Burns became a literary sensation after his arrival in Edinburgh. He was helped along the way by his Masonic connections and

patronage from men like Dugald Stewart. Burns died aged only 37, and his popularity was confirmed by the fact that around 10,000 people attended his funeral.

The pub is named after William Brodie (1741-88), who was a respected member of the establishment in Edinburgh until it was discovered he was leading a secret life as a burglar. Brodie was convicted in 1788, and hanged in front of 40,000 people very near to here. His secret life inspired Robert Louis Stevenson's *The Strange Case of Dr Jekyll and Mr Hyde*.

Continue on and look for **40** **Lady Stair's Close** on the right (there is a sign above referring to Burns' residence near here). If you walk down here you can visit the **Writers' Museum**, situated in Lady Stair's House. This contains a wealth of information on the lives and work of Scotland's writers, including Robert Burns, Sir Walter Scott, and Robert Louis Stevenson.

Just up from here on the Royal Mile is **41** **Gladstone's Land** on the right. This 17th-century high-tenement house is open to the public and run by the National Trust for Scotland (see p.77) for details).

Close by is **㊷ James Court** (it has three different entrances – take the middle one called 'Mid Entry'). James Court was built in 1727 and – at the time – was seen as a spacious and innovative development compared to what existed up to that point in the Old Town. However, the construction of town houses in the New Town from the late 1760s meant James Court soon became unfashionable.

Before then, James Court attracted upmarket residents including David Hume and the lawyer and biographer James Boswell (1740-95). David Hume later moved from here to Paris and wrote 'I am sensible that I am misplaced, and I wish twice or thrice a-day for my easy-chair, and my retreat in James's Court'. Hume later abandoned the Old Town to live on St David Street at the site visited earlier.

Boswell is best known for his biography of Dr Johnson, and Johnson visited him at James Court. Boswell's diaries also provide a fascinating insight into life in Edinburgh during the Enlightenment period, when everyone seemed to know everyone else. By way of example, on 27 June 1774 Boswell went to see 'the foundation stone of the Register House laid' and two days later attended a dinner with 'Bob [Robert] Adam the architect who was lively enough, though vain'. On 7 July 1776 Boswell talked with Hume as the philosopher lay dying at his house in the New Town. And on 3 December 1782 he went to Lord Kames' house and there found 'Mr [James] Craig the architect showing him plans of the New Town'.

Boswell was by profession a lawyer, and was obsessed by his social standing. While he liked David Hume, he had reservations about being associated publicly with an atheist who was regarded as being immoral by the church and many others: 'I was not clear that it was right in me to keep company with him'. Boswell perhaps was not aware of the irony of such a view, given that he frequently recorded in his diary the details of his mammoth drinking sessions, encounters with prostitutes and subsequent painful bouts of gonorrhea. He also found time to write a poem in favour of slavery.

In return, Hume was fond of Boswell, but obviously had his own concerns – he once described Boswell as 'very good-humoured, very agreeable, and very mad'.

Leave James Court and cross over the Royal Mile to visit ❸ **Riddle's Court**. Dating from 1590, it was built for John McMorran, Edinburgh's wealthiest merchant. Eight years later, James VI hosted a lavish royal banquet here. David Hume lived here for a few years from 1751, and after moving in wrote to a friend that he was now head of a household of 'two inferior members – a maid and a cat'. The walk ends here.

To return to the start point, you can walk back down the Royal

Mile and right along George IV Bridge. If you continue along, you pass ❹ **Greyfriars** – covered in more detail by a separate walk (see p.125). A number of people mentioned on this walk are buried here including William Adam and his son John (brother of Robert Adam), Joseph Black, James Hutton, William Smellie, Allan Ramsay and William Creech.

From Greyfriars you can turn up Chambers Street (passing the National Museum of Scotland) and soon return to Old College, where the walk began. ●

**43**

44 *Greyfriars*

## SHOP...

**Grassmarket Market**
39 Grassmarket, EH1 2HS
*www.stockbridgemarket.com*

## VISIT...

**Surgeons' Hall Museums**
Nicolson Street, EH8 9DW
*www.museum.rcsed.ac.uk*

**Museum of Edinburgh**
142 Canongate, EH8 8DD
*www.edinburghmuseums.org.uk*

**The People's Story**
*The Royal Mile, 163 Canongate,*
*EH8 8BN*
*www.edinburghmuseums.org.uk*

**The Scott Monument**
East Princes Street Grdns, EH2 2EJ
*www.edinburghmuseums.org.uk*

**Old City Observatory**
*38 Calton Hill, EH7 5AA*
*www.edinburghmuseums.org.uk*

**Mary King's Close**
2 Warriston's Cl, High St, EH1 1PG
*www.realmarykingsclose.com*

**St Gile's Cathedral**
High St, EH1 1RE
*www.stgilescathedral.org.uk*

**The Writers' Museum**
Lawnmarket, Lady Stair's Close,
EH1 2PA
*www.edinburghmuseums.org.uk*

**Gladstone's Land**
477b Lawnmarket, EH1 2NT
*www.nts.org.uk/gladstones-land*

**National Museum of Scotland**
Chambers Street, EH1 1JF
*www.nms.ac.uk*

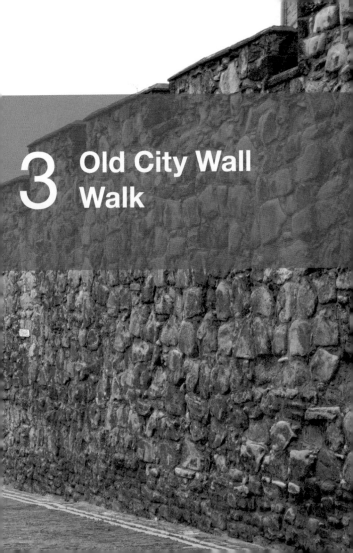

# 3 Old City Wall Walk

# Old City Wall Walk

1. Granny's Green Steps
2. Grassmarket
3. Castle Wynd South
4. Flodden Wall
5. Flodden Wall tower
6. Telfer Wall
7. George Heriot's School
8. Tefler Wall
9. Oddfellows Hall
10. Flodden Wall
11. Flooden Wall plaque
12. Bristo Port
13. Bedlam Theatre
14. Potterrow Port
15. Old College
16. Rutherford Bar
17. Flodden Wall tower
18. Flodden Wall
19. Old Surgeons' Hall
20. Cowgate Port
21. Boyd's Entry
22. Netherbow Port
23. Scottish Storytelling Centre
24. World's End public house
25. Tweeddale Court
26. Carving of Netherbow Port
27. Waverley Station

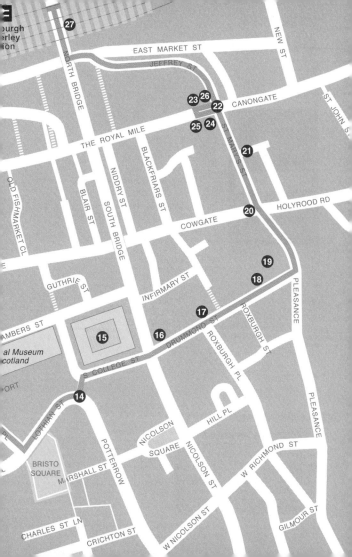

# Old City Wall Walk

Start: Johnston Terrace
Finish: Waverley Station
Distance: 1.8 miles

GRANNY'S GREEN STEPS

This walk begins on Johnston Terrace on the south side of Edinburgh Castle (see p.99). Look out on the south side of Johnston Terrace for some steep stairs known as ❶ **Granny's Green Steps** and pause for a couple of minutes to read a little about the history of the city walls before continuing.

Before the 15th century there already existed some fortified walls around Edinburgh, but not a great deal is known about them. In 1450, King James II, fearing an English attack, authorised a fundamental overhaul of the city's defences. The resulting wall became known as the King's Wall, and was completed by 1475. It began at the castle and ran eastwards, parallel with the High Street on the north side and the Cowgate to the south. It ended just before modern St Mary's Street in the east and turned up slightly to join the High Street.

After the English army inflicted a terrible defeat on the Scots at Flodden in 1513, the town council realised that the King's Wall was no longer adequate to protect the city from an English attack. The following year the council ordered a levy to be taken from citizens to finance the construction of a new fortified wall. This was intended to extend further out than the King's Wall, and to protect

ERECTED ON A SITE NEAR THE
EXTREMITY OF THE ANCIENT TOWN
WALL BUILT IN THE REIGN OF JAMES II
KING OF SCOTS A.D. 1450 FOR THE
PROTECTION OF EDINBURGH
AGAINST INVASION

a number of important religious institutions and newer streets that had grown up outside the older fortifications.

This new wall – known as the Flodden Wall – was largely completed by 1560. In the 17th century Edinburgh had again

View of Edinburgh Castle from Granny's Green Steps

*Granny's Green Steps*

increased in size and so a further extension of the city wall was planned. This extension, which took place between 1628 and 1636, is known as the Telfer Wall.

Sadly, the 15th-century King's Wall has all but disappeared, and only sections of the 16th-century Flodden Wall and 17th-century Telfer Wall remain today. This walk will largely follow the route of the Flodden and Telfer Walls.

Before you walk down Granny's Green Steps, look up to see a sign on the wall of the structure on the corner which recalls that this was once the site of a fortification built during the reign of King James II. This is the fortification that became known as the King's Wall.

Walk down the steps, the line of which follows the route of the Flodden Wall. Most of the Flodden Wall was designed to ensure a clear space of approximately 24 feet on the outside and 12 feet on the inside. It reached a height of up to 25 feet at some places and was around 4 feet thick.

The wall was punctuated by six substantial gates – or 'ports'. These (in the order you visit each site on the walk) were the West Port, Bristo Port, Potterrow Port, Cowgate Port, Netherbow Port and New Port – all demolished before 1800. There were also a number of fortified towers built at strategic points along the wall, but only one survives today.

At the bottom of the stairs you reach the ❷ **Grassmarket**, where for hundreds of years a number of markets were held and public executions took place. The history of the Grassmarket is covered by a separate walk, (see walk p.101).

Walk along the north side of the Grassmarket until you reach ❸ **Castle Wynd South** on the left. Walk up the Wynd for about 20 yards. Parts of the current wall may incorporate remnants of the original 15th-century King's Wall, which ran east to west ahead of you. This gives a sense of how much smaller Edinburgh was in the 15th century as only the area to the north of here was deemed worthy of protection behind the city wall.

Retrace your steps and continue along the west side of the Grassmarket. On the pavement you can see different-coloured paving slabs (punctuated by a long thin bench) that mark the direction of the ❹ **Flodden Wall**. Stop at the junction with West Port Road on the south-west corner. The West Port gatehouse in the Flodden Wall, built in 1514, was located just here. All traffic in and out of the west side of the Grassmarket would have gone through the West Port; the area outside to the west used to be known as Wester Portsburgh.

*Vennel*

Political union with England in 1707, and the final defeat of the Jacobite uprising led by Bonnie Prince Charlie in 1746, signalled a new era of peace in Scotland from the mid-18th century. At the same time, the population of Edinburgh had grown from around 10,000 in the 16th century to five times that number by 1750. This led to the inevitable conclusion that a city wall no longer served any purpose and in fact was proving a hindrance – particularly as increasing levels of traffic struggled to get through the narrow city gates.

As a result, by 1800 all six of the main gates in the wall had been demolished, and over the next few decades large sections of the wall itself were pulled down. West Port survived until 1787, though its name continues to be used for the gap left behind.

Follow the map up the steep stairs of the Vennel, its name derived from the Old French word *venelle*, meaning a small street or passage. The Vennel follows the line of the Flodden Wall, which continued south of the West Port gate. About half way up on the left, stop to look at the only remaining **5 tower** in the

Flodden Wall that survives today. This part of the Vennel features in a scene from the 1969 film *The Prime of Miss Jean Brodie* starring Maggie Smith and based on the novel of the same name by Muriel Spark.

From the tower, the Flodden Wall originally ran eastwards, parallel with the south side of the Grassmarket and along the north side of George Heriot's School. It then joined Greyfriars (seen later). Today it is not possible to walk along this route because of the buildings that have since sprung up.

Instead, continue up the Vennel. On the left is a section of the ❻ **Telfer Wall**. As mentioned earlier, this was an extension of the Flodden Wall and was built between 1628 and 1636. The reason for the extension was that in the early 17th century the town council acquired a further 10 acres of land south of the Flodden Wall, and wanted the city wall to protect this new district. The extension wall is named after John Telfer (or Taillefer), the master mason responsible for its construction.

Continue on to Heriot's Row. George Heriot's School lies to your left. George Heriot (1563-1624) was a wealthy goldsmith and money-lender whose principal client was James VI of Scotland. After the death of Elizabeth I, James became James I of England. Heriot joined the King in London and amassed a huge fortune. He bequeathed money on his death to found a charitable school (then called a hospital) for the orphans of burgesses and freemen of Edinburgh, which opened in 1659.

At the top turn left onto Lauriston Place, and continue past **7 George Heriot's School**. The distinctive shape is said to have inspired JK Rowling when she was creating Hogwarts' school attended by Harry Potter. As you walk on the north side of Lauriston Place you are following the route of the Telfer Wall extension – just before the shops on the left, look out for another surviving section of the **8 Tefler Wall** (there is a sign).

On the north side of this surviving section stands Greyfriars Kirk and kirkyard (visited shortly). A charity poorhouse that was built in the 1740s also stood on the other side of the wall.

Turn left down Forrest Road – again following the direction of the Telfer Wall. (If you turn down Forrest Hill on the left you can see on the north side some remaining walls from the poorhouse that date from the first half of the 19th century.)

On the right-hand side, almost opposite the entrance to Forrest Hill, is a pub that occupies the former **9 Oddfellows Hall**. The origins of the Oddfellows movement are obscure, but it probably began in the 17th century as a reaction by lower-ranking members of trade guilds – apprentices and fellows – to the way the guilds were being run by their senior members. These lower ranks decided to set up their own self-help organisations, originally meeting in taverns. As the members were drawn from an 'odd' assortment of different trades, they became known as 'odd fellows'.

By the 19th century the Oddfellows movement had grown substantially, and a large network of Oddfellows' grand lodges were built throughout the country. Many lodges had their own unique traditions, customs and ranking systems that appear to be modelled on the Masonic movement. Each provided social activities, accommodation, assistance and support for members.

This hall dates from 1870 and was used by three different Orders of Oddfellows. After the creation of a larger welfare state after WWII, many Oddfellows organisations began to close. This hall stopped being used by the Oddfellows by 1960.

Shortly on the left, you reach the entrance to Greyfriars Kirk. Greyfriars is covered by a separate walk (see p.124), but you may wish to extend your visit now to look around the kirkyard in more detail.

Follow the map right over to the west side of the kirkyard (passing the kirk on your left). With George Heriot's School visible ahead, you should now be able to see an original section of the ❿ **Flodden Wall** (there is a sign). Originally the Flodden Wall ran eastwards from the tower on the Vennel you visited earlier and met the west side of Greyfriars. It then ran south until it reached the bottom of the kirkyard before turning east again until it reached the next major gate, the Bristo Port.

FLODDEN · WALL

Flodden Wall & Greyfriars Kirk

To visit the site of Bristo Port, retrace your steps out of Greyfriars and turn right. Walk around the bend of Forrest Road and just by No 5 on the wall look out for a ⑪ **plaque** that commemorates the location of the Flodden Wall. There is a **line in the pavement** that shows the direction the Flodden Wall then took. This line continues over the traffic island opposite, so cross at the traffic lights (remembering to look down to see the line but also being careful of traffic!).

Ahead of you is the National Museum of Scotland (see p.99). Inside, in an area not open to the public, is another section of the Flodden Wall. Ask politely and a member of staff may show you. Try to find the unusual sundial on the museum's corner by Bristo Port.

Walk down Bristo Port – a short road that leads up to the museum. This is approximately where the city gate named ⑫ **Bristo Port** once stood (it is also sometimes called Society Port or Greyfriars Port). The gate was built in around 1515 and was demolished in the late 18th century.

From Bristo Port, the route of the Flodden Wall ran eastwards to another gate in the wall – Potterrow Port. However, the creation of Chambers Street and the museum to the immediate east of here means the original route of the Flodden Wall cannot be followed. (A section of the wall is visible within a corridor inside the museum; however, you can only see this by prior appointment.)

Opposite Bristo Port you will see a gothic church on the corner. This dates from 1849 and is today the ⑬ **Bedlam Theatre**,

home of the excellent Edinburgh University Theatre Company. The former church stands near the site of the Edinburgh Bedlam Mental Institute, originally attached to the poorhouse mentioned earlier. It was here that one of Scotland's great poets, Robert Fergusson, died in October 1774 aged just 24. In Fergusson's time, inmates were treated badly, more like inmates in a prison. Many would have been kept chained to walls, and sleeping on straw.

Follow the map along Bristo Place and at the end turn left along the pavement that skirts the south side of Lothian Street. Shortly you will see on your right an underpass (going under Lothian Street) that contains a sign for ⑭ **Potterrow Port** – a fairly uninspiring reminder of the third city gate that stood just to the north of here in the vicinity of West College Street (which you pass on the left-hand side).

Potterrow Port was demolished in the 1780s. It is sometimes referred to as the 'Kirk o'Field' Port on account of it having been near the site of the old medieval church of St Mary in the Fields, otherwise known as 'Kirk o'Field'. This is where Lord Darnley

was murdered with his servant in 1567 after a massive gunpowder explosion. His wife, Mary, Queen of Scots, was suspected of being involved in the murder plot and it ultimately led to her abdication.

The Kirk o'Field later became the site of the first College in Edinburgh in the 16th century. This was later founded as the University of Edinburgh in 1582.

Continue along South College Street, with ⑮ **Old College** on your left (see Enlightenment Walk p.45). The route of the Flodden Wall ran along the south side of Old College and where you are walking now. The foundation stone of Old

15

College (originally New College) was laid in 1789. By this time, Edinburgh University was world famous, and the city authorities wanted a new, grand building to reflect this prestige. The original design was by the famous architect Robert Adam. It took several decades to complete the construction, by which time another famous architect, William Henry Playfair, had taken over from Adam. If you have time take a moment to visit the grand courtyard of Old College.

Cross over Nicolson Street to enter Drummond Street – previously called Thief Raw. You are back on the original route of the Flodden Wall. In medieval times the area to the north of here was dominated by one of the religious institutions that the town council of the 16th century wanted the Flodden Wall to protect – the Dominican Priory of Blackfriars.

On the left-hand side look out for an usually shaped building, with the date 1834 above the window. Today a restaurant, this was until a few years ago the famous **⓰ Rutherford Bar**. Founded in 1834, Rutherford's was a spit-and-sawdust establishment popular with generations of University students, including Robert Louis Stevenson and Arthur Conan Doyle. *Peter Pan* author JM Barrie once imagined a meeting with Stevenson: 'he led me away from the Humanities to something that he assured me was much more humane – a howff called Rutherford's where we sat and talked'. You can see what the bar once looked like if you watch the gritty, Edinburgh-based film *16 Years of Alcohol* (2003), directed by Richard Jobson.

The Blackfriars Priory was founded in the 13th century and dominated this part of Edinburgh until it was largely destroyed in 1559 during the upheavals caused by the Scottish Reformation. By the 18th century a number of important Edinburgh institutions were located on the site of the priory, including the Royal Infirmary, the Royal High School and the Surgeons' Hall.

Many notable figures associated with the Scottish Enlightenment (see Walk 2) attended the Royal High School when it was based here in the late 18th century. Old Surgeons' Hall is where Dr Robert Knox gave private lessons at the school of anatomy. His career was ruined when it was discovered he had purchased corpses from the notorious murderers William Burke and William Hare (Burke was hanged in 1828 for his part in the murders; Hare and Knox remained free men).

Continue along Drummond Street. It meets Roxburgh Place on the right and this is where another **⑰ tower in the Flodden Wall** used to be located. Carry on, and after a few minutes on the left you will see a substantial section of the **⑱ Flodden Wall**, with **⑲ Old Surgeons' Hall** (see p.99) visible on the north side.

This surviving section of wall extends around the corner as you turn left into the Pleasance, and gives the best impression of how the fortification would have appeared in the early 17th century. Follow the map northwards, with the wall to your left. All the land inside the wall would have once been part of Blackfriars Priory.

Shortly you reach the junction with the Cowgate on the left. This is the location of the fourth city gate – **⑳ Cowgate Port** (also known as Blackfriars' Port). Another port was later built just beside it across St Mary's Wynd that became known as St Mary's, or Pleasance, Port.

The Cowgate was the first large street in Edinburgh to be built after the High Street, and by the 16th century had become very fashionable and popular with wealthier residents. However, it lay outside the 15th-century King's Wall and was therefore vulnerable to attack. The Flodden Wall solved this problem by running to the south of the Cowgate.

Continue to follow the route of the Flodden Wall by walking up St Mary's Street – originally St Mary's Wynd before a major redevelopment of the area took place in the late 19th century. The city wall ran up the west side of this route and local householders were obliged to raise their garden walls as part of the defensive lie.

On you right look out for ㉑ **Boyd's Entry**. In the 18th century this was the site of James Boyd's Inn, also known as the White Horse Inn. Look out for a memorial on the corner that records the arrival at the inn of Dr Samuel Johnson (1709-84) on 14 August 1773. He had come to Edinburgh to meet his friend (and later biographer) James Boswell (1740-95) before they set out on a tour of the Hebrides. Boswell's account of the trip was later published in *The Journal of a Tour to the Hebrides* (1785), and Johnson published his own account in 1775.

Boswell went on to write the renowned biography *The Life of Samuel Johnson* (1791). He recalled that while staying at the inn here, Johnson 'asked to have his lemonade made sweeter, upon which the waiter with his greasy fingers, lifted a lump of sugar, and put it into it. The indignant Doctor threw it out of the window.'

Boswell and Johnson later left the inn to walk up to Boswell's house (in James Court off the Royal Mile). Boswell recorded that 'it was a dusky night: I could not prevent his being assailed by the evening effluvia of Edinburgh'. During Boswell's era it was still normal for residents in Edinburgh's multi-storey tenements to empty their rubbish and toilet waste onto the street. The warning call to those below was 'Gardy loo!' – from the French 'prenez garde à l'èau'.

The Netherbow Port

Stop by the junction with The Royal Mile. The fifth city gate was called the ㉒ **Netherbow Port** and was situated just here. It was the largest and best known of all the entrances

23 *Scottish Storytelling Centre and John Knox House*

into Edinburgh, and strategically important as it restricted access to and from Canongate (which runs down the hill and towards Holyrood). For many centuries Canongate was a separate administrative and political district (or 'burgh') outside of Edinburgh.

A number of gates were built in this location. The last one was constructed in 1603 and demolished in 1764. Brass bricks on the cobbled surface trace the outline of the Netherbow, so do not forget to look down.

In 1544, Netherbow Port was attacked by the English during a campaign known as the 'Rough Wooing' (on account of Henry VIII wanting to marry his son Edward to the infant Mary, Queen of Scots – then aged only three). The gate was blown open and the city was burned and pillaged. This contributed to the general view that the city walls and gates were not actually very useful in preventing attacks. However, they did serve other purposes – facilitating the collection of duties from those going in and out of the city, and helping to control crime and the outbreak of diseases.

Head left, uphill. On the right-hand side is the  ㉓ **Scottish Storytelling Centre**, which features an old sign (with the date 1606) and a bell, both from the original Netherbow Port. Next door (and part of the Storytelling Centre) is John Knox House, which dates back to 1470. John Knox (c.1513-1772) is probably

Scotland's most famous clergyman, and one who did more than anyone to ensure the Protestant Reformation swept through the country. Whether he actually lived here or not is a moot point (there is a plaque in nearby Warriston Close that may indicate the site of his dwelling place).

If you look back you will see the ㉔ **World's End public house**. This area was known as the World's End for many poor people living in the Old Town because this

part of Edinburgh was literally the end of their world as they could not afford to pay entrance fees to go in and out of the Netherbow Gate and so stayed inside the walls.

Almost opposite the old sign of 1606 is **㉕ Tweeddale Court**, which you enter to reach a courtyard. On the west side is a high stone wall which may be a rare remnant of the 15th-century King's Wall that also ended at Netherbow, though the gate in those days was about 50 yards to the west of the site just visited. The stone shed is thought to be an example of a sedan-chair storage house dating back to the Georgian period.

Tweeddale House directly in front of you dates from the 16th century and some of its occupants would have no doubt seen the Flodden Wall being completed. The unusual name Tweeddale comes from the Marquess of Tweeddale, adviser to King Charles II, who bought the house in 1670.

In 1806, a notorious murder took place here when a little girl discovered the body of a bank messenger named William Begbie, who had been stabbed to death. He had been carrying a package of £4,000 in banknotes to a bank in Leith. No one was ever caught, but months later the bulk of the money was discovered hidden in a wall.

Retrace your steps to the High Street and towards the junction. Up high on a building on the left is a **㉖ carving** that shows what the Netherbow Port looked like. The heads and body parts of executed prisoners were regularly left on spikes above the gate to serve as a deterrent.

The clock from the Netherbow Port can been seen today in the frontage of the Dean Gallery, part of the National Gallery of Modern Art that houses the Paolozzi collection.

Return to the junction again and now continue north along Jeffrey Street. This was laid out in the late 19th century after the passing of the Improvement Act of 1867 which removed unsafe buildings and swept away slums in parts of Edinburgh. When the Flodden Wall ran along this part of the route it was known as Leith Wynd.

Follow the map and head north past **㉗ Waverley Station**. This follows the route of the last section of the Flodden Wall and the station stands on the approximate site of New Port – the sixth of the main gates in the city wall. Just to the west of here lay the Nor' Loch (or North Loch) – an expanse of water created in medieval times which formed a natural defensive barrier to the north. The loch was drained in the 18th century and today is the location of Princes Street Gardens.

This is the end of the walk. You can continue north to reach Princes Street which has a number of bus and tram connections. ●

## VISIT...

**Edinburgh Castle**
Castlehill, EH1 2NG
*edinburghcastle.scot*

**Greyfriars Kirk & Museum**
Greyfriars Place, EH1 2QQ
*www.greyfriarskirk.com*

**Surgeons' Hall Museums**
Nicolson Street, EH8 9DW
*www.museum.rcsed.ac.uk*

**National Museum of Scotland**
Chambers Street, EH1 1JF
*www.nms.ac.uk*

**Scottish Storytelling Centre & John Knox House**
43-45 High Street, EH1 1SR
*www.scottishstorytellingcentre.com*

**Edinburgh University Anatomical Museum**
University Medical School, Teviot Place, EH8 9AG
*www.ed.ac.uk/biomedical-sciences/anatomy*

## SHOP...

**Grassmarket Market**
39 Grassmarket, EH1 2HS
*www.stockbridgemarket.com*

Maggie Dickson's pub (see p.119)

# 4 Grassmarket Walk

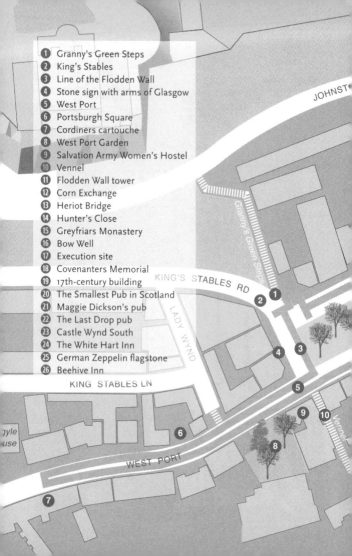

1 Granny's Green Steps
2 King's Stables
3 Line of the Flodden Wall
4 Stone sign with arms of Glasgow
5 West Port
6 Portsburgh Square
7 Cordiners cartouche
8 West Port Garden
9 Salvation Army Women's Hostel
10 Vennel
11 Flodden Wall tower
12 Corn Exchange
13 Heriot Bridge
14 Hunter's Close
15 Greyfriars Monastery
16 Bow Well
17 Execution site
18 Covenanters Memorial
19 17th-century building
20 The Smallest Pub in Scotland
21 Maggie Dickson's pub
22 The Last Drop pub
23 Castle Wynd South
24 The White Hart Inn
25 German Zeppelin flagstone
26 Beehive Inn

JOHNST

Granny's Green Steps

KING'S STABLES RD

LADY WYND

KING STABLES LN

Vennel

West Port

yyle
use

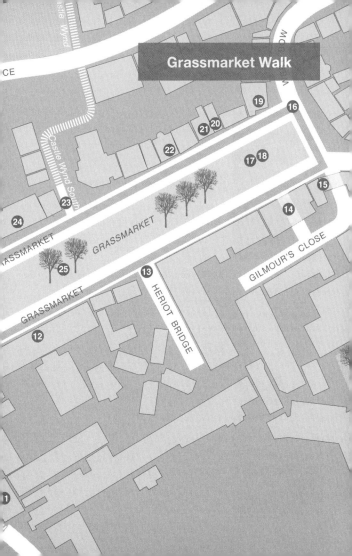

Castle Wynd

CE

Castle Wynd South

GRASSMARKET

GRASSMARKET

GRASSMARKET

GRASSMARKET

HERIOT BRIDGE

GILMOUR'S CLOSE

19

16

21 20

22

17 18

15

14

23

24

25

13

12

# Grassmarket Walk

Start: Granny's Green Steps
Finish: Beehive Inn
Distance: 0.5 miles

This short walk around the Grassmarket takes about an hour, though there are plenty of cafés, restaurants and pubs to delay you along the way! Each Saturday there is also an excellent food, gifts and crafts market that runs between 10am and 5pm.

The walk begins on the north-west corner by King's Stables, at the foot of ❶ **Granny's Green Steps**.

One of Edinburgh's liveliest spots, the Grassmarket was probably laid out to its current dimensions by the end of the 14th century. It comprises a 230-yard-long rectangle, situated below the dramatic lines of Edinburgh Castle.

Today it is largely dominated by the entertainment and tourist industries, and is at its most vibrant (or irritating) at weekends, when the hordes of hen and stag parties are very much in evidence. However, in the past this is where for centuries a number of major markets were held – right up until 1911. It was also where many hundreds of public executions took place.

To begin the walk, pause at the junction with ❷ **King's Stables**, named after the horse stables originally established here by an English garrison occupying the castle in the 14th century. This is where the late-medieval kings such as James IV would have kept horses used for hunting or in jousting tournaments. When the monarchy began to live in Holyrood Palace rather than the castle, the stables became less important and were sold in the 16th century.

*Foot of Granny's Green Steps*

Look down on the floor near the bottom of the steps to see a line marked on the ground. This follows the ❸ **line of the Flodden Wall** – a fortified city wall that was built after 1514 to protect the south side of Edinburgh. It was named after the Battle of Flodden of 1513, in which the Scots were heavily defeated by the English – a disaster that caused Edinburgh's town authorities to plan for better defences in case the English attacked. The wall started from the castle before cutting along the west side of the Grassmarket and continuing up the Vennel – visited shortly (see also Old City Wall Walk p.77).

Turn around and on the opposite side of the road is a ❹ **stone sign** with the words 'Let Glasgow Flourish' and the arms of that city. The tree at the centre of the arms relates to St Mungo, Glasgow's patron saint. It is said that a holy fire he was guarding was put out by some boys, but St Mungo managed to get the fire going again using wood from the hazel tree.

Seeing the arms of Glasgow in the centre of Edinburgh is perhaps surprising, particularly given the traditional rivalry between Scotland's two greatest cities. The explanation is that this building, dating from c.1880, was once occupied by the Edinburgh and Glasgow Bank, hence the arms of each city were set up above the entrance. The bank, once

independent, was taken over by the Clydesdale Bank in the 1850s and as a brand name has long since disappeared.

Walk on, stopping by the pedestrian crossing. The road leading away from the Grassmarket is called ❺ **West Port**, named after the former fortified entrance gate in the Flodden Wall that was built in the 16th century and remained here until the 1780s.

Follow the map about 200 yards along West Port on the north side. In the 19th century this area was blighted by slums, often populated by the families of Irish labourers who came to Edinburgh to work on new constructions such as the Union Canal between Edinburgh and Falkirk.

Two of the most notorious characters in Edinburgh's history, William Burke and William Hare, are closely associated with this area. They originally came to Edinburgh from Ireland for labouring work, but when Hare chanced upon an old man in a lodging house who had died from natural causes, he decided to make some money by selling the corpse to Dr Robert Knox, a prominent anatomist who taught medical students.

*Lady Wynd and King's Stables Lane*

The money was so good that Burke and Hare wanted to continue this illicit trade, but as there were not enough fresh corpses available to be stolen from Edinburgh's graveyards, they decided to murder the weak and vulnerable whom they came upon in the slums. During 1828 they killed some 16 people, with Knox choosing not to ask too many questions. Scotland's antiquated laws made it very difficult to source fresh corpses for medical examination, so anatomists were often reduced to dealing with 'body snatchers'.

Some of the victims were lured to their deaths at Hare's lodgings in nearby Tanner's Close. The Close has long disappeared but was approximately on the site of today's King's Stables Lane and Argyle House (seen shortly).

Eventually Burke and Hare were caught, though Hare escaped death by giving King's evidence against Burke. Burke was hanged before a crowd of around 25,000 on the Lawnmarket, with hundreds of onlookers paying for the privilege of getting a better view from one of the overlooking windows.

In a cruel final twist of fate, Burke's own corpse was displayed to the public and later dissected in front of medical students. Hare, having avoided execution, fled, and various myths grew up around his fate. Dr Knox's career never recovered thanks to his association with what became known as the West Port Murders and an Edinburgh mob even burned his effigy in the streets. If you visit the Anatomical Museum within Edinburgh University you can see Burke's skeleton on display. A 19th-century children's rhyme about the West Port Murders went as follows:

> *Up the close and down the stair,*
> *In the house with Burke and Hare.*
> *Burke's the butcher, Hare's the thief,*
> *Knox, the boy who buys the beef.*

Carry on walking up West Port, looking out for a sign on the right for ❻ **Portsburgh Square**. The name recalls a burgh named Wester Portsburgh that lay outside the city proper until 1856. This square was built in 1900 on the site where a tannery once operated – a reminder that this area was once home to a number of industrial and manufacturing businesses.

Further up West Port on the right is Argyle House, mentioned earlier because of its Burke and Hare connection. It is regarded as one of the ugliest buildings in Edinburgh; however, behind the 'brutalist' surface it is home to the UK's largest technology-firm incubator, housing dozens of innovative companies. Walk back down West Port on the south side, where there are several second-hand book shops – definitely worth a browse.

Nestled between the bookshops, a sign for 'Cordiners Land' can be seen above a doorway. Above it is an old ❼ **cartouche** from 1696 that was once used to mark premises controlled by the Cordiners – a trade incorporation or guild that controlled the production of leather goods and shoes in Edinburgh. You can see a depiction of the knife use to cut the leather. The name of the guild is derived from Córdoba, which produced the finest leather then available.

Retrace your steps towards the Grassmarket, passing along the same route as the farmers would have taken into the city through the West Port gate. King Charles I also arrived through the gate in 1633, the year of his Scottish Coronation.

Argyle House

On the south side is ❽ **West Port Garden** – opened in 1910 and one of a number founded in slum areas of the city during the early 20th century, inspired by the work of the pioneering urban planner Patrick Geddes (1854-1932). It was primarily intended to provide local children in the slums around Grassmarket with somewhere to play safely and is a reminder of the area's bleak past.

Re-enter the Grassmarket along the south side. On the right (just by the pedestrian crossing) is a former **❾ Salvation Army Women's Hostel**, built in a distinctive art nouveau style. It also dates from 1910, a period when the social conditions in this area were still very poor and various missions sought to alleviate the suffering. It remained in operation until the 1980s.

On the south side you will see a foundation stone dating from 1911 that refers to Mrs Bramwell Booth of the Salvation Army. Florence Soper was born in 1861, and joined the Salvation Army in London. She met and later married Bramwell Booth – son of the army's founder General William Booth. Bramwell went on to lead the Salvation Army after his father died and Florence herself held very senior roles within the organisation.

Florence's marriage to Bramwell in 1881 was unusual. William Booth himself conducted the ceremony in a public hall with 6,000 members of the Salvation Army in attendance. The audience had paid money at the entrance and this was then used to purchase a pub in London (the Eagle which features in the rhyme 'Pop Goes the Weasel'), which was then converted into a Salvation Army hall.

Continue along the south side, stopping by the entrance to the ❿ **Vennel** whose steps climb steeply up to Lauriston Place. The Vennel follows the line of the old Flodden Wall mentioned earlier and if you have time you can walk up to see a rare remaining ⓫ **tower** (about half way up). The Vennel – a Scots corruption of the old French word 'venelle' meaning small street – features in a scene from the 1969 film *The Prime of Miss Jean Brodie* starring Maggie Smith and based on the novel of the same name by Muriel Spark. In the book the schoolgirls and Brodie approach the Grassmarket, 'which none of the girls had properly seen before, because none of their parents was so historically minded as to be moved to conduct their young into the reeking network of slums which the Old Town constituted in those years'.

As you walk along the south side, stop to look around the Grassmarket, with a superb view up to Edinburgh Castle. Many of the buildings on this south side are fairly modern, with those to the north, east and west being mainly Victorian. From 1477, after a charter was granted by James III, the Grassmarket became one of Edinburgh's official market places. This was initially for cattle, and later horses, corn and timber were also sold here.

The Grassmarket was attractive as a market venue because it sits in a valley. This meant cattle and horses could be sold here without having to drive the animals up the steep climb to the Old Town. Other kinds of goods could be transported here and offloaded before being hauled up the hill by carters using barrows. All this activity led to many inns and stables being established here. It is almost impossible to imagine how busy the Grassmarket was in the past, when all manner of goods and animals were sold here, but if you look online for a picture entitled *The Horse Fair in the Grassmarket*, painted by James Howe in the 1830s, you will get a pretty good idea.

*View of castle sketched by JMW Turner*

In later years a number of places the carters once slept in were converted into hostels for the homeless, and during the 19th century the Grassmarket become notorious as a slum. The western side was used for stables and yards in which animals could be kept before being sold and slaughtered. The origin of the name Grassmarket itself is thought to be derived from the hay, corn and seed once sold here by farmers.

Continue along the south side, reaching a modern hotel complex on the right. This stands on the site of a ⑫ **Corn Exchange** that was erected in 1849. It replaced an earlier corn market that had stood since 1716 on the east side of the Grassmarket. This older corn market was sketched by the famous painter JMW Turner in 1818.

If you stand in front of the hotel and look towards the castle, you see another view that Turner sketched of the north side of Grassmarket – he probably stood (or sat) just where you are now. Another of Turner's Edinburgh sketches is titled *Figures Carrying Goods and a Hand-Cart* – most likely inspired by the carters he would have seen moving goods around the Grassmarket.

The Corn Exchange building of 1849 would have been an imposing sight, but sadly it was demolished in 1965. It was designed by David Cousin (1809-78), who was also responsible for building a number of churches and cemeteries in Scotland, including Dean and Warriston Cemeteries in Edinburgh. He learnt his craft under the famous Edinburgh architect William Henry Playfair. The trade activities carried out here were transferred out to a new Corn Exchange in Gorgie in 1912.

Saturday market

Just after the hotel is ⓭ **Heriot Bridge** – although as you can see, there is no actual bridge to be found! George Heriot's School lies just to the south of Grassmarket and opened in 1659. The main approach to the school used to be from a bridge along this street from the Grassmarket, but it was removed in the 1760s as it was blocking other traffic.

The Heriot Brewery was once based here. It was just one of around 40 breweries that operated in central Edinburgh during the 19th century. A brewery may have been founded here as early as the 16th century, and during the 19th century it traded under the name John Jeffrey & Co. The site here became very cramped and brewing moved away to Roseburn in the 1860s. Selling its products around the world, the Heriot Brewery continued there until 1900.

Continue along and stop outside ⓮ **Hunter's Close** – named after Alexander Hunter (1729-1809), a physician. By the entrance look out for a plaque that recalls that this is where in 1736 Captain John

HUNTER'S CLOSE

*Bow Well and West Bow*

Porteous (c.1695-1736) was hanged from a dyer's pole. The events that led up to the lynching of Captain Porteous began that same year, when two smugglers named Andrew Wilson and George Robertson were sentenced to death for attacking a collector of customs. In those days smugglers were tolerated by many members of the public, who saw the customs men as servants of oppressive English rule.

Many citizens of Edinburgh were therefore delighted when Robertson managed to escape his guards before the day of execution. Wilson was not so fortunate and was hanged at the Grassmarket. The vast crowd watching the execution became agitated and threw missiles at the town guard, which was under the command of Captain Porteous – a figure already deeply unpopular with many in the city because of his high-handed behaviour. Porteous and the town guard tried to retreat but he soon lost his temper and ordered his men to fire back. About six people were killed, and another dozen injured. Porteous was found guilty of murder but political pressure applied from England saw him receive an official pardon.

The Edinburgh mob, however, saw things differently and he was dragged from the Tolbooth prison to the Grassmarket and lynched. He was buried in Greyfriars kirkyard nearby (see Walk 5). The authorities in London were furious, one result being that the Lord Provost of Edinburgh was arrested and held for three weeks, while the city itself was fined £2000.

Shortly you reach the south-east corner. Just beyond here lies the Cowgate and Candlemaker Row. The latter was home to the candlemakers whose manufacturing workshops once added to the bustle and noise of the Grassmarket area.

At this junction – just to the south – once stood the ⓕ **Greyfriars Monastery**, which was founded in the 15th century and survived until 1559 when it fell victim to the upheavals of the Scottish Reformation. The monastery's garden was later donated by Mary, Queen of Scots, to the city for use as a graveyard, with a kirk being built in the early 17th century (see Walk 5, p.125).

In medieval times the Knights Templar also had a property near here in the long-demolished Temple Close (near to where the Apex Hotel now stands). After the Templars were suppressed in the early 14th century, their property was taken over by the Knights of Saint John, a similar military-religious order founded during the era of the Crusades (see p.14).

Cross over to the middle of the east side of the Grassmarket. To your right, the West Bow runs up to become Victoria Street. In the middle of the street stands ⓖ **Bow Well**, which dates from 1681. It provided local residents with fresh water from the city's first piped water supply which had its source in Comiston (about 3 miles to south of here), where there were twenty-seven spring heads, many named after animals.

Walk over to the former ⓗ **execution site** – the shape of a gallows is helpfully marked out on the ground. Public executions began here in the mid-17th century and continued right up until the late 18th century. The large sandstone block, in which the gallows-tree was secured, could still be found here until 1823.

Nearby is the ⓲ **Covenanters Memorial**, which recalls another dark period in Edinburgh's history. The Covenanters were a religious and political movement, their named derived from the National Covenant signed by the movement's followers in 1638 at Greyfriars. By signing, they were confirming their opposition to interference by the Stuart Kings in the affairs of the Presbyterian Church of Scotland.

The Covenanters unsurprisingly sided with Parliament against Charles I during the Civil War. However, when Charles II became King, he exacted his revenge. During what became known as the 'Killing Time', thousands of Covenanters in Scotland were executed by forces loyal to the monarchy. The memorial marks the spot where over 100 Covenanters were executed between 1661 and 1688.

Walk over to the north-east corner. On the left is a rare surviving ⓳ **17th-century building**. On its eastern side (facing West Bow), you can see a sign above what was once a doorway, with the date 1616. This is probably the oldest building in Grassmarket, though it has been rebuilt in later centuries.

The architect James Craig (1739-95) lived very near here from 1773 until his death. His greatest moment was in 1766, when he won

the competition to produce a plan for the New Town while he was still in his twenties. He went on to design a number of individual buildings but his career never lived up to this early promise. He died in poverty, the grand New Town he had designed still being laid out over a 100-acre site (see Walk 6 and 7).

In 1775 an anonymous guide to prostitutes was published called *Ranger's Impartial List of the Ladies of Pleasure in Edinburgh*. This included a listing for Miss Stewart, who lived in the Grassmarket. She

16 _Bow Well & 19  17th Century building_

was described as 'extremely fond of the game, but observes a great deal of decency when she approaches the altar of Venus. We would advise her to accept the offer which a gentleman lately made her, to enter into the honourable state of matrimony.'

Continue along the north side of the Grassmarket. Stop outside ⑳ **The Smallest Pub in Scotland**, which measures just 17feet by 14feet. Above the pub is a sign for 'Mission Hall' and a plaque below the sign for Curries Close. This commemorates the Grassmarket Mission that was once located here, which was founded by James Fairbairn in 1886. The Mission provided food and clothing for the residents of the Grassmarket slum dwellings, and Fairburn would organise talks here by some of the most prominent people in Edinburgh in order to raise donations.

After WWII many missions like this began to decline as the growing welfare state provided the poor with increasing levels of assistance. In addition, the number of people living in the Grassmarket area began to fall, so in 1989 the original trust behind the Mission sold the halls here. However, the Grassmarket

Mission trust continues to this day to support various initiatives to tackle poverty, and has an office just near here in Candlemaker Row.

Continue along, passing the ㉑ **Maggie Dickson's pub**. This is named after a fishwife from Musselburgh who was hanged in the Grassmarket in 1724 for murdering her illegitimate baby. However, after her body was taken away, she regained consciousness in her coffin as it lay on a cart returning to her home town. This apparent resurrection caused the authorities a problem as they were not allowed to execute someone twice for the same crime under the rule of 'double jeopardy'. She was therefore allowed to remain free and became known as 'half-hangit Maggie'.

Shortly after this is ㉒ **The Last Drop public house**, named for the drop suffered by prisoners who were hanged from the gibbet that once stood nearby. It is said to be haunted by the spirit of a small girl wearing medieval garments, and ghosts in the cellar apparently call out the names of members of staff while they are up in the bar serving. Beside the pub (on the left) you can see a lintel above the door that came from an original house here dated 1634 now incorporated into the current early 20th-century structure. The inscription reads 'Blessed be God for all his Giftis'.

Continue along the north side and stop by ㉓ **Castle Wynd South**. Parts of the Wynd may incorporate remains of the 15th-century city wall – known as the King's Wall – that once protected the south of Edinburgh. It was superseded in the 16th century by the more extensive Flodden Wall mentioned earlier.

Back on the Grassmarket, look out for the Petit Paris restaurant, which offers an excellent French-themed menu and is just one of many pleasant places to eat at on this walk.

The Crawley Tunnel (or Aqueduct), built in 1821, ran north from The Meadows, right under the Grassmarket, before ending near the foot of The Mound. Some think it went much further, crossing Princes Street to end right in the heart of the New Town. Designed to bring fresh water into the city, significant sections of the underground tunnel survive and sections continue to be uncovered – most recently during excavations for the city's new tram system in 2009.

A few doors down is **24 The White Hart Inn**, which has a claim to be Edinburgh's oldest pub, with parts of the structure such as the cellar dating back to 1516. Most of the building above ground level dates from the 1740s. It is named for the incident in 1128 when King David I encountered a white hart (hart being an old English word for a stag) while hunting. Fearing for his life, he tried to grab the antlers but instead found himself holding a cross. This encounter inspired him to found Holyrood Abbey in Edinburgh.

The White Hart is often described as one of the most haunted pubs in Scotland, with numerous apparitions sighted in the cellar over the years. A psychic researcher conducted a formal report into the sightings here in 2004. The area investigator concluded: 'I do feel that there is something strange going on in the White Hart Inn'.

For many centuries the inn would have been one of the busiest places in Edinburgh, as generations of farmers, carriers and coach travellers stayed here on their way to and from the city. The Grassmarket was a major arrival and departure point for passenger coaches and goods wagons, and the White Hart was just one of a number of coaching inns located in this area.

The inn would also have benefited from the trade of those coming to witness public executions, or to bet at the cock-fighting pit that stood near here in the late 18th century. In the 1700s, the White Hart was notorious for hosting marriages of eloping couples who wanted a cheap, secret ceremony performed with no unnecessary questions being raised. For a while the inn even had its own resident priest who would preside over the marriage ceremonies.

It is said that Burke and Hare got some of their victims drunk in the White Hart before luring them back to the lodging houses of the West Port, where the murders took place (see p.107). The poet Robert Burns (1759-96) stayed here for a week in 1791 during his last visit to Edinburgh. It was here that he had his third and final meeting with his muse, Agnes Maclehose. She was married

and about to leave Edinburgh for Jamaica to seek a reconciliation with her estranged husband. In their love letters, Burns used the pseudonym 'Sylvander' and she used 'Clarinda'. Their parting inspired one of Burns' most famous works – *Ae Fond Kiss*. 'Clarinda' was later buried in Canongate Kirk (see Canongate Walk p.23).

In front of the White Hart in the central section is a **25** **flagstone** whose inscription records that this is where a bomb a German Zeppelin bomb fell in April 1916. One person was killed here and a further 12 people died across the city in the same raid. The next World War also had an impact on life in the Grassmarket. In 1940, a number of cafés were owned by local Italian residents, and several had their windows smashed in by a mob after Mussolini declared war on Britain.

Just past the White Hart is the **26** **Beehive Inn**, also a former coaching inn. In 2008 archaeologists discovered signs of human habitation near to the Beehive that have been dated to between 1500 and 1300 Bc. Previously it had been thought this part of Edinburgh had remained uninhabited until the 13th or 14th century. Inside, the door of the condemned cell from Calton Jail (see p.62) can be seen – a grim reminder of Edinburgh's darker past. It is likely that the murderer Burke walked through this door when he left Calton Jail on his way to execution in front of thousands of onlookers in 1829. Continue west to reach the starting point and the end of the walk. ●

*Grassmarket*

## SHOP...

**Grassmarket Market**
39 Grassmarket, EH1 2HS
*www.stockbridgemarket.com*

## EAT/DRINK...

**Petit Paris**
38-40 Grassmarket, EH1 2JU
*www.petitparis-restaurant.co.uk*

## VISIT...

**Scottish Genealogy Society**
15-16 Victoria Terrace, EH1 2JL
*www.scotsgenealogy.com*

**Edinburgh Castle**
Castlehill, EH1 2NG
*www.edinburghcastle.gov.uk*

**Greyfriars Kirk & Museum**
Greyfriars Place, EH1 2QQ
*www.greyfriarskirk.com*

**National Library of Scotland**
George IV Bridge, EH1 1EW
*www.nls.uk*

**National Museum of Scotland**
Chambers Street, EH1 1JF
*www.nms.ac.uk*

*Elizabeth Paton's tomb, p.138*

# 5 Greyfriars Cemetery Walk

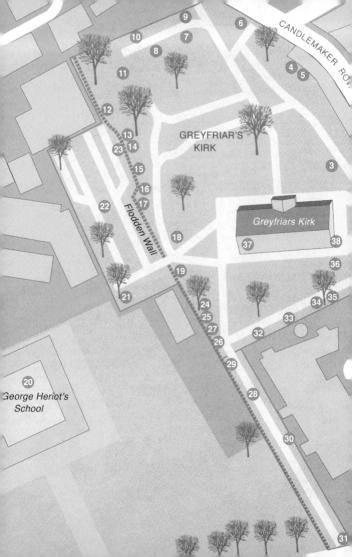

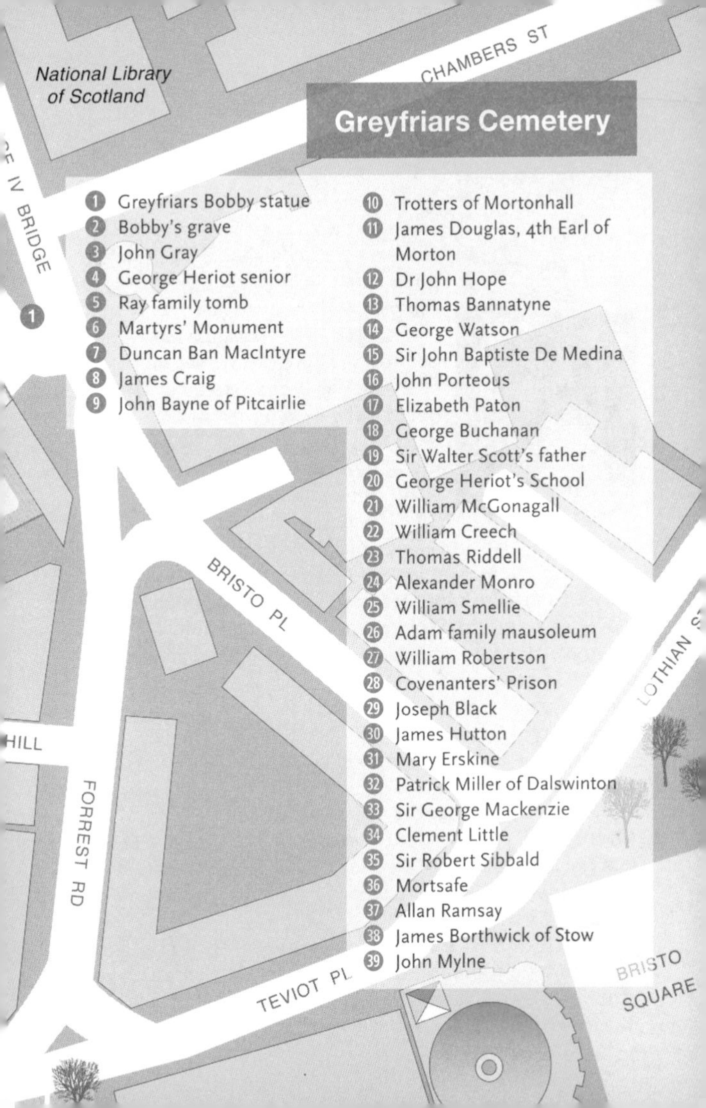

National Library of Scotland

CHAMBERS ST

## Greyfriars Cemetery

1 Greyfriars Bobby statue
2 Bobby's grave
3 John Gray
4 George Heriot senior
5 Ray family tomb
6 Martyrs' Monument
7 Duncan Ban MacIntyre
8 James Craig
9 John Bayne of Pitcairlie
10 Trotters of Mortonhall
11 James Douglas, 4th Earl of Morton
12 Dr John Hope
13 Thomas Bannatyne
14 George Watson
15 Sir John Baptiste De Medina
16 John Porteous
17 Elizabeth Paton
18 George Buchanan
19 Sir Walter Scott's father
20 George Heriot's School
21 William McGonagall
22 William Creech
23 Thomas Riddell
24 Alexander Monro
25 William Smellie
26 Adam family mausoleum
27 William Robertson
28 Covenanters' Prison
29 Joseph Black
30 James Hutton
31 Mary Erskine
32 Patrick Miller of Dalswinton
33 Sir George Mackenzie
34 Clement Little
35 Sir Robert Sibbald
36 Mortsafe
37 Allan Ramsay
38 James Borthwick of Stow
39 John Mylne

IV BRIDGE

BRISTO PL

LOTHIAN ST

HILL

FORREST RD

TEVIOT PL

BRISTO SQUARE

# Greyfriars Cemetery Walk

Start: Greyfriars Cemetery
Finish: Greyfriars Cemetery
Distance: 0.5 miles

This short walk takes you on a tour of some of the most notable burial places and tombs within the Greyfriars kirkyard. It can be completed in about an hour.

As you walk towards the entrance of Greyfriars you are likely to see tourists posing by the lifesize bronze statue of ❶ **Greyfriars Bobby** – the Skye terrier that has done more to spread the name of Greyfriars around the world than any of the eminent men and women buried here.

The best-known version of the Bobby story has it that he belonged to John Gray, an Edinburgh night-watchman. Gray died in 1858 and was buried in Greyfriars. For the next 14 years, Bobby returned again and again to his master's grave, fed by a local restaurant owner named John Traill. Traill also stood up for Bobby when the town council required all dogs to be either licensed or terminated. Eventually the sympathy created for Bobby ensured that the Lord Provost of Edinburgh himself paid for Bobby's licence.

After the dog's death, it was secretly buried here by Traill and his friends, and the legend continued to grow – perhaps best told in the 1961 Disney film *Greyfriars Bobby* and in a film from 1949 in which Lassie stands in for the terrier. It has also been suggested that when the real Bobby died, local businessmen replaced him with a succession of terriers that lay by Gray's burial spot in order to keep the tourist trade going.

The memorial and fountain were unveiled in 1873, funded by the wealthy philanthropist Baroness Angela Burdett-Coutts (her family money was largely derived from Coutts, the Queen's bank). The memorial was the work of the eminent Scottish sculptor William

*Statue of Greyfriars Bobby*

Brodie (1815-1881) and is Edinburgh's smallest listed structure. A reminder of the days when a fresh water supply was still uncertain for many residents of Edinburgh, the fountain served more than just a decorative purpose. Fittingly, it had an octagonal lower drinking basin for dogs. The words *'Greyfriars Bobby. From the life just before his death'* are inscribed around the base of Bobby's statue.

As you enter Greyfriars itself, the kirk lies directly ahead. Between you and the kirk is the ❷ **burial place of Bobby**. You will often find sticks or other tokens on his grave. People's affection for this little dog doesn't appear to be diminishing despite the passing years.

The kirk is usually open to visitors Monday to Saturday from April to October, subject to services taking place. Before you begin a walk around the kirkyard, it is worth reading a little about the history of Greyfriars itself. In the 15th century this area became home to a Franciscan monastery known as Greyfriars after the colour of the habits worn by the friars. In fact, the habits were actually more of a brown colour, but in medieval times the shade of brown worn was commonly described as being grey.

The Franciscans provided medical care for the poor, a role they fulfilled until they were forced out of Edinburgh in 1559 during the Scottish Reformation. The friars then fled to the Netherlands.

In 1562, the monastery's garden was gifted by Mary, Queen of Scots, to the people of Edinburgh to be used as a burial ground. Up until then most burials had taken place in the churchyard of St Giles on the Royal Mile, but that site had become overcrowded. Mary's gift was not just an act of kindness – during the summer months the putrid smell of rotting corpses at St Giles kirkyard was making life unbearable for the local residents.

*17th-century monuments*

A kirk (a Scottish name for church) opened here in 1620, the first to be built in Edinburgh after the Reformation. A second kirk opened in 1721 and the buildings became known as Old and New Greyfriars. The two kirks were later amalgamated. The kirkyard was used for around 100,000 burials, although only a fraction are represented by the gravestones that you can see today. New burials largely ceased after the 1870s because Greyfriars was itself 'full'.

Turn right, with the kirk to your left. Walk along the path that runs parallel with the outer wall on the east side of the kirkyard. Also on the left-hand side is the gravestone of Bobby's owner ❸ **John Gray**.

To your right along the wall are a number of mainly 17th-century monuments and tombs for prominent Edinburgh men and their families – largely merchants, lawyers and noblemen. Many are embellished with *memento mori* – symbols to remind the viewer of the inevitably of death. The most commonly seen are the skull and crossbones, hourglasses and skeletons representing death. The 17th century was the heyday of such embellishments, which were meant to be interpreted by those who were illiterate or perhaps could not understand the Latin inscriptions on many of the tombs.

Continue along to where you find, by the wall, the tomb of ④ **George Heriot senior** (c.1540-1610), a goldsmith. Today he is best known for being the father of the George Heriot who left a legacy for the foundation of George Heriot's School, bordering Greyfriars. Heriot junior was the court goldsmith to James VI of Scotland, later James I of England, and made a great fortune from lending money to the King. He died in 1624 and left a substantial sum to found the school (known then as a 'hospital') for 'puir, faitherless bairns'. You will see the school later on in the walk.

Just beside Heriot is the ⑤ **Ray family tomb**. It is fascinating not for the fact that any of the Ray family were particularly famous, but because it lists so many family members from 1616 up to the 1880s. Those buried here include surgeons, writers, schoolmasters and merchants.

Continue on, and on the right, by the boundary wall, is the ⑥ **Martyrs' Monument**. This commemorates the Covenanters who died for their cause, many of whom are buried nearby. They formed a Scottish Presbyterian religious movement that opposed the approach to organised religion taken by the Stuart kings, principally Charles I and Charles II. The result was a bitter conflict that formed one of the darkest chapters in Scottish history.

The famous National Covenant – essentially an oath taken by supporters of the Scottish Presbyterian faith – was signed at Greyfriars in 1638. Charles I failed to subdue the movement before he was executed. Later, during the reign of Charles II, the troubles flared again as the King sought to re-impose his authority in Scotland.

This became known as the 'Killing Time'. After a vicious battle at Bothwell Brig in 1679, many hundreds of captured Covenanters were brought back to Edinburgh and imprisoned for around five months in the grounds of Greyfriars. Hundreds died because of the harsh conditions they were kept in, while others were executed or died during transportation to the colonies. You will see later the site often described as the 'Covenanters' Prison'.

Continue on to an obelisk which commemorates ❼ **Duncan Ban MacIntyre** (1724-1812), a once famous Gaelic poet who travelled throughout the country in Highland dress selling his poems. He fought against the Jacobites in 1746 before becoming a gamekeeper. After being forced from his job, he arrived in Edinburgh and served in the town guard.

Nearby to the north is a stone lying on the ground that commemorates ❽ **James Craig** (1739-95). Craig is famous for having submitted in 1766 the winning design for the New Town (see Walk 6 p.149). This development doubled the size of Edinburgh through the creation of new streets and housing to the north of the castle from the late 1760s. Despite having achieved this while still in

his mid-twenties, Craig failed to live up to his early promise. He died in poverty and today very little remains in Edinburgh of his architectural work.

Just by Craig's grave are two large tombs on the northern edge of the kirkyard. One is a neo-classical construction for ❾ **John Bayne of Pitcairlie**, a 17th-century lawyer and landowner. An almost life-size statue of him stands in the shadows – a spooky sight when first encountered. He appears to be holding a purse – perhaps symbolising his wealth or, more likely, that as a lawyer he was a keeper of the King's signet used to seal official documents. This late-Renaissance tomb is possibly styled on a Roman example, and has been described as one of the most architecturally significant in Greyfriars – an 'extraordinary example of Scottish classicism'.

Beside Bayne is another impressive mausoleum, dating from 1709, for the ❿ **Trotters of Mortonhall**. During the 1600s the Trotter family had a house in Trotter's Close off the Royal Mile, approximately where 107 High Street is today. The family owned an estate at Mortonhall on the south side of Edinburgh. The tomb was designed by the prominent architect Robert Mylne (who designed the Mylne family tomb seen at the end of the walk).

Walk up the path towards the kirk, and almost immediately on your right is an oddly shaped, stubby column. It has the initials J.E.M. carved on the top and may mark the grave of ⑪ **James Douglas, 4th Earl of Morton** (1516-81).

Douglas is best known for acting as Regent when James VI was a child. He was involved in the brutal murder of Mary, Queen of Scots' secretary, David Riccio, and was beheaded after being found guilty of his part in another murder – of Mary's second husband, Lord Darnley (blown up just a short distance from Greyfriars). Ironically, he was killed by the Maiden – an early version of the guillotine – that he himself had introduced to Scotland. After Douglas was executed, he was secretly buried at night here, although his head was put on a spike on the roof of Netherbow Port. It would be over a year before James VI would allow the head to be reunited with the body.

Walk over to the wall on the west side. ⑫ **Dr John Hope** (1725-86) is buried by the wall. A prominent botanist, he amalgamated two botanic gardens that existed in Edinburgh during the 18th century, moving them to a new site near Leith Walk. This became the Royal Botanic Garden, which moved to its current home in Inverleith in the 1820s.

Beside Hope is the impressive tomb of ⑬ **Thomas Bannatyne** (1570-1635), a prominent merchant. It is richly and dramatically decorated, featuring a chubby baby and numerous skulls.

Just further along the wall (going south) is the final resting place of ⑭ **George Watson** (1654-1723), another wealthy Edinburgh merchant. He left a large sum of money for a school to educate the sons of other merchants who faced financial difficulties. Today, George Watson's College is one of

Edinburgh's best schools, with recent old boys including the cyclist Sir Chris Hoy and rugby players Gavin and Scott Hastings.

Go back to the path, and just as you ascend some steps, look down. There is a grilled entrance low down (and easy to miss). This is the tomb of **15** **Sir John Baptiste De Medina** (1659-1710), a Spanish portrait painter who found fame in Edinburgh. Baptiste was the last person to be knighted in Scotland before the Act of Union in 1707.

Go up the steps, and just before you draw level with the kirk, look right. Very low down is the grave of **16** **John Porteous** (c.1695 -1736), one of the most controversial figures in Edinburgh's history. As an officer in the town guard, he had a bad reputation among Edinburgh's citizens. This came to a head after he ordered his men to fire into a rowdy crowd during the execution of a smuggler in Grassmarket (see Grassmarket Walk p.114).

Six people were killed by Porteous' troops, with another dozen or so wounded. Porteous was subsequently found guilty of murder, but pardoned after political pressure from London was applied. However, the mob was not going to stand for this and so pulled Porteous from his cell and lynched him. In the following months there was a bitter political battle between those in London who wanted to, among other things, get rid of Edinburgh's post of Lord Provost, and the Scots who were desperate to defend Edinburgh's institutions.

A plain stone with just the single letter 'P' was the only reminder of Porteous for many years. The current headstone was erected fairly recently, bearing the inscription, '*John Porteous, a captain of the City Guard of Edinburgh, murdered September 7, 1736. All Passion Spent, 1973.*'

Behind Porteous by the wall is yet another magnificent 17th-century tomb, this one for ⑰ **Elizabeth Paton**. She died in 1678 aged 40, and this was erected by her husband John Cunningham. You can see the figure of Death, with a crown, wearing robes and holding a sceptre and tablet. Father Time, with wings, kneels and holds out an hourglass to Death.

On the other side of the path, towards the kirk, is a memorial pillar to ⑱ **George Buchanan** (1506-82). Buchanan, described as the greatest Scottish writer of the Renaissance, excelled as a scholar, poet, dramatist and political historian. He served as tutor to Mary, Queen of Scots, and her son James VI, and also acted as Moderator of the General Assembly of the Church of Scotland. His criticism of the Catholic church made him a controversial figure and he was imprisoned for his beliefs for a while on the Continent.

From here walk towards the archway on the west side. This leads away from the kirk and into an extension of the kirkyard. Look out for a sign for the Flodden Wall. This defensive wall was built in the 16th century around the south side of Edinburgh and this is a rare section that has survived (see Walk 3, p.79).

Just by the arch (on the south side) look for a simple stone that commemorates ⑲ **Sir Walter Scott's father**, also Walter Scott (1729-99). Scott senior practised as a lawyer in Edinburgh, as did his more famous son, and was an elder at the kirk here.

*View towards Edinburgh Castle*

Carry on through the arch. You now get a good view of ⑳ **George Heriot's School**, mentioned earlier. The first major building to be constructed in Edinburgh outside the city wall, it is said to have helped inspire JK Rowling when she was creating the fictional Hogwarts school in the Harry Potter books. Rowling wrote much of the first Harry Potter book while sitting in the Elephant House café nearby – its rear room overlooks Greyfriars – and she often used to walk in the kirkyard. As you will see shortly, some of people buried here may have been used by her for character names

In the south-west corner facing George Heriot's School, look for a plaque on the wall that recalls ㉑ **William McGonagall** (1825-1902), a failed actor and poet known by the title of 'the world's worst poet'. If you are not convinced, read the lines on the plaque.

From here walk north. On the right is a line of tombs and headstones that mark the boundary of the cemetery's extension and on the west side is the grave of ㉒ **William Creech** (1745-1815). Creech was probably the most prominent bookseller and publisher of 18th-century Edinburgh, working with many of the great figures of the Enlightenment. He served as Lord Provost – the leader of the Edinburgh town council – and the location of his offices on the Royal Mile, which he occupied for over 40 years, became known as Creech's Land.

He fell out for a while with Robert Burns over 100 guineas he owed the poet for the sale of rights to Burns' works. While they later settled their dispute, Burns immortalised Creech by describing him as: 'A little pert, tart, tripping wright/And still his precious self his dear delight; Who loves his own smart shadow in the streets/Better than e'er the fairest she he meets'.

Burns also wrote about Creech in the poem *Willie's Awa!*, his publisher being one of the very few people Burns bothered to write more than once about.

Creech also published the works of the economist Adam Smith and philosopher David Hume, and his famous literary parties and breakfasts were popular with many prominent figures during the great era of the Scottish Enlightenment.

Continue down the hill, and at the bottom bear right and walk over to the north-east corner of this extension. On the wall is the headstone of ㉓ **Thomas Riddell**, who died in 1806 aged 72. He was not famous, but in recent years there has been much speculation that JK Rowling may have borrowed the name for the Harry Potter books. Within the series, the boy Tom Marvolo Riddle grows up to become the evil

Lord Voldemort. Harry Potter fans have also linked William McGonagall with another character in the books – Professor Minerva McGonagall of Hogwarts school.

Walk back up the slope and return under the arch to the main kirkyard. Continue up the path by the west wall.

Shortly on the right is a fairly plain headstone remembering **24** **Alexander Monro** (1697-1767) and his son – also Alexander (1733-1817). These two Monros, together with Alexander junior's own son (buried in Dean Cemetery), succeeded each other to the post of Professor of Anatomy at the University. This meant the Monro family held this important position for an amazing period of 125 years. During this time their efforts helped Edinburgh's medical school to become one of the best in the world.

Just past here is the gravestone of **25** **William Smellie** (1740-95). A close associate of Creech, he was also a printer who acted as editor of the first edition of the *Encyclopaedia Britannica*. He was good friends with Robert Burns, and the poet's description of Smellie appears on the gravestone – 'Here lies a man who did honour to human nature'. Smellie also printed some of Burns' poems and the poet would sit on a stool in Smellie's office correcting the proofs.

Smellie founded the Crochallan Fencibles, a drinking club that met in a tavern off Anchor Close (see p.69). Burns was also a member and presented new works to his friends – over several whiskies, no doubt.

Continue on to the  **26** **Mausoleum of the Adam family**. Inside there is a bust of William Adam (1689-1748). William, a leading Scottish architect of his day, was responsible for a large number of mansions and public buildings, including the Royal Infirmary in Edinburgh (now demolished). William also designed Hopetoun House near Edinburgh, often described as the finest stately home in Scotland. William passed his trade on to his sons, Robert, John and James, who together developed the 'Adam' style of neo-classical architecture. James is also buried here and John Adam designed this mausoleum.

Beside the Adam family is another fine tomb, this one built for **27** **William Robertson** (1721-93). He was a historian who also served as Moderator of the General Assembly of the Church of Scotland as well as Principal of Edinburgh University. In this role Robertson was instrumental in developing the University's worldwide reputation for excellence, and also helped the creation of a new central building known as New College (today called Old College, see p.44 and largely designed by Robert Adam, mentioned earlier). He was a prominent member of the fairly small group of individuals connected to Edinburgh who were seen as being at the heart of the Scottish Enlightenment movement.

Head south and ahead of you is a southern extension of the kirkyard that is often described as the site of the **28** **Covenanters' Prison**, mentioned earlier. However, it was used for burials only after the Covenanters were held here in 1679, so the more likely area where the prisoners were confined, is just to the south-east of here. Unfortunately the extension is usually locked, though you can visit by prior arrangement with the kirk office. Some walking tours also have access (see p.147).

Prominent people buried in the extension include the scientist ㉙ **Joseph Black** (1728-99). Among his many great contributions to science was the discovery of latent heat – helping the development of the steam engine – and the identification of carbon dioxide. He served as a professor at both the University of Glasgow and the University of Edinburgh and was a friend of other leading figures of the Scottish Enlightenment including David Hume and Adam Smith.

Nearby is the final resting place of ㉚ **James Hutton** (1726-97), known as the 'Father of Modern Geology' because of his revolutionary work on understanding how the earth was formed. He was friends with Black and they attended many social gatherings together during the heady days of the Scottish Enlightenment.

㉛ **Mary Erskine** (1629-1707) is buried right at the end of the extension. Mary was a wealthy philanthropist who gifted money to the Company of Merchants of the City of Edinburgh and who founded the Merchant Maiden school in 1694. The school was renamed after her in the 1940s and it remains one of the city's main independent schools.

Continue along the south wall away from the extension gates.

Just here is the tomb of ㉜ **Patrick Miller of Dalswinton**, in Dumfries and Galloway (1731-1815). He was a wealthy banker who served as the deputy governor of the Bank of Scotland for nearly 30 years. He was also an inventor, and his many projects included a new type of threshing machine and drilling plough. Miller also collaborated on an early version of the steam-powered boat and he tried to interest a number of European countries in buying an innovative warship he had designed.

Miller became friends with Robert Burns shortly after the poet arrived in Edinburgh. In December 1786 Burns wrote, 'An unknown hand left ten guineas for the Ayrshire Bard in Mr Sibbald's hand, which I got. I have since discovered my generous unknown friend to be Patrick Miller, Esq. Brother to the Justice Clerk; and drank a glass of claret with him by invitation at his own house yesternight.' Their relationship became severely strained after Burns leased a farm from Miller but later abandoned the farming life and the property.

Continue on and just ahead is the tomb of ㉝ **Sir George Mackenzie** (1636-91). Known as 'Bluidy Mackenzie' for his zealous prosecutions of criminals and the Covenanters, he was generally reviled by the citizens of Edinburgh. It is said that his tomb is haunted, with poltergeist attacks a regular occurrence. Indeed, Greyfriars is often described as one of the most haunted places in Scotland and the family tombs on this stretch of the kirkyard are particularly atmospheric when it is getting dark.

A little further along is the tomb of ㉞ **Clement Little** (d. 1580) and his brother **William Little** (d.1601), who served as Lord Provost

of Edinburgh. Both men helped to found the University of Edinburgh in the 1580s, and Clement donated books that formed part of the first library. Look for the female figures representing the virtues of Justice, Mercy, Faith and Love. The reclining figure on the tomb depicts William Little. The tomb dates from 1683 and was commissioned by later members of the Little family.

Beside this is the tomb of **35 Sir Robert Sibbald** (1641-1722), physician to Charles II and the first Professor of Medicine at the University of Edinburgh. He was also a founder of Edinburgh's Royal College of Physicians. His interests were not confined to medicine – the blue whale was originally called 'Sibbald's rorqual' after he described a whale stranded in the Firth of Forth in 1692.

Walk towards the kirk and at you will see a **36 'mortsafe'** – a grave protected by an iron cage. The device was invented in around 1815 and was designed to prevent the attentions of the body snatchers who kept the city's anatomy classes supplied with corpses for dissection. Often the structure would stay in place only for around six weeks until the body was so decayed it was of no use for medical examination. The trade in bodies largely ended after the Anatomy Act of 1832 legalised the sale of corpses to medical schools.

Walk over to the edge of the kirk to see a memorial stone to **37 Allan Ramsay** (1686-1758), a prominent Edinburgh publisher, wig-maker and poet. He was responsible for setting up the country's first lending library, and the first professional theatre in Edinburgh.

From here walk back along the path by the kirk. Just as you reach the east wall, look out for the headstone of an apothecary and surgeon named ㊳ **James Borthwick of Stow** (1615-1676). This dramatic memorial features a near full-size dancing skeleton carrying a scythe. Below its foot is a crown, said to symbolise righteousness. Borthwick served as a surgeon with foreign armies fighting in Europe for many years, and also served as an MP for Edinburgh in the Scottish Parliament.

The final tomb seen on the walk is on the east side, just up from the entrance. This is for ㊴ **John Mylne** (1611-67), a master mason and noted architect. He was responsible for many works in Edinburgh including the Tron Kirk on the High Street, significant parts of George Heriot's School, and the reconstruction of the kirk here. Mylne was also involved in the construction of fortifications and the Citadel fort in Leith. The tomb was designed by his son Robert (1633-1710), another prominent architect, who is also buried here. From here you can exit Greyfriars via the entrance you came through at the start of the walk. ●

## VISIT...

**Greyfriars Kirk & Museum**
Greyfriars Place, EH1 2QQ
*www.greyfriarskirk.com*

**Greyfriars Cemetery Tours**
Tours by appointment
*contact@greyfriarskirk.com*

**National Museum of Scotland**
Chambers Street, EH1 1JF
*www.nms.ac.uk*

## EAT/DRINK...

**The Elephant House**
21 George IV Bridge, EH1 1EN
*www.elephanthouse.biz*

Thistle Court p.172

# 6 First New Town Walk

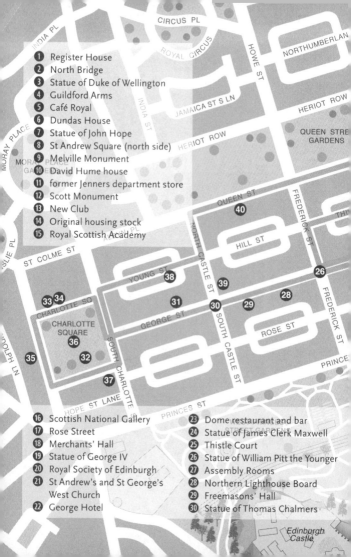

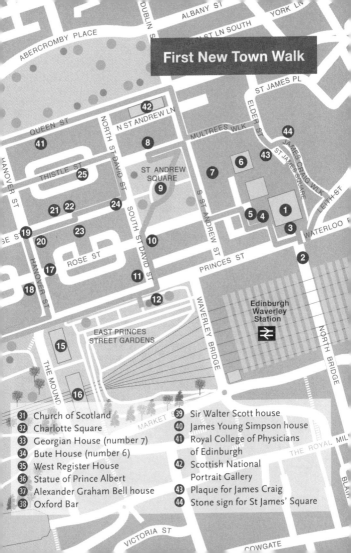

# First New Town Walk

**41** Royal College of Physicians
**42** Scottish National Portrait Gallery
**8** St Andrew Square
**9**
**6**
**7**
**43** Plaque for James Craig
**44** Stone sign for St James' Square
**1**
**5** **4**
**3**
**2**
**25**
**21** **22** **24**
**23**
**19**
**20**
**17**
**18**
**10**
**11**
**12**
**15**
**16**

Edinburgh
Waverley
Station

EAST PRINCES
STREET GARDENS

**31** Church of Scotland
**32** Charlotte Square
**33** Georgian House (number 7)
**34** Bute House (number 6)
**35** West Register House
**36** Statue of Prince Albert
**37** Alexander Graham Bell house
**38** Oxford Bar

**39** Sir Walter Scott house
**40** James Young Simpson house
**41** Royal College of Physicians of Edinburgh
**42** Scottish National Portrait Gallery
**43** Plaque for James Craig
**44** Stone sign for St James' Square

# First New Town Walk

Start: North Bridge / Princes Street
Finish: Waterloo Place
Distance: 3.1 miles

*Duke of Wellington and North Bridge*

This walk takes you on a journey around the original New Town of Edinburgh as it was developed between the late 1760s and the 1820s. It is often called the First New Town, to distinguish it from later extensions (see the Northern New Town Walk p.187).

The walk begins outside **❶ Register House**, facing the North Bridge. Before moving on, it is worth reading a little about the origin of the First New Town.

By the 18th century, Edinburgh – centred on the Old Town you can see to the south – was severely overcrowded. Largely confined within the city walls, rich and poor lived side by side in cramped, often unsanitary conditions. Developers, who were restricted by the space available, built shoddy multi-storey dwellings that were prone to collapse. Visitors to the

city were often appalled by the poor living conditions, and the author Daniel Defoe remarked: 'I believe that in no city in the world so many people have so little room'.

By about 1750, the city's population had grown to around 50,000 – a fivefold increase since the 16th century. George Drummond (1688-1766), who served six times as Lord Provost of Edinburgh, applied considerable pressure on the town council to begin a major modernisation of the city. His efforts were helped by the collapse of a tenement building on the Royal Mile in 1751. This led to an enquiry and the publication of a report in 1752 entitled *Proposals for carrying on certain Public Works in the City of Edinburgh*.

The report was highly critical of Edinburgh's shortcomings compared to London and other European cities, and recommended that as the capital of 'North Britain', substantial improvements should be made. The report recommended two new public buildings, the extension of the city to the north, and the draining of the Nor' (or North) Loch. The recommendations formed the basis of new public architecture and projects that were begun from the 1750s. Most notable of these were Register House (where you are now), the North Bridge and the Royal Exchange (on the site of the collapsed tenement). However, it was not until 1766 that plans for the New Town really began. That year a competition was held to design a new residential district that would occupy a 100-acre site to the north. This competition was won by a fledging architect named James Craig (1739-95) – then still in his twenties.

Craig originally proposed a street plan based on the Union Jack, but his design was considerably modified by the planning committee before being approved in 1767. Even watered down, the plan remained very patriotic, and was designed to curry favour with the Hanoverian court in London.

Many of the original street names were chosen to celebrate the political union between Scotland and England that had taken place in 1707 and created 'Great Britain'. The two principal squares would represent Scotland (St Andrew Square on the east side) and England (St George Square on the west side). Most of the other streets were to be named after King George III, his immediate family, and other national figures, emblems and patron saints.

The plan reflected the spirit of the Scottish Enlightenment in that it was both rational and highly ambitious. This contrasted sharply with the seemingly chaotic, haphazard sprawl of the Old Town.

Look over to the ❷ North Bridge, whose construction was an important part of the town council's attempt to persuade inhabitants of the Old Town that the extension of the city northwards would be easily accessible. The foundation stone was laid in 1763 by George Drummond, although various problems with the construction, including a collapse that killed five people, meant it did not open until 1772. The original bridge was replaced by the current structure in the 1890s.

Enter Register House (today referred to as General Registry House). Construction began in 1774 and its purpose was to house Scotland's public records. Its location at the end of the new bridge and facing the Old Town was intended as a clear statement that Edinburgh's future lay on this side of the city.

Register House was principally designed by Robert Adam (1728-92), the best known member of a family of architects whose neo-classical 'Adam' style became hugely influential during the Georgian era. The building was not completed until 1822, the costs of the Napoleonic Wars having dented public finances and forced a delay in construction. During the intervening years the empty shell was called 'the most magnificent pigeon house in Britain' – an early sign that the creation of the New Town was not always a straightforward process.

Today, the building still serves its original purpose of housing public records, and is one of the oldest archives in the world. Construction was partly funded by the sale of estates owned by wealthy Jacobites, who were punished after the rebellion of 1745. Enter Register House to see Adam's magnificent domed rotunda, taking particular note of the open stonework on the first floor, showing the simplicity and honesty of Adam's design style.

At ground-floor level there is a striking statue of George III which dates from 1787 and was sculpted by Anne Seymour Damer (1749-1828). Damer led an extraordinary life in an age when it was still difficult for women to achieve their ambitions. Born into an aristocratic Whig family, she mixed with figures such as David Hume, Lord Nelson and Horace Walpole and her many adventures included being captured by pirates and having an audience with Napoleon.

Outside Register House look for the statue of the ❸ **Duke of Wellington** that was unveiled on 18 June 1852, the anniversary of the Battle of Waterloo (1815). Thousands of people attended the ceremony, with soldiers of the 79th Highlanders standing along North Bridge. Wellington personally sat for the sculptor Sir John Steell (1804-91). Steell was also responsible for three other statues seen along this walk. To the rear of Register House is the Archivist's Garden, a tranquil spot that contains 57 varieties of plant with a Scottish connection.

Opposite Register House once stood the Theatre Royal which opened in 1769. This became Edinburgh's leading theatre and reflected how the city's cultural life was gravitating to the New Town. It was demolished in 1860.

Follow the map and stay by the railings along Gabriel's Road (look for the sign). This historic road once ran from near Calton Hill right across the undeveloped land upon which the New Town was built before reaching Silvermills and the Water of Leith. (You can find a remaining section of Gabriel's Road in Stockbridge, see p.253). Before the New Town was built, Gabriel's Road was known as a 'lovers' lane', with courting couples walking along it from the Old Town into what was still largely countryside. It is said they would stop for strawberries and cream at a small cottage named 'Peace and Plenty' that once stood on the east side of St Andrew Square.

You pass on your left two fine examples of Victorian bars – the ❹ **Guildford Arms** (opened 1898) and the ❺ **Café Royal** (opened 1863). Their opulent interiors are prime examples of the great age of Victorian design. The Café Royal (which has a separate oyster bar) features in the Oscar-winning film *Chariots of Fire* (1981) – it is where Harold Abrahams dines with singer Sybil Gordon after she performs in *The Mikado*. Some of the furnishings, including Doulton ceramic murals, came from the International Exhibition of Industry, Science and Art that took place on Edinburgh's Meadows in 1886.

Continue along West Register Street to enter St Andrew Square then walk up the right-hand (east) side to reach **6 Dundas House** – today the registered office of the Royal Bank of Scotland.

Craig's First New Town is rectangular in shape, measuring approximately two-thirds of a mile long and one-fifth of a mile wide. Craig's original plan envisaged St Andrew Square (on the east side) and St George Square (on the west) connected by George Street – named for the reigning monarch George III (1738-1820). The area lying between the two opposing squares was split into eight large blocks – with major roads running to the north and south of the development, parallel with George Street in the middle.

It was a relatively simple plan, and for some rather too plain. However, complications were to arise, the first caused by Dundas House. (You can go inside during normal banking hours.) Dundas House was originally a grand villa, completed in 1774, and commissioned by Sir Lawrence Dundas (1710-81). Dundas had made his fortune supplying the British army with provisions, as well as from banking and canals. The building was designed by Sir William Chambers (1723-96) – best known for Somerset House in London.

Craig had wanted a church dedicated to St Andrew to be located here (with a corresponding church dedicated to St George on the square on the west side of the New Town). However, Dundas got there before him, having benefited from a preview of Craig's plan. The construction of Dundas House forced Craig and the town council to place the church on George Street instead (seen later).

The noted Edinburgh lawyer and biographer James Boswell (1740-95) described Dundas as 'a cunning shrewd man of the world', evidenced when he was nearly forced to leave the Square after betting his house during a high-stakes game of cards. He lost the game, and Dundas House, to General John Scott, but managed to persuade Scott to accept instead a new house – financed by Dundas – in nearby Dublin Street. After Dundas' death his villa became an Excise Office in 1794 – hence the royal arms outside. It was bought by the Royal Bank in 1825. Once inside, you can ask to see the magnificent domed interior, peppered with stars.

The Royal Bank of Scotland was founded in 1727, a development that was encouraged by the government in London which suspected that senior elements in the Bank of Scotland (founded in 1695) were sympathetic to the Jacobite cause.

Outside Dundas House is an equestrian statue featuring ❼ **John Hope, 4th Earl of Hopetoun** (1765-1823). He served as an officer during the Napoleonic Wars and was later Governor of the Royal Bank. According to Edinburgh folklore, the sculptor, Thomas Campbell, did not receive his fee because of his error of making the horse shorter than the Earl. Hopetoun House, which remains the family seat of the Earl of Hopetoun, can be found a few miles outside Edinburgh near Queensferry.

Walk up the east side of the Square. Beneath your feet lies the Scotland Street Tunnel, built in the mid-19th century. It originally ran between Canal Street Station (near today's Waverley Station) and Scotland Street Station by Canonmills. Around 1,000 yards long, it was used for public trains until 1868. It was then used for goods traffic and other purposes, including a bomb shelter during WWII, a mushroom farm, a place for radioactive experiments and a car storage facility. Today, it lies abandoned and is not usually accessible.

Follow the map to the north side of ❽ **St Andrew Square**. This contains the best surviving examples of houses built when the Square was originally laid out – numbers 23 to 26 date from the early 1770s.

No 22 is where Dr Joseph Bell (1837-1911) was born. An eminent physician of his day, his ability to diagnose patients from tiny details became legendary and he helped the police with a number of investigations. Arthur Conan Doyle (1859-1930) studied under Bell and also worked as his clerk. Doyle later acknowledged that Bell was the chief inspiration for the great detective Sherlock Holmes.

Henry, Lord Brougham (1778-1868), was born at 21 St Andrew Square. Brougham became a distinguished lawyer and MP, also serving as Lord Chancellor. In 1802 he was one of the founders of the influential *Edinburgh Review* magazine and he also designed the famous horse carriage that bears his name. Brougham was a controversial, difficult character, but one who became a leading figure within the movement that helped to end slavery in the British Empire.

Slavery existed as the New Town was being built. No 36 (now 37) was the address registered to Thomas Corrie (1790-1859) – a banker. One of many slave-owners who lived in Edinburgh, he claimed compensation from the British Government when slavery was finally abolished in 1833. Corrie owned slaves, but probably never met the slaves he owned in the Carribean and elsewhere. Other Scots were closer to the problem; Liverpool port records show that one-fifth of captains working on slave ships were Scottish. Today Harvey Nichols stands approximately where Corrie's property was once located. The fourth floor restaurant in Harvey Nichols is where Renton gives his updated 'choose life' speech in Trainspotting 2 (2017).

The north-east side of St Andrew Square is near to Edinburgh Bus Station, originally St Andrew Square Bus Station when it opened in 1957. As a schoolboy, John Lennon arrived here on a bus from Liverpool, playing a cheap harmonica all the way.

When the bus arrived in St Andrew Square, the impressed conductor gave the future Beatle a much better-quality harmonica which had been left on the bus the week before. Lennon treasured the instrument, playing it on the single *Love Me Do*, and when he returned years later to play a concert in Edinburgh with The Beatles at the ABC Cinema on Lothian Road. Lennon's aunt and cousin lived at 15 Ormidale Terrace in Murrayfield, and for five summers – from the age of nine – John stayed with his relatives in Edinburgh, getting to know the city very well.

Return to walk through the heart of St Andrew Square. During WWI American troops camped here while awaiting deployment in France. Today the Square is dominated by the **❾ Melville Monument**, which dates from 1823 and was modelled on Trajan's Column in Rome. It is topped by a statue of Henry Dundas (1742-1811), 1st Viscount Melville. This Dundas (relative of the man who commissioned Dundas House) was a lawyer who became an influential politician serving as Minister of War for his great friend William Pitt the Younger. Pitt became Prime Minister aged only 24 and occupied the office from 1783-1801 and 1804-06.

It is said that Dundas' stubborn opposition to the abolition of slavery held back reform by around 15 years. Owing to his huge influence in Scotland's affairs, he had a number of nicknames including 'Harry the Ninth, uncrowned King of Scotland' and (according to Lord Cockburn) 'the absolute dictator of Scotland'. His career never really recovered after he was implicated in a financial scandal, though his tarnished reputation evidently did not discourage the sponsors of this monument.

Walk down through the heart of the Square to its south-west corner. The Square was one of the first areas of the New Town to be built, from the late 1760s. From here, the development spread slowly westwards, coming to an end in Charlotte Square (begun in 1792 and completed by 1820). It is worth noting that St Andrew Square Garden was not made open to the general public until 2008, 238 years after it was completed. It is still a subject of heated debate that many of the New Town parks and squares remain private, including Queen Street Gardens seen later in the walk.

Stop at the junction with South St David Street. No 21 is where the house of the philosopher ⑩ **David Hume** (1711-76) once stood. Hume, a leading figure of the Scottish Enlightenment (see p.66), became one of the first people to move here from the Old Town. It was a risky decision as in the early years of the New Town development there was a chance the whole enterprise might fail and residents could have been left stranded on a huge unfinished building site.

Hume was a notorious atheist – and according to Edinburgh legend, one of his friends added a 'St' to the street sign for 'David Street' as a joke when the philosopher moved in. Though a great story, this was always meant to be St David Street and was named for the patron saint of Wales in 1772. This was an extension of the patriotic street-naming convention proposed by Craig which was intended to emphasise the unity of the kingdom.

The naming of streets in the First New Town took place before Ireland became part of Great Britain in 1801. This helps to explain why there is no St Patrick Street in the First New Town. There is, however, a Dublin Street in the later extension (called the Northern New Town) that was built after 1801.

Continue down South St David Street to reach Princes Street. You pass the former ⑪ **Jenners department store** on the right. Founded by Charles Jenner and Charles Kennington, it was known as the 'Harrods of the North' and had a presence on Princes Street from 1838 until its closure in May 2021. The current ornate structure dates from the 1890s, after a fire destroyed the original buildings. It was designed by William Hamilton Beattie (1842-1898), who was also responsible for the Balmoral Hotel (opposite Register House). There are plans by the site's owners to restore the building and reopen a department store here, so the fine building looks destined to survive.

The site to the west of Jenners was once home to the Royal Hotel, and it was here that ex-Confederate President Jefferson Davis stayed during his visit to Edinburgh in 1869. Davis had lost the American Civil War to his arch-enemy Abraham Lincoln, and had even been charged for a while with playing a part in Lincoln's assassination. Davis was received with warmth by many during his visit to Scotland, perhaps oddly to modern eyes given that he was a disgraced White Supremacist who had supported slavery and had helped to prolong a terrible war that resulted in nearly three quarters of a million deaths.

Cross over Princes Street to reach the vast **⓬ Scott Monument**, which dominates the view ahead.

In Craig's plan, Princes Street was meant to be called St Giles Street, after the patron saint of Edinburgh. However – in another unexpected change of plan – George III was invited to review and approve the design. He objected on the grounds that the name would remind him of a notorious slum district in London named St Giles. Instead, the street was named Prince's Street after the Prince of Wales (later George IV). It only became 'Princes Street' in the 1830s.

The 200-foot-high Scott Monument dates from the 1840s and commemorates the great Scottish writer Sir Walter Scott

(1771-1832). Originally due to be sited in Charlotte Square, it was described by Charles Dickens as 'the spire of a gothic church taken off and stuck in the ground'. The statue of Scott sitting with his faithful deerhound Maida was also sculpted by Sir John Steell. The Monument was completed in 1846, though its designer George Kemp never saw it completed after he fell and drowned in the Union Canal.

Scott's historical novels became hugely popular in the early 19th century (see p.67), and he is credited with creating a growth of interest in Scottish culture and history both here and abroad. He also stage-managed the visit of George IV to Scotland in 1822, the first by a British monarch since the mid-17th century.

You may wish to climb up the stairs to get an excellent view of central Edinburgh (see p.185). Scott lived as a child in the Old Town and would have watched the New Town being built. Like Hume, he later moved here (his house is seen later on).

Continue along Princes Street. It was originally intended to be largely residential, with buildings on just the north side so residents could enjoy the views up to Edinburgh Castle and the Old Town. However over the years the street became increasingly commercialised, and dominated by shops, hotels and offices. As a result, much of the original Georgian housing stock was demolished or substantially redeveloped.

Continue westwards, with Princes Street Gardens on your left. These lie on the site of the Nor' (or North) Loch, which was formed in the 15th century after the Craig Burn that flowed from the north side of Castle Rock was dammed. The Nor' Loch served as a natural defensive barrier on the north side of the Old Town, while the city walls protected the south side (see Walk 3, p.79).

Princes Street Gardens

From the mid-18th century the threat of invasion ceased. The city walls were pulled down and the Nor' Loch drained. Princes Street Gardens were laid out on the drained site of the loch and were originally open only to the residents of Princes Street.

Though it is hard to imagine it now, in the 1770s the town council was concerned that developers would not wish to build houses in the New Town in case they remained unsold. The council therefore used incentives to attract investment, for example promising that the first person to build a house on Princes Street would be exempt from tax. This encouraged John Neale, a silk dealer, to build a house here and very soon others followed.

A link with the period when the New Town was laid out survives with the **⓭ New Club** at No 86. It was founded in 1787 and has been based on this site since 1837, though the current building dates only from the 1960s. Some of the internal rooms such as the dining room contain the original wooden panelling from the earlier structure. It remains one of the most prestigious institutions in Edinburgh.

Continue along Princes Street. It was along here that the opening scene of the film *Trainspotting* (1996) was located, showing the main character Renton (played by Ewan McGregor being chased by store detectives.    Surprisingly for a film set principally in Edinburgh, many scenes were shot elsewhere, particularly Glasgow.

The building to the left of Primark gives a rare glimpse of what the **⓮ original housing stock** looked like when Princes Street was still residential. It is surprisingly plain, with a rare example of a basement. It was only later on – principally during the Victorian era – that more ornate façades were added to many of the Georgian buildings.

Retrace your steps slightly to the junction with Hanover Street. The area to the south is dominated by the 19th-century neo-classical buildings of the ⑮ **Royal Scottish Academy** and (to its rear) the ⑯ **Scottish National Gallery** (see p.185). Both were designed by William Henry Playfair (1790-1857) and were built after the First New Town was largely completed. Both buildings are located on the Mound – a man-made feature created from soil excavated from the New Town site as foundations were dug out.

When you have finished, follow the map up Hanover Street, which was largely constructed by 1790. Its name is a reminder of a bygone age when Britain and part of modern-day Germany were linked by a common ruler. George I (1660-1727) was already the ruler (or 'Elector') of Hanover when he became King of Britain and Ireland in 1714, following the death of Queen Anne with no Protestant heir on this side of the Channel to succeed her.

The House of Hanover would supply Britain with its monarchs from George I through to Queen Victoria, and the creation of the New Town took place during the heyday of the Georgian era (principally through the reigns of George III and IV). As a woman, Victoria was not permitted to rule Hanover, thus breaking the link between that dominion and the British throne.

As you head north up Hanover Street, you cross over **17 Rose Street** – maintaining Craig's patriotic theme by being named after the English national emblem. Today this is a lively street, full of shops, restaurants and bars. It was originally designed for wealthier artisans and was under construction by the early 1780s. However, it later degenerated into a notorious Red Light area, with one Victorian book on the issue of prostitution in the city noting how 'tenants [would] subscribe for the payment of a man to hold a burning torch in the entrance to some of the brothels in Rose Street, on the supposition that visitors to these dens of infamy would thereby feel ashamed of their conduct'.

On the west side of Hanover Street is **18 Merchants' Hall**, which dates from the mid-1860s. The merchants of the city were hugely influential in the way Edinburgh developed over many centuries, protecting their own commercial interests and having significant political power through their right of representation on the town council. In 1681 the Merchant Company of Edinburgh received a Royal Charter from Charles II.

By the mid-19th century the Merchant Company, as with most other trade guilds, lost its monopoly over commercial matters and focused increasingly on education and charitable purposes. The Merchant Company is still an influential business forum, and is still involved in the operation of a number of the city's best-known private schools – George Watson's College, the Mary Erskine School, and Stewart's Melville College.

Continue uphill to reach George Street – named after George III. The street is the central thoroughfare of the New Town – linking St Andrew Square with Charlotte Square. At the junction is a statue of  **George IV** (1762-1830). When his father George III became incapacitated by bouts of mental instability, George, already the Prince of Wales, acted as Regent from 1811 until he became King in 1820.

Though he was often ridiculed for his extravagant behaviour (and girth) in England, George IV became reasonably popular in Edinburgh, particularly after his historic visit in 1822. This greatly improved relations between the House of Hanover and Scotland. As mentioned earlier, the visit was managed by Sir Walter Scott. Scott, who even persuaded the King to dress in tartan – a politically charged move given that Scotland's national dress had recently been banned following the Jacobite uprisings. No doubt the patriotic naming convention adopted by the New Town planners helped to convince the monarchy that subjects north of the border were loyal after all.

Turn right and walk eastwards down George Street. Almost directly on the right-hand side (numbers 22-24) is the home of the **Royal Society of Edinburgh**. Established at the height of the Scottish Enlightenment era in 1783, the Society's main purpose today is as an educational charity. Its list of founding fellows includes some of the most notable men of the Enlightenment era such as Adam Smith, Joseph Black, Lord Kames, James Hutton and Benjamin Franklin. The Society has been based here since 1909.

Continue along George Street, aiming for the church spire on the left-hand side. This street was the only main thoroughfare on Craig's plan that was expected to have houses on both sides. Princes Street to the south, and Queen Street to the north, were designed so residents would have an uninterrupted view over the other side of the road.

Shortly you reach ㉑ **St Andrew's and St George's West Church**. As mentioned earlier, Craig originally planned that St Andrew Square should have a church dedicated to the patron saint of Scotland on its east side. The construction of Dundas House put paid to that plan, and as a result the church was built here instead. It opened in 1784 and was the first place of worship to be built in the New Town.

Charlotte Square on the west side of the New Town did end up with a church as originally planned – named St George's. However, in 1964 that church merged with St Andrew's and left Charlotte Square to come here.

The eight church bells are the oldest complete peal of bells in Scotland and were cast in the 18th century at the famous Whitechapel Bell Foundry in London. The Foundry – still in operation – was established in the 15th century and produced both Big Ben and the Liberty Bell of Philadelphia. The church's bells were recently returned to Whitechapel for maintenance.

A key event in the so-called 'Disruption' of 1843 took place here. For years there had been unhappiness within sections of the Church of Scotland about the right of wealthy landowners to install ministers of their choosing in a parish, even if the local congregation disagreed. This, and other issues, resulted in a break-away movement that formally began at this church on 18 May 1843.

On that day, 121 ministers and 73 elders stood up and walked out of the Church of Scotland General Assembly being held in the church. They then walked along a pre-planned route through Edinburgh to Tanfield Hall near Canonmills (see p.243), where they formally established the Free Church of Scotland. Thomas Chalmers (1780-1847) acted as the first Moderator of the new church (his statue is seen later). Within the next few months, hundreds more would follow them, creating a schism in Scotland's religious life that would take many decades to heal. The church has an undercroft café which is worth a visit if you need a break before continuing.

Beside the church is the ㉒ **George Hotel**. It incorporates three separate town houses that were built in the 1780s.

Opposite the church is the ㉓ **Dome restaurant and bar**. Once a bank, this grand neo-classical building dates from 1847. This was

originally the site of the Physicians' Hall, home to the Royal College of Physicians of Edinburgh. The hall was designed by James Craig – winner of the New Town design competition – and built in 1775. The hall was demolished to make way for the building you see today.

Today there are in fact very few remaining examples of Craig's architectural work in Edinburgh. After winning the prize for the overall lay-out of the New Town, Craig did not receive many commissions to design individual buildings. In 1786 he published *A Plan for Improving the City of Edinburgh*, which suggested changes to the Old Town that were not accepted by the town council. Rather sadly, Craig's moment in the sun had passed, and he died a few years later in relative poverty.

Continue along George Street until you reach the statue of ㉔ **James Clerk Maxwell** (1831-1879). This renowned physicist established the theory of electromagnetism and is often referred to as the father of modern physics (see p.195).

From here, follow the map north and then left into Thistle Street, named for the flower that has long been a symbol of Scotland. According to legend, a member of an enemy army was sneaking up on the Scottish forces when he stood on a thistle

and screamed out in pain. The Scots were alerted to the imminent attack and the day was saved. The planners of Thistle Street, as with Rose Street, originally intended to attract workers and shopkeepers; however, the developers who built the houses were aiming instead to attract wealthier merchants and professionals.

On the left stop at ㉕ **Thistle Court** which is home to the first buildings constructed in the New Town. A developer named John Young received a financial incentive to buy

*Thistle St*

the first plot of land here. Possibly uncomfortable about breaking with old habits, he built two houses facing each other rather than terrace houses facing the street as the authorities had expected.

The buildings date from c. 1768 – just two years after James Craig won the design prize. Craig came here to lay the foundation stone in front of a large crowd of onlookers – the symbolic birth of the New Town. Young was also responsible for developing nearby Young Street, obviously named after him. This might have come as a pleasant change for residents of the city after the doggedly patriotic names used for many of the other streets of the New Town. The building on the west side of the Court cleverly encloses an electricity substation.

Continue along Thistle Street. It has a mews lane to the rear which would originally have contained stables, carriage houses and living quarters for servants. East Thistle Street was once home to the Six Feet High Club, established in 1826, and – as its name suggests restricted to those people who were at least six feet tall. An exception was made for Sir Walter Scott, who was allowed to join despite not quite measuring up!

Cross over Hanover Street and continue eastwards along Thistle Street until you reach Frederick Street. This is named after George III's second son, Prince Frederick Augustus (1763-1827). Also known as the Duke of York and Albany, he was immortalised in the children's song *The Grand Old Duke of York* as the man who marched his soldiers to the top of the hill and down again.

It is worth noting that at approximately the same time as the town council of Edinburgh was seeking favour with George III by laying out streets named after him and his immediate family, the King's subjects in America were heading in a very different direction.

The American colonies declared their independence in 1776, accusing George III of many things including 'He has abdicated Government here... He has plundered our seas, ravaged our Coasts, burnt our towns, and destroyed the lives of our people.' An equestrian statue of George III in New York was destroyed by a revolutionary mob.

Follow the map towards George Street. At the junction of Frederick Street and George Street stands a statue of **26 William Pitt the Younger**. He served as Prime Minister during much of the period during which the New Town was being built.

Stop and look at the statute of Pitt for a moment. You are now at the very heart of Craig's New Town development – however, this was almost a very different place.

There is some evidence that Craig's original design for the New Town was modelled on the Union Jack flag, but the planning committee rejected this. Instead, they took Craig's more orthodox revised plan and adapted it – quite how, we will probably never know, though some prominent architects sat on the committee. Craig separately came up with an alternative design – the so-called 'Circus Plan' – that envisaged a huge circular space at the heart of the New Town, just where you are standing today. It was to be called George's Circus, with a statue of George III in the centre of the circle.

Craig was clearly very proud of the Circus Plan, choosing to hold it rather than the final 'Adopted Plan' in a painting of him painted by David Allan some years after the first buildings began to spring up.

Head left on George Street, today one of the most upmarket shopping districts in Scotland. Unlike Princes Street, it has managed to retain a fair number of its original Georgian buildings. Cross over to visit the  **❷ Assembly Rooms**.

Opened in 1787, the Assembly Rooms soon became the most prestigious place for entertainments in the New Town. The first major event held here was a ball for the Caledonian Hunt on 11 January. It was attended by around 340 of the great and good of the Scottish upper classes, and proved to any doubters that the New Town could provide entertainments superior to anything that existed in the Old Town.

This also marked a significant change in the social fabric of Edinburgh. For centuries different classes had co-existed in the Old Town, often living on different floors of the same tenement buildings. However, only the better-off could afford to live in the New Town, and when they moved on the less well-off inhabitants of the Old Town were left behind, both physically and socially. Few probably felt much affection for the new exclusive residential district.

However, this 'social cleansing' impacted on the educated, wealthy classes as well. Perhaps it was no coincidence that the great age of the Scottish Enlightenment came to an end as the New Town was completed in the 1820s. The Old Town had its faults, but it had always been a great social and intellectual melting pot, and arguably helped to shape the ideas of the Enlightenment's key figures.

On 23 August 1822, the Assembly Rooms hosted the glittering Peers' Ball that was attended by George IV. The painter JMW Turner was also there and drew a couple of sketches. Charles Dickens and William Thackeray separately came here to read extracts from their novels to the public, and in 1827 (during a dinner) Sir Walter Scott finally confirmed to a cheering audience that he was indeed the (previously anonymous) author of the hugely popular Waverley novels.

Return westwards along George Street. Shortly on the left at No 84 is the headquarters of the ㉘ **Northern Lighthouse Board**. The board was established in 1786 to operate lighthouses around Scotland. This early New Town building is a good example of the elegant design of the original George Street. As a rule of thumb, anything in the New Town that is more ornate than this dates from the 19th century or later. Look out for the model lighthouse on the frontage.

Walk westwards, passing ㉙ **Freemasons' Hall** on your left (No 96). The current building was completed in 1912 replacing an earlier Masonic building founded here in 1858. It is the home of the Masonic Grand Lodge of Scotland, which has been representing Freemasons in Scotland since 1736. There is a small museum. Public tours are possible (see p.185).

The statue at the junction of Castle Street is of ㉚ **Thomas Chalmers** (1780-1847) – a leading figure in the 'Disruption' of 1843 that began in St Andrew's Church (as was) which you visited earlier. It is often mentioned that he is looking disdainfully away from the headquarters of the ❸❶ **Church of Scotland** (at No 121 George Street – north side). The statue is another by Sir John Steell.

Continue on to reach ❸❷ **Charlotte Square**. It was originally intended that the square be named after St George as an English-themed counterbalance to St Andrew Square. However – in yet another change to Craig's original plan – the authorities decided this would cause confusion given that there was already a George Square in the south of Edinburgh. This square was instead named after George III's wife.

Walk around the north side of the square first. This contains the best remaining examples of the original houses. By the time Charlotte Square was being built, the New Town was clearly a success and this square has been described as the 'grand finale'.

As a result, the town council no longer had to offer generous incentives to encourage developers to build here, but instead could lay down stricter conditions to ensure a consistency of architectural design. The council employed the renowned Robert Adam to produce the overall design – the only major section of the New Town created as a single unified piece.

The commissioning of Adam by the council may have been a reaction to criticism from some quarters that earlier parts of the New Town development were rather plain. Adam drew up the plans in 1791, just a year before he died, so he never saw Charlotte Square completed.

To see inside one of these grand houses, you may wish to visit the ❸❸ **Georgian House** at No 7 (north side). Restored by the National Trust for Scotland, it is open to the public, with each room ordered the way it would have been at different stages in history (see p.185).

177

*Ashlar stonework*

**❸❹ Bute House (Number 6)**, designed by Adam, embodies the changing political landscape of Scotland. Between 1970 and 1999 it was the official residence of the Secretary of State for Scotland; however, the creation of the Scottish Parliament in 1999 led to this becoming the official residence of the First Minister of Scotland. Prime Minister Theresa May and Scottish First Minister Nicola Sturgeon met at Bute House in July 2016, just a few days after May had replaced David Cameron in the aftermath of the Brexit referendum. It was May's first official trip since entering 10 Downing Street, and Sturgeon tweeted a message: 'I hope girls everywhere look at this photograph [of both leaders outside Bute House] and believe nothing should be off limits to them'. Some press reports instead concentrated on the poor state of the pavement outside Bute House.

In recent years a controversy has raged over whether the chandelier at No 6 was looted by the Nazis and then illicitly brought here after WWII ended. The captain in the British Army who provided the chandelier to the Marchioness of Bute, then owner of the house, claimed to have found the chandelier abandoned on the streets of Cleves.

No 5 was where Elizabeth Grant of Rothiemurchus was born in May 1797. She later wrote a fascinating memoir about her life that documented how high society behaved in Georgian Britain. When her family first moved to Charlotte Square, it was still largely empty – her father bought one of only three houses that stood here.

In her memoir, Grant speculated on why her husband, a wealthy landowner, wanted to bother to try to establish a career as a lawyer in London. She concluded that 'the French Revolution, in the startling shake it had given to the aristocracy of all Europe... while it was annihilating its own, had made it a fashion for all men to provide themselves with some means of earning a future livelihood, should the torrent of democracy reach to other lands'. Evidently even the richest residents of the New Town still suffered from insecurity about their futures.

Look out for the decorative fanlight above a number of the front doors – a particularly Georgian feature that allowed light into the hallway in the age before electricity. If you look down, you can also see that the stonework by the basement where the servants once lived is often rougher, with a smoother finish (known as ashlar) used higher up.

Walk around to the west side to reach **35** **West Register House**. Today (like Register House, seen at the start of the walk), it is part of the National Archives of Scotland. Robert Adam originally designed a church dedicated to St George for this site, but after he died the design was taken forward by another eminent architect named Robert Reid (1774-1856). The result, completed by 1814, was a simpler, more austere structure. The congregation moved away in the 1960s to merge with St Andrew's Church on George Street (visited earlier). Reid was responsible for a number of other streets in the later extension to the First New Town, as well as the façade of Parliament Square in Edinburgh and the Customs House in Leith.

Walk around the south side of the square. Underneath lie the remains of a WWII air-raid shelter – no longer accessible.

In the centre of the Square you can see a statue of **36** **Prince Albert** by Sir John Steell. Steell was knighted here by a grateful Queen Victoria when she attended the unveiling ceremony in 1876. It is not

generally possible to visit the garden; however, it is the site of the Edinburgh International Book Festival which takes place every August.

Continue along the south side of the square and when you reach the junction with South Charlotte Street look out for No 16. This is where **37 Alexander Graham Bell** (1847-1922), inventor of the telephone (and many other devices), lived as a child. His mother's deafness had a huge impact on Bell, and much of his life was spent investigating ways to help the deaf. Like Sir Walter Scott, he was educated at the Royal High School.

Continue along the east side of the Square. Houses of other notable figures who once lived on the Square or nearby include No 9 – Joseph Lister (1827-1912), surgeon and pioneer of antiseptic surgery; No 13 – Sir William Fettes (1750-1836), whose legacy funded the famous Fettes College in Edinburgh (alumni include Tony Blair and James Bond); No 44 – architect Robert Reid; and No 24 – Field Marshal Earl Haig (1861-1928).

Continue northwards up North Charlotte Street and then right along Young Street

– named after John Young, one of the developers who built this part of the New Town in the 1790s. The land was 'fued' to him in 1779 – a Scottish term that means the landowner grants someone else their land in return for agreed conditions and fees. Hill Street – in the block to the east of here – was named after another developer called James Hill.

As you walk along Young Street, you pass two well-known Edinburgh pubs – the Cambridge Bar and then the ❸❽ **Oxford Bar**. The 'Ox' is one of the cosiest pubs in the city and a favourite haunt of John Rebus – the Edinburgh detective created by Ian Rankin. Rankin is also seen at the bar from time to time and held his stag night here. He write of how the 'Ox' is 'Edinburgh in microcosm – a city that seems very public and yet very private at the same time'.

Soon you reach North Castle Street, named for its view of Edinburgh Castle to the south. ❸❾ **Sir Walter Scott** lived with his wife at No 39 – a house he had built from 1802 to 1826. It features in a sketch by JMW Turner.

Scott was hugely popular during his lifetime and became very wealthy. He owned this house and also a huge country mansion named Abbotsford House. However, a banking crisis in 1825 caused the collapse of the printing and publishing business he had a financial interest in. Rather than face the public disgrace of bankruptcy, Scott worked himself into an early grave trying to pay back his creditors. He was forced to sell this house to help raise funds.

Continue along North Castle Street to reach Queen Street – named for George III's wife Queen Charlotte. It was originally meant to be called Forth Street on account of the great views northwards to the Firth of Forth, and Frederick Street was to be called Queen Street. However, after discussions between the town planners and Queen Charlotte, the plans were changed and this became Queen Street instead.

*North Castle Street looking south*

Turn right on Queen Street. This street marked the northern limit of the First New Town. What you see to the north is part of a later extension which began in the early 1800s and which is often called the Northern New Town (and is covered a separate walk (see p.187). Queen Street was never commercialised in the same way as Princes Street or George Street, and as a result it retains the most complete set of late-18th-century Georgian buildings in the New Town. It also gives a fair idea of how Princes Street must originally have looked.

To the north are the private Queen Street Gardens. When Queen Street was first laid out these were mainly open fields, and maps of the late 18th century still list the names of individual landowners. Queen Street Gardens are almost as large as their near-neighbour, Princes Street Gardens, which were once private too. The only way to access them is through private tours (see p.185).

Follow the map to No 52. This was the home of **40 Sir James Young Simpson** (1811-1870), a Scottish obstetrician who pioneered the use of chloroform as an anaesthetic. This town house became a gathering point for intellectuals as well as people from all walks of life who were of interest to Simpson.

Simpson's provision of chloroform to Queen Victoria during the birth of her eighth child did much to popularise its use among an initially sceptical medical profession. During early experiments with the drug the doctor and some colleagues fell unconscious in the dining room here, causing a great shock to his wife when she entered the room.

Continue along Queen Street and after the junction with Hanover Street on the right look out for the ㊶ **Royal College of Physicians of Edinburgh** at No 9. This grand building was designed in a late Greek Revival style by Thomas Hamilton (1784-1858) and finished in 1844.

The history of the College goes back to the 17th century when physicians in the city would hold meetings at home with colleagues to discuss how best to organise the medical profession. An official representative body was formed in 1681 and its efforts would help Edinburgh become a world-leading centre for medical research and training.

The College's first hall was located in the Old Town. However, like many other institutions, the College joined the exodus to the New Town. Its later hall (designed by James Craig) stood between 1781 and 1843 on the site of the Dome restaurant, seen earlier on George Street. No 8 Queen Street was designed by Robert Adam in around 1771 for Baron Orde and incorporated into the Physicians' building in the 1950s.

Continue on to the ㊷ **Scottish National Portrait Gallery** on Queen Street (see p.185). It was built in the 1880s and its neo-gothic design contrasts sharply with the simple style of the New Town's Georgian architecture. You will find many portraits here of notable figures mentioned during this walk, including David Hume and Sir Walter Scott. It also contains the statue of Robert Burns that was once located at the Burns Monument on Calton Hill. The statue was removed here because

of fears it was being destroyed by pollution from the gas works down below in Canongate.

From here, follow the map south along North St Andrew Street and turn left along the pedestrianised Multrees Walk. Continue through this modern shopping centre and bear right at the end (along Elder Street) before turning left into James Craig Walk. Look out on the right-hand side for a ❹❸ **plaque on the wall** remembering James Craig. It is placed on the only buildings that remain from the original St James' Square that was designed by Craig in 1773.

Opposite the plaque, by the entrance to the new St James Quarter shopping mall, and behind a window, is the historic ❹❹ **stone sign for St James' Square** with the date of 1779. It would no doubt have been familiar to Robert Burns, who lived on the Square when it was still in its prime. He once wrote to his secret love 'Clarinda' that he thought he had seen her walking past one day while he was in his room looking through the window.

What was initially an elegant square of Georgian tenements had become very run down by the 20th century. Together with neighbouring Greenside, this area was described as representing 'the lowest depths of Edinburgh vice and poverty' by the Scotsman in 1905. In the mid-1960s the Square made way for the woeful St James Centre and New St Andrew's House. This whole area has recently undergone another controversial development with the new St James Quarter. Its tower - described as 'the

Walnut Whip' and other less complimentary terms – is now a new feature on Edinburgh's famous skyline.

Continue directly ahead to reach Leith Street, with Register House to your right. This is the end of the walk. As you will now have realised the First New Town is not a huge place, but in just a few years it doubled the residential capacity of Edinburgh. James Craig, who died aged just 55 in 1795, would have seen his original plan slowly grow and take shape in front of him, albeit in a modified fashion. In recent years both the Old and New Town have been recognised as World Heritage Sites by UNESCO. They stated that the two sites 'represent a remarkable blend of two urban phenomena: organic medieval growth and 18th-and 19th-century town planning'. ●

## VISIT...

**Scott Monument**
East Princes St Grdns, EH2 2EJ
*www.edinburghmuseums.org.uk*

**Royal Scottish Academy**
The Mound, EH2 2EL
*www.royalscottishacademy.org*

**Scottish National Gallery**
The Mound, EH2 2EL
*www.nationalgalleries.org*

**Freemasons' Hall & Museum**
96 George Street, EH2 3DH
*www.grandlodgescotland.com*

**Scottish National
Portrait Gallery**
1 Queen Street, EH2 1JD
*www.nationalgalleries.org*

## EAT/DRINK...

**Guildford Arms**
1 West Registry Street, EH2 2AA
*www.guildfordarms.com*

**Café Royal**
19 West Registry Street, EH2 2AA
*www.caferoyaledinburgh.co.uk*

**The Dome restaurant & bar**
14 George Street, EH2 2PF
*www.thedomeedinburgh.com*

**The Oxford Bar**
8 Young Street, EH2 4JB

**Urban Angel (café)**
121 Hanover Street, EH2 1DJ
*www.urban-angel.co.uk*

Moray Place see p.196

# 7 Northern New Town & Moray Estate Walk

# Northern New Town & Moray Estate Walk

## Map labels

KING GEORGE V PARK

BELLEVUE CRES
BELLEVUE PL
E LONDON ST
BROUGHTON ST
ROYAL CRESCENT
DUNDONALD ST
CUMBERLAND ST
TES ROW
SCOTLAND ST
DRUMMOND PL
LONDON ST
BARONY ST
GREAT KING ST
NELSON ST
ALBANY ST
YORK
DUBLIN ST
UMBERLAND ST
ABERCROMBY PLACE
DUBLIN ST LN SOUTH
YORK PL
QUEEN ST
NORTH ST DAVID ST
THISTLE ST
GEORGE ST
ROSE ST
HANOVER S
PRINCES ST

① Greek temple
② Abercromby Place
③ Robert Louis Stevenson House
④ St Stephen's Church
⑤ Kay's Bar
⑥ James Clerk Maxwell Foundation
⑦ Moray Place
⑧ Ainslie Place
⑨ 28 Moray Place
⑩ Gloucester Lane
⑪ Royal Circus
⑫ Sir Henry Littlejohn house
⑬ 3 South East Circus Place
⑭ St Vincent's
⑮ Circus Lane
⑯ Mews houses
⑰ George V Park
⑱ Scotland Street Station
⑲ Scotland Street
⑳ Drummond Place
㉑ 15 London Street
㉒ Dublin Meuse
㉓ Star Bar
㉔ Polish Ex-Servicemen's Club
㉕ JM Barrie house

# Northern New Town & Moray Estate Walk

Start: Queen Street
Finish: Dundas Street
Distance: 2.45 miles

The walk begins at the junction of Queen Street and Hanover Street, at the northern edge of the First New Town (see First New Town Walk, p.149). It explores the extension that was created to the north of here, known as the Northern New Town, and also a neighbouring but separate development on land owned by the Earl of Moray.

Edinburgh's First New Town had a massive impact on the city, effectively doubling its size. It stretched (south to north) from Princes Street to Queen Street, and (east to west) from St Andrew Square to Charlotte Square. It followed, broadly, James Craig's winning design of 1766, and the main construction took place from the late 1770s to the early 1800s.

The success of the First New Town encouraged further development, aimed mainly at attracting the wealthier inhabitants of Edinburgh. The obvious place to begin building was immediately to the north – an area that in the 1790s mostly comprised open land interrupted by small villages and industrial sites near the Water of Leith. Much of this land was owned by the Heriot Trust, a charitable body responsible for managing the legacy of James VI's chief goldsmith and money-lender, George Heriot (see p.87).

Cross over Queen Street, named for Charlotte, wife of George III. It contains the most complete set of Georgian houses in the First New Town. Begin walking downhill, with Queen Street Gardens on either side. This continues into Dundas Street, which was named for Henry Dundas, 1st Viscount Melville (1742-1811). He came to be regarded as the unofficial ruler of Scotland thanks to his close political alliance with Prime Minister William Pitt the Younger. A monument to him dominates the centre of St Andrew Square (see p.161).

The genesis of the Northern New Town (also known as the Second New Town) dates back to the early 1790s. A landowner named David Stewart, a former Lord Provost, sent a proposed development plan to the Heriot Trust. Stewart later had to withdraw because he suffered financial problems, but the Trust, with cooperation from the town council, decided to proceed. In 1801 the architects Robert Reid and William Sibbald submitted a further plan – not dissimilar to Stewart's proposal – which was approved.

Reid (1774-1856) was the King's architect and surveyor for Scotland and was responsible for many works in Edinburgh, particularly the exterior of Parliament Square. Sibbald (1760-1809) was another Scottish architect and builder who served as Superintendent of Public Works in Edinburgh from 1790 until his death.

As you go down the hill you should (on a clear day) be able to get a view to the Firth of Forth and beyond. On the left-hand side, obscured by trees, is a small ❶ **Greek temple** inside the gardens. It originally served as a grand shed for garden equipment and today is a gas-regulation station. The gardens – split into three sections – are sadly not open to the public, a subject which has stirred up much debate in recent years as pressure has grown to open up areas like this to common use.

Soon you reach a junction. To your right is ❷ **Abercromby Place**. It was designed by Robert Reid in 1805, and you can see that it curves northwards. This is because the original landowner refused to sell up to the developers, who were then forced to build around his land. It is sometimes described as the first crescent-shaped street in Edinburgh, but this was more by accident than design.

Turn left to enter Heriot Row, named after George Heriot. This quickly became, and remains today, one of the most exclusive and expensive addresses in Scotland. The terraces were largely completed by 1808. The street soon became known as Advocates' Row because many prominent lawyers lived or had their offices here, the legal profession at one point accounting for around 40 per cent of all residents.

Walk over to No 17 Heriot Row. This was the childhood home of ❸ **Robert Louis Stevenson** (1850-1894). One of Scotland's greatest writers, he is best known for *Treasure Island*, *Kidnapped* and *The Strange Case of Dr Jekyll and Mr Hyde*. A sickly child, he was often confined to his bed and would wait to see the 'Leerie' – or lamplighter – arrive at dusk outside the house. His poem *The Lamplighter* includes the lines:

> *My tea is nearly ready and the sun has left the sky;*
> *It's time to take the window to see Leerie going by;*
> *For every night at teatime and before you take your seat,*
> *With lantern and with ladder he comes posting up the street*

Heriot Row

Sadly, Stevenson was never in good health, suffering from what is thought to have been tuberculosis. As he got older he sought better climates to live in; he died, aged only 44, in the Samoan Islands.

Continue along Heriot Row and then walk north up Howe Street. It is named after Richard, Earl Howe, who served as Admiral of the Fleet in the 1790s.

Ahead of you, down the hill, is the impressive sight of ❹ **St Stephen's Church**. It dates from 1828 and was designed by William Henry Playfair (1790-1857). Playfair is one of the most influential architects in the history of modern Edinburgh and is best known today for neo-classical works such as the Scottish National Gallery and the Royal Scottish Academy. The church has a 160-ft tower, and the longest clock pendulum in Europe. If you go up the main steps and look up at the entrance, you can see Playfair's name listed as the architect above the doorway.

In recent decades the church building has been used for a variety of purposes, and split into three levels. In 2014, it was announced that Leslie Benzies, then president of Rockstar North (responsible for *Grand Theft Auto*), was purchasing the former church for use by the local community. The Great Hall of St Stephen's features in *Trainspotting 2*, the scene when Spud attends a recovery group. You will pass St Stephen's later on in the walk.

Turn left into Jamaica Street, the only place in the Northern New Town designed to provide accommodation for workers. Most of it was demolished in 1960. This street – as with India Street visited later – was named after what were then British colonies.

Walk through Jamaica Street South Lane and shortly on your right you see ❺ **Kay's Bar** – one of the city's most atmospheric pubs. It began as a coach house, and in the early 19th century became a wine shop run by John Kay. The wine shop continued to operate until the 1970s before becoming a public house. Kay's Bar is definitely worth a visit if you have time.

5 Kay's bar

Follow the map into India Street – built from around 1820. Cross over to stop outside No 14. The renowned physicist  **James Clerk Maxwell** (1831-1879) was born here. Maxwell is credited with establishing the theory of electromagnetism, one of the most significant discoveries in scientific history. As a result he is often described as the father of modern physics, whose achievements rank with those of Newton and Einstein. Einstein also acknowledged that 'the special theory of relativity owes its origins to Maxwell's equations of the electromagnetic field'.

Today the James Clerk Maxwell Foundation is based here, a charity that promotes the teaching of science and also commemorates Maxwell's work. Visits to the house can be made by prior appointment (see p.207).

Continue up India Street, bearing right into Heriot Row and then along Darnaway Street into Moray Place. You have now entered the Moray Estate development, which began in the 1820s. It was instigated by the 10th Earl of Moray, who decided in around 1822 to develop his 13-acre estate and cash in on the residential housing boom that was sweeping through Edinburgh.

If you had walked this exact route in 1820, you would now be in open fields lined by trees, with nothing north of here until the Water of Leith that flows along on its way to the Firth of Forth. Only Moray House – the Earl's grand family house – stood on the 13-acre site (situated approximately where Randolph Crescent is today).

The family history of the Earls of Moray goes back a long way, but the first Earl was Lord James Stuart (or Stewart). He was the eldest (and illegitimate) son of James V of Scotland, and a half-brother of Mary, Queen of Scots. He became one of her main advisers and was created 1st Earl of Moray by her in 1562. James later ruled Scotland as Regent until he was assassinated in 1570.

The 1st Earl's daughter married James Stuart of Doune, uniting the two families, and James Stuart became the 2nd Earl of Moray. The estate where you are standing now was acquired by the 9th Earl of Moray in 1782 and feued out by the 10th Earl in the early 1820s in accordance with a design by James Gillespie Graham (1776-1855).

Gillespie Graham was better known for his neo-gothic designs but was able to work in the neo-classical style that you see today. The unusual shape of the Moray Estate is a welcome change from the rigid grid pattern of the First New Town. Strict conditions were set down by Gillespie Graham as to how the houses would be designed, thus ensuring a consistency across the area.

Robert Reid, designer of much of the Northern New Town, and Gillespie Graham, responsible for the neighbouring Moray Estate, were bitter enemies. Gillespie Graham – described as 'ambitious, self-seeking and perhaps unscrupulous' – awarded himself the title 'Architect to His Majesty for Scotland' when George IV visited Scotland in 1822. However, Reid had already secured the official title 'Master of Work to the Crown of Scotland' a few years earlier, a role that gave him official responsibility for royal buildings in Scotland. Reid took offence at Graham's rudeness and a feud developed.

Walk around the south side of ❼ **Moray Place**. This 12-sided site named for the earldom is the central feature of the Moray Estate. From around 1825 the upper classes of Edinburgh began to move into the huge houses built here, and some descendants of these original families still reside here today. After nearly 200 years it remains arguably Scotland's grandest street and its rich history featured in the 2014 BBC documentary *The Secret History of Our Streets*.

Over time many of the big houses became uneconomic to run, even for very wealthy families, and were thus gradually converted into premises for commercial companies such as firms of lawyers and architects or made into flats. However, this tranquil place still has a surprisingly large number of private residents.

Follow the map along Great Stuart Street (another nod to the Moray family tree). Alexander Monro (1773-1859), Professor of Anatomy, lived at number 1 on this street. He was known as

'tertius' to distinguish him from his father Alexander ('secundus') and grandfather Alexander ('primus'). All three held the same post at the University's medical school for a continuous period of 125 years.

Monro tertius was regarded as the least gifted of the dynasty. One of his students was Charles Darwin, who wrote in 1825: 'I dislike him and his lectures so much that I cannot speak with decency about them. He is so dirty in person and actions'. He also thought Monro 'made his lectures on human anatomy as dull as he was himself'.

Monro's poor reputation caused many of his students seeking practical experience through the dissection of bodies to go elsewhere. Many paid for private lessons with the gifted surgeon Dr Robert Knox.

Knox's ruthless ambition saw him purchasing the corpses of several murder victims from Scotland's most infamous serial killers – William Burke and William Hare.

Monro had the last laugh, however. Burke was convicted for murder, and his corpse was dissected by Monro himself in front of students of the University. Knox, his great rival, was lucky to escape with just his reputation ruined. Monro even dipped his quill pen into Burke's blood, writing, 'This is written with the blood of Wm Burke, who was hanged at Edinburgh. This blood was taken from his head'.

Continue into ⑧ **Ainslie Place**. This oval-shaped site, much smaller than Moray Place, was named after the 10th Earl's wife, who was the daughter of Sir Philip Ainslie of Pilton. Just to the west of here is Randolph Crescent and the edge of the Moray Estate. As mentioned earlier, the large estate house of the Earl of Moray stood where the Crescent is today. The great architect William Henry Playfair worked and lived at 17 Great Stuart Street (which connects Ainslie Place to Randolph Crescent) from 1831 until his death in 1857.

You can visit Randolph Crescent, which lies on the western edge of the Moray Estate, if you have time. No 3 on the Crescent was the home for many years of the prominent publisher John Blackwood (1818-1879). He was the friend and publisher of many prominent writers including William Makepeace Thackeray (who stayed at the house for two months in 1857) and George Eliot. Blackwood recognised Eliot's talent very early on in her career, and read her manuscripts while living here. From this western edge of the estate, retrace your steps to Moray Place.

Follow the map along the north side. The 10th Earl kept one magnificent house for himself after his lands were developed here – ⑨ **No 28**. It covered around 11,000 square feet and at least a dozen staff looked after the Earl when he stayed in Edinburgh.

Continue past No 28 and take the next left to reach Doune Terrace, dating from 1822. It was named for the heir to the Earl of Moray (known as Lord Doune) and after the family's estate in Doune in Perthshire. This curves down to the right and shortly you reach Gloucester Place.

Just on the right, look out for ⑩ **Gloucester Lane**. This used to be Church Lane and people from Stockbridge to the north would have walked up here to attend services at the parish church of St Cuthbert's near the Lothian Road. Once a country lane through open fields, it is now just a minor road on the border between the Northern New Town and the Moray Estate development. The current name was adopted only in the 1960s after the city authorities decided to cut down on the number of streets in Edinburgh with 'Church' in their name.

Turn right onto India Street and then left along Circus Gardens to reach ⑪ **Royal Circus**. You are back within the boundaries of the Northern New Town, and this is the focal point on the development's western edge.

Royal Circus was designed by William Henry Playfair in the early 1820s. No 24 was home to ⑫ **Sir Henry Littlejohn** (1826-1914), who served as the city's first Medical Officer of Health. His efforts to tackle the terrible conditions endured by many of the poorer residents of the city helped change the lives of thousands of people and gave momentum to the growing public health movement that flourished in the late Victorian age.

He also co-founded the Royal Hospital for Sick Children in Edinburgh and worked closely with another eminent Edinburgh medical figure – Dr Joseph Bell (1837-1911). Both Bell and Littlejohn taught the author Arthur Conan Doyle when he was a medical student at the University, and while Bell's amazing powers of deduction inspired Doyle to create the character of Sherlock Holmes, it is almost certain that Littlejohn influenced the author as well. Littlejohn certainly worked as a forensic expert for the Edinburgh police. Both he and Bell are buried in Dean Cemetery in Edinburgh (see Walk 12).

For 50 years, the original Mrs Doubtfire – Annabella Coutts – ran a second-hand clothes shop in the basement of ⑬ **No 3 South East Circus Place**. Coutts (1887-1979) was married four times, and her surname Doubtfire most likely came from one of her husbands named Dofur – a French army captain who died fighting in WWI. Coutts became known as Madame Doubtfire, and sold mostly high-quality cast-offs provided by the local wealthy residents.

Madame Doubtfire was a feisty, pipe-smoking eccentric who kept dozens of cats. She certainly made an impression on the writer Anne Fine, who moved into Dundas Street in the early 1970s and visited Doubtfire's shop. Years later, having left Edinburgh, Fine decided to write a book with the title *Madame Doubtfire*. She returned to the city to ask Doubtfire's permission but discovered the old lady had died, aged 92.

Fine's 1987 book *Madame Doubtfire* was later adapted (and re-named) by Hollywood. *Mrs Doubtfire* (1993), starring Robin Williams, was a huge world-wide hit. Today the premises are home to the Doubtfire Gallery (see p.207).

Follow the map northwards along the top side of Royal Circus. No 4 Royal Circus was where musician Roy Williamson (1936-90) was born and lived with his family. He studied at the Edinburgh College of Art and founded the famous folk group The Corries with Ronnie Browne. He was responsible for *Flower of Scotland* – Scotland's unofficial national anthem sung before international rugby matches.

Slightly further along, No 6 North East Circus Place was used for the external shots of the flat that features in *Shallow Grave* (1994). The black comedy was the first film directed by Danny Boyle and included Ewan McGregor and Ken Stott among its cast.

St Stephen's Church

Walk along North East Circus Place and turn left down St Vincent Street. Continue downhill to reach St Stephen's at the bottom (mentioned earlier, see p.193).

On the corner is another church – ⑭ **St Vincent's**. It was designed in a neo-gothic style by the brothers John, William and James Hay in 1856. Between 1971 and 1996 it also served as the home of the Commandery of Lochore and of the Military and Hospitaller Order of St Lazarus.

The little-known Order of St Lazarus traces its history back to the Crusades. In 1142, the King of Jerusalem granted land to a church and convent dedicated to St Lazarus, the patron saint of lepers. Members of the Knights Templar stricken by leprosy were required to join the convent, and the Lazarites for a while became a religious-military force.

The Knights of the Order of St Lazarus were forced from the Holy Land and by the late 18th century were settled in France. The Order was suppressed during the French Revolution and revived in 1910, though different factions were then formed, making the modern history of the Order very complex.

Just behind the church is ⑮ **Circus Lane** – a charming curved road that contains a number of pretty mews houses. It is worth spending a few minutes walking down here to explore it a little.

When you have finished, cross over into Cumberland Street, most probably named for Ernest Augustus, younger brother of the Prince of Wales, who was created Duke of Cumberland in 1795. This contains more modest houses that were aimed at artisans, shopkeepers and tradesmen.

To see more examples of ⑯ **mews houses**, turn right into South West Cumberland Street Lane and continue along – it re-joins Cumberland Street at the end. Here turn left into Dundas Street and then right along Fettes Row – the northern edge of the Northern New Town. This soon becomes Royal Crescent, which was laid out from the 1820s in an elegant Greek classical style.

You pass on your right Dundonald Street (but do not go up it). This was named for Rear Admiral Cochrane, Earl of Dundonald (1775-1860). Cochrane was a colourful figure, a Scottish naval officer and politician who was nicknamed 'The Sea Wolf' by the French navy for his exploits during the Napoleonic Wars. He was expelled from the navy for committing fraud, and went on to help the rebel navies of Chile, Brazil and Greece as they fought in wars of independence. Later reinstated to the navy, Dundonald is said to have been one of the inspirations for the fictional hero Horatio Hornblower.

Further down on your left, take the steps to reach ⑰ **George V Park**, and the former site of the ⑱ **Scotland Street Railway Station**. The Scotland Street Tunnel – closed to the public since the 1860s – still runs underground from here right up to Waverley Station (see p.241).

The area to the north of here was once dominated by the industrialised villages of Canonmills and (to the west) Silvermills. During the early 19th century a number of commercial enterprises were based there, including a tannery, distillery, brewery and flour mills. They all used water drawn from the Water of Leith nearby and fed the waste products back into the river. The tannery in particular would have meant the area would have been fairly smelly, and this all contributed to the halting of the Northern New Town at this point.

Continue along Royal Crescent to reach ⑲ **Scotland Street**. The naming of Scotland Street was part of a wider patriotic naming policy for the new streets of the Northern New Town. When Ireland joined the United Kingdom in 1801, the street names in the Northern New Town were just being settled. As a result, a number of streets were diplomatically named to reflect this union, though the original street names of Caledonia Street, Anglia Street and Hibernia Street were changed in 1806 to Scotland Street, London Street and Dublin Street.

Writer Alexander McCall Smith has created a popular series of stories based around this road, the first book called *44 Scotland Street* (2005). One of the main characters is a student named Pat who becomes a tenant at No 44 (there is no such number in real life). In the publicity blurb for the series, it is written that 'Scotland Street occupies a busy, Bohemian corner of Edinburgh's New Town, where the old haute bourgeoisie finds itself having to rub shoulders with students, poets and portraitists'. In between writing books, McCall Smith is also a Professor of Medical Law at Edinburgh University.

Walk up Scotland Street to reach ⑳ **Drummond Place**. This is named after Lord Provost George Drummond (1688-1760), who owned several acres here and lived in a large house named Drummond Lodge. Drummond was perhaps the figure most responsible for galvanising the town council into agreeing to develop the First New Town in the mid-18th century and as a result his importance to the history of Edinburgh is immense.

Drummond Place began to be laid out in 1804 and was not completed until the early 1820s. It was designed to form the main east end of the Northern New Town, much as St Andrew Square formed the eastern focal point of the First New Town.

Drummond Lodge used to stand here (where the gardens are today) in the 18th century. After George Drummond died, it was sold and then rebuilt in the 1770s as a mansion called Bellevue to a design by the great architect Robert Adam. This building was later used as a customs house before having to be demolished in the 1840s during the creation of the Scotland Street Tunnel that ran directly below.

Compton Mackenzie (1883-1972), best remembered as the author of *Whisky Galore* and *The Monarch of the Glen*, lived at numbers 31 and 32. He was also one of the co-founders of the Scottish National Party in 1928.

Bear left around Drummond Place to enter **London Street** on the east side. Cross over to the south side to stop by **21** **No 15**. There is a plaque outside that recalls the curious fact that the Icelandic national anthem was composed in the house in 1874, the lyrics by Matthías Jochumsson and the music by Sveinbjörn Sveinbjörnsson.

Retrace your steps to Drummond Place and walk along the south side and then head left into Dublin Street. Walk uphill and

*Nelson Place*

cross over to turn right up **22 Dublin Meuse**. This is a pretty, tranquil place, despite being so centrally located, that contains a number of mews houses. Turn right along Northumberland Place and Nelson Place.

On the left, not immediately obvious, is the **23 Star Bar**. It is located in a category 'B' listed building designed by Robert Reid and William Sibbald dating from 1804. It is a cosy pub with a great juke box that is said to have a clause in its lease forbidding the removal of a male human skull found inside...

Continue on, bearing right onto Nelson Street, and walk northwards, staying on the left-hand side. You now re-join Drummond Place on its west side. On the left at No 11 is the **24 Polish Ex-Servicemen's Club** – a legacy of the first wave of Polish migrants to come to Scotland during WWII. Many were unable to return to Poland under the communist regime that took control of the country after WWII ended.

Continue north, just past the junction with Great King Street. If you look down at the pavement to your left, you should be able to see the substantial blocks of stone that were laid here to allow wealthy residents travelling by horse or carriage to reach the pavement without getting their shoes dirty on the untreated roads.

Head down Great King Street. Designed by Robert Reid, it was laid out from 1804; however, many of the buildings were not completed for another decade. This was partly as a result of the Napoleonic Wars, which caused great economic problems that had a severe impact on many developers. Great King Street was planned to be as prestigious as Heriot Row but it never quite managed to attain the same level of exclusivity.

Named after George III, it was always intended a grand central thoroughfare through the heart of the Northern New Town connecting Royal Circus to Drummond Place, just as George Street linked Charlotte Square and St Andrew Square in the First New Town.

Famous past residents include **25** **JM Barrie** (1860-1937), best known as the author of *Peter Pan*, who lived at No 3 when he was a student at the University (there is a plaque), and Thomas de Quincey (1785-1859), author of *Confessions of an English Opium-Eater*, who lived at No 9.

Continue along and after a few minutes you reach Dundas Street, where the walk ends. From here you can head up the hill to where the walk began. ●

## VISIT...

**James Clerk Maxwell Foundation**
14 India Street, EH3 6EZ
*www.clerkmaxwellfoundation.org*

**Doubtfire Gallery**
3 North West Circus Place,
EH3 6TP
www.doubtfiregallery.com

## EAT/DRINK...

**Kay's Bar**
39 Jamaica Street, EH3 6HF
*www.kaysbar.co.uk*

**Star Bar**
1 Northumberland Pl, EH3 6LQ
*www.starbar.co.uk*

**The Pantry (café)**
1 North West Circus Pl,
EH3 6ST
*www.thepantryedinburgh.co.uk*

## SHOP...

**Stockbridge Market**
Saunders Street, EH3 6TQ
*www.stockbridgemarket.com*

Well Court and Water of Leith p.215

# 8 Dean Village & Stockbridge Walk

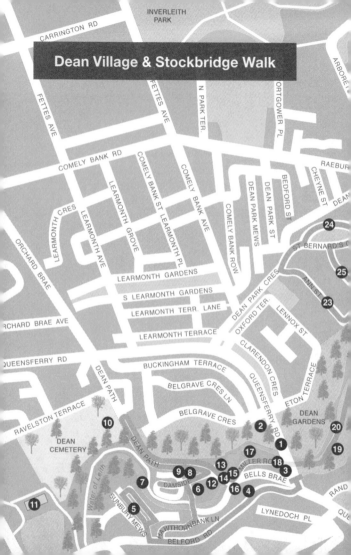

# Dean Village & Stockbridge Walk

1. Dean Bridge
2. Holy Trinity Church
3. Kirkbrae House
4. Drumsheugh Baths
5. Sunbury Street
6. Well Court
7. Dam
8. Dean Path Buildings
9. Tenement building
10. Dean Cemetery
11. Scottish National Gallery of Modern Art
12. Old village school
13. West Mill
14. Old bridge
15. Sign of the Baxters
16. Baxters' Tolbooth
17. Lindsay's Mill
18. Mar's Flour Mill
19. Greenland Flour Mill
20. St George's Well
21. St Bernard's Well
22. St Bernard's Bridge
23. Ann Street
24. St Bernard's Crescent
25. Danube Street
26. Clock tower
27. Water of Leith pathway
28. Stockbridge Colonies
29. Glenogle Baths
30. Stockbridge Parish Church
31. Stockbridge Library
32. St Stephen Place
33. Red-brick building (former church hall
34. St Stephen's School
35. Stockbridge Farmers' Market
36. Duncan's Land

# Dean Village & Stockbridge Walk

Start: Dean Bridge
Finish: Gloucester Street
Distance: 3.45 miles

Dean Bridge, Holy Trinity Church and Kirkbrae House

This walk begins on the south side of Dean Bridge by the junction with Bells Brae and Belford Road. It begins with a stroll through Dean Village before exploring parts of Stockbridge.

❶ Dean Bridge was built in 1831-32 and was designed by the famous Scottish civil engineer Thomas Telford (1757-1834), known as the 'Colossus of the Roads'. This was Telford's last major work, having left a legacy of canals, bridges and roads throughout Britain.

The financing of the bridge came largely from John Learmonth (1789-1858), a local landowner who served as Lord Provost of Edinburgh in 1831. He had purchased the Dean Estate from the Nisbet family in the 1820s, and wished to develop a new residential district to the north that would attract the wealthier classes. However, first he needed a better transport link as traffic at the time had to go down into the steep valley below and cross a small bridge over the Water of Leith located in Dean Village (seen shortly).

While the new Dean Bridge helped with this problem, its great height also ensured that it became a popular suicide spot – known as the 'Bridge of Sighs'. Later raising of the parapets helped to end this reputation.

On the other side of the bridge is the substantial ❷ **Holy Trinity Church**, built in a neo-gothic style in the 1830s. In the 1950s it was converted for use as an electricity transformer station before being redeployed once again as a church in recent years.

Just on the south-west side of the bridge stands ❸ **Kirkbrae House**. This has its origins in the 17th century when it was a tavern for the millers and bakers who worked down in Dean Village. The Incorporation of Baxters (or bakers) was a powerful trade guild that controlled the baking industry in Edinburgh for many centuries. The guild also ran many of the flour mills by the edge of the Water of Leith.

Their tavern here was extended in a baronial style in the late 19th century and is now a private home. Look out for the trade arms and sundial, and some stones from Dean House – a grand building that was demolished in the early 1840s to make way for Dean Cemetery (seen later).

Follow the map down Belford Road, passing the ❹ **Drumsheugh Baths** on the right – the oldest private swimming club in Edinburgh. It was built in a Moorish style in the 1890s (replacing a structure from 1882 that was destroyed in a fire).

You are walking on the south side of Dean Village. For centuries this was called the Water of Leith Village – so named because it was located by the Water of Leith that flows

View of Dean Village

from the Pentland Hills before exiting into the Firth of Forth by Leith. The village was the centre of Edinburgh's milling industry for around 800 years. The name 'Dean' is derived from 'dene', meaning a deep valley.

Belford Road is possibly named after a ford that once existed near here by Bell's Mills. The road, today fairly quiet, was part of the old road to Queensferry. Follow the map, getting a good view of Dean Village to your right. Take the right-hand turn into Sunbury Street and continue your descent.

Milling began in this area by the Water of Leith in the 12th century after the monks of Holyrood Abbey were granted rights by King David I. The strong current meant this was a good place for flour mills, then powered by water wheels.

Around 11 flour mills were run by the Incorporation of Baxters (or bakers) by the 17th century, and during the 19th century there was also a chemical works, distillery and tannery operating in the village. Hundreds of factory workers, millers and bakers would have thronged this area, a far cry from the quiet streets you see today.

While the opening of Dean Bridge in the 1830s took traffic away from the village, it was more profoundly affected in the latter half of the 19th century when large steam-powered flour mills began to open in Leith. The smaller mills along the Water of Leith struggled to compete and began to close.

By the end of the 19th century the village was facing severe economic and social problems. This never really improved and the low point for the village in terms of social decay was probably in the 1950s. After this, the area was slowly regenerated into what is now a prosperous and tranquil residential neighbourhood close to the heart of Edinburgh.

**❺ Sunbury Street** and the surrounding area is named after Sunbury House, and an associated distillery that once occupied several acres here. The Sunbury Distillery was founded in 1813 by James Haig, a member of the Haig whisky dynasty. It soon became one of the biggest distilleries in Scotland.

In the 1830s Graham Menzies bought part of the business, later taking over from the Haig family. Menzies moved production to the Caledonian Distillery (north of Dalry Road – see p.290) and the distillery here closed in 1856. The distillery complex included a mill and mash house, a molasses storehouse, huge boilers, four warehouses, workmen's cottages, a stables and a piggery.

Walk down to the end, then around the corner and back along Belford Mews. These streets contain good examples of mews buildings and 19th-century artisan housing. Return to Belford Road and then turn left, taking another left down the steep Hawthornbank Lane which leads you into the heart of Dean Village.

You reach a footbridge from which you get an excellent view of the village and the Water of Leith that runs through it. Cross over the footbridge, with the vast **❻ Well Court** on the right as you cross. The footbridge stands approximately were there used to be a ford across the river – the original crossing point over the Water of Leith until the construction of the old bridge, which you will see shortly. You may spot some unusual stone

6 Well Court

sculptures – stacked stones made into a tower. These are the work of a local resident and add a touch a quirkiness to an already unusual part of Edinburgh.

Bear left into Damside and walk through an archway at the end to see (over the wall) a ❼ **dam** (or 'cauld') by the river. These were built to create a greater drop to increase the flow of water. By the 18th century there were three such dams along this stretch of the river. Water was also diverted from the river into man-made channels (known as 'lades') that led to the mills and powered the water wheels.

Water of Leith

Damside stands on the site of a large chemical works that operated in the early 19th century before being replaced by a tannery. The tannery continued until the 1970s. When it closed, it marked the end of any significant industrial activity in Dean Village – a historic moment given that milling began here in the 12th century.

Walk back to visit Well Court (you can walk into the courtyard). This was designed in 1884 for John Ritchie Findlay (1824-98), owner of the *Scotsman*, and its purpose was to provide accommodation for working-class tenants. Many of the less well-off residents of Dean Village were badly affected by the decline in the fortunes of the milling industry. Findlay was a prominent philanthropist, responsible for providing the funds that created the Scottish National Portrait Gallery, on Queen Street in Edinburgh, and helping to secure the admission of women to the University

Medical School. However, it is said in the case of Well Court that Findlay's motives were slightly selfish, and that he wanted not only to help the less fortunate, but to improve the view from his huge house at number 3 Rothesay Terrace over the industrial buildings of Dean Village that lay down below.

Turn left up Dean Path. Before the construction of Dean Bridge, this would have been a bustling place, full of passenger coaches and other traffic making its way to and from Edinburgh.

On the left you pass **8 Dean Path Buildings**, dating from 1885 and also built for Findlay. This is a classic Victorian tenement block designed by Findlay's son James L Findlay. Just beside Dean Path Buildings (as you continue up the hill) is a **9 tenement building** from the late 18th century on the left at number 29. This is a style of building that would have been common in Dean Village at the time when the mills were at their busiest.

Continue uphill and around the bend. Shortly on your left you find the entrance for **10 Dean Cemetery**, subject of a separate walk (see p.313). If you do not have time to do that walk, it is worth spending half an hour strolling through the cemetery, which contains some of the most fascinating tombs and headstones to be found in Edinburgh. Prominent people buried here include architect William Henry Playfair, lawyer and conservationist Lord Cockburn, controversial Major General Sir Hector MacDonald and Dr Joseph Bell – the inspiration for Sherlock Holmes.

The cemetery opened in the mid-1840s. It stands on the former site of Dean House which was founded in the early 17th century and owned for many years by the Nisbet family. On the other side of the entrance gates (east side) is approximately where the original Village of Dean and Dean Farm once stood. From the mid-19th century the original buildings and open fields around them began to disappear as the area was developed for residential housing. As the Village of Dean became just a memory, its name was co-opted by the Water of Leith Village, which became known as Dean Village.

The cemetery is adjacent to the ⓫ **Scottish National Gallery of Modern Art** – and if you have time you may wish to visit one or both of the gallery buildings here (see p.233). You can access one of the two galleries – known as Modern Two – through a gate on the west side of the cemetery (very near a distinctive pink pyramid tomb).

Modern Two is housed in what was originally built as the Dean Orphan Hospital in 1833 by Thomas Hamilton. Its sister gallery – Modern One (on the other side of Belford Road) – dates from the 1820s and was originally John Watson's School for fatherless children.

Otherwise, retrace your steps down Dean Path, on a clear day enjoying a good view of Edinburgh through the trees. Pass Well Court on your right again and stop by the ⓬ **old village school** that stands beside it, which dates from 1875. In recent years it has been converted into residential flats.

On the other side of the road, just before the bridge, is **⓭ West Mill**. Once used for flour production, this is a rare example of a surviving mill building in Dean Village. A mill stood on this site for centuries, though this structure dates from 1805. Look up to see a roundel plaque high on the south-west wall that displays a wheatsheaf as well as the names of the Deacon and other officers of the Baxters guild. The Baxters bought this and other mills in the village from the town authorities in the 1730s. West Mill has also been converted for residential use.

Cross the **⓮ old bridge**, which dates from the 18th century and was the main crossing over the Water of Leith until the Dean Bridge opened. Originally traffic crossing the bridge would have continued up the steep incline of Bells Brae ahead of you (reaching the starting point of the walk).

Stop on the bridge to get one of the best views of Dean Village. On the south side of the bridge – just by the wooden bench on the left – look out for the **⓯ sign of the Baxters**. The sign shows the paddles used to get the loaves out of the hot ovens, with the loaves themselves sitting in the middle.

Directly ahead of you as you cross the bridge is a yellow building known as **⓰ Baxters' Tolbooth**, which dates from 1675. This was once the headquarters of the Baxters and also served as their granary. Above the doorway is an old sign which reads, 'God bless the Baxters of Edinburgh who built this hous 1675' (sic).

Follow the map eastwards on the path beside the Water of Leith. You will hear the roar of another dam beside you.

Shortly on the left is a small open space that was part of the site of **17** **Lindsay's Mill**, used for corn. All that remains today are the mill stones, which are made of orthoquartzite and were imported from France. The material is particularly hard and was needed because at one time coarser American corn was being imported requiring a stronger millstone to process it effectively. There are useful information boards here giving you more history of the village and its milling industry.

Carry on, passing underneath the great span of Dean Bridge. Just here (before you pass under Dean Bridge) was the site of **18** **Mar's Flour Mill**. Like many of the mills near here, this closed in the late 19th century. Continue eastwards, beginning to leave Dean Village. In Ian Rankin's book *Strip Jack* (1992), a woman is found dead in the river underneath the bridge and the case is investigated by Detective Inspector John Rebus.

Up on the right-hand side stand substantial walls and behind them the fine houses of the Moray Estate. In the early 1820s the Earl of Moray's estate comprised Moray House and surrounding fields.

However, within the next decade this was all replaced by upmarket houses designed for the wealthier classes (see Walk 7). It was a dramatic transformation of the area south of the Water of Leith, and typified Edinburgh's growth beyond the original New Town.

As you walk around the gentle bend after the bridge you pass the site of **19** **Greenland Flour Mill**. In the 19th century a great 'lade' – or man-made channel – carried water at head height from Dean Village to mills like this situated further downstream.

*Riverside walk*

Shortly on the left you will see a modest stone building which houses ⑳ **St George's Well** and dates from 1810. It was named also to celebrate George III (whose jubilee was the year before) and is one of two wells on this part of the river that were once popular with visitors. It was claimed that the mineral waters here could cure various ailments.

Continue on. On your left you can see the beautiful Dean Gardens and then the classical columns of ㉑ **St Bernard's Well**. Just before the well you can take some steps on the left that lead down to a pathway right beside the Water of Leith – you can return up to the main path further along.

The natural spring around which St Bernard's Well was constructed is said to have been discovered by three boys from George Heriot's School who were fishing on the river. The original well-house was built on the spring in around 1760, and the current structure (incorporating a pump room) dates largely from around 1789, when it was built for a prominent lawyer and judge named Francis Garden, Lord Gardenstone (1721-93).

21. St Bernard's Well

Garden was an unusual man, so fond of pigs he kept them in his bedroom (and occasionally in his bed). He was also friends with Robert Burns, both part of a small group of Edinburgh men who would meet each other in order to plan how best to progress the cause of political and electoral reform in the last years of the 18th century. In 1788, he was also one of the judges in the case of Joseph Knight, an African slave who was brought to Scotland by his 'owner' and who then ran away, arguing that slavery was not permitted

under Scottish law. Knight showed enormous bravery in taking on the whole conservative, pro-slavery establishment of Scotland, and was supported in his case by Dr Samuel Johnson and James Boswell. Lord Gardenstone and his fellow judges ruled in Knight's favour, setting a precedent that the laws of Scotland did not allow slavery.

The main structure you can see was designed by Alexander Nasmyth as a circular Greek temple supported by Doric columns. Nasmyth (1758-1840) was a famous painter, and his sons were buried at Dean Cemetery (one son, James, invented the steam-hammer). Nasmyth's portrait of Robert Burns is perhaps the most reproduced image of the poet in history. The statue at the centre of the temple is of Hygieia, the Greek goddess of health.

The well was very popular, and its waters were said to cure blindness and all sorts of other illnesses. The 18th-century poet Claudero wrote that the water 'cleans the intestines and an appetite gives while morbific matters it quite away drives.' Another person thought the water tasted like 'the washings from a foul gun barrel'.

According to Edinburgh lore, St Bernard of Clairvaux (d. 1153) lived in a cave near here, although there is no biographical evidence he ever came to Scotland. One of Edinburgh's 'lost' football teams was St Bernard's FC, which began in the 1870s and continued until 1943. The team was based for many years where the George V Park in Canonmills is found today (see p.239-40) and was named after this well. The well finally closed to the public in 1940 due to health concerns about the quality of the water. The famous painter JMW Turner sketched a view of Edinburgh in 1818 that featured St Bernard's Well.

Follow the map to **㉒ St Bernard's Bridge**, which dates from the early 1820s. You are now approaching Stockbridge. For many centuries this was a small village best known for its mill and a crossing point over the river used by herdsmen bringing cattle to market. The name of the village itself is derived from the Scots 'stock brig', meaning a timber bridge.

Cross over the bridge, but pause to look at the tidy Edinburgh allotments on the south side with their doors set into the wall.

Cross over to the north side and enter Upper Dean Terrace, turning left up the hill. The actress and ballet dancer Moira Shearer (1926-2006) lived at number 3 Upper Dean Terrace with her husband, the broadcaster Ludovic Kennedy (1919-2009). Shearer is perhaps best

known for her leading role in the Powell and Pressburger film *The Red Shoes* (1948), and she also acted in two other films directed by Michael Powell – *The Tales of Hoffmann* and *Peeping Tom*. Kennedy's career as a journalist was also highly successful, and his investigative work into miscarriages of justice helped to bring about the abolition of the death penalty in Britain.

Stockbridge's fortunes changed dramatically after the famous painter Sir Henry Raeburn (1756-1823) married a rich widow named Ann Edgar in 1780. She had inherited the Deanhaugh Estate and Raeburn later acquired the neighbouring St Bernard's Estate, developing the fields for residential housing in the early 1800s.

New streets began to be laid out here from around 1813, although the size of the development was much more modest than the New Town. Follow the map into **23 Ann Street** – named after Mrs Raeburn. It was most likely designed by the architect James Milne. One of the earliest streets to be completed in the new development of Stockbridge, it is often described as the most attractive in Edinburgh. It features front gardens, noticeably absent in most other houses built in this period.

Follow the map eastwards into **24 St Bernard's Crescent**, which dates from the mid-1820s. This is one of the grandest parts of Stockbridge and is frequently used as a location for period film and television dramas; from here, turn right into pretty **25 Danube Street**. Number 17 on this street was the location of perhaps Edinburgh's most notorious brothel, run for over 30 years by Dora Noyce.

Noyce was an Edinburgh character, often seen in furs and pearls. She was charged nearly 50 times with living off immoral earnings; however, she retained a wry sense of humour, able to quip that her brothel was just a 'YMCA with extras'. She also said, 'in my profession there is no such thing as bad publicity, so do make sure you print the correct address in your newspaper'. When American navy ships were in dock at Leith, it is said that the sailors queued up outside the brothel as far as Ann Street. Noyce died in 1977, aged 76.

At the end turn left, walking along the north bank of the Water of Leith via Dean Terrace. You pass Carlton Street on the left, which stands approximately on the site of St Bernard's House, once occupied by Raeburn.

Continue on to reach the heart of Stockbridge at Deanhaugh Street. This and Raeburn Place have lots of cafés, up market restaurants and shops, and Stockbridge has long had a reputation as one of the most interesting parts of Edinburgh (although perhaps not so bohemian as it once was). There are also a number of fine charity shops, some containing a wide selection of second-hand books. You may also want to pay a visit to the Stockbridge Tap, awarded the title of the best pub in Scotland in 2015. In 2016, Stockbridge was voted the best place to live in Scotland by a survey conducted in *The Sunday Times*.

One notable resident of Stockbridge is the physicist Peter Higgs. Higgs (b. 1929) became a professor at Edinburgh University, and in the 1960s first published his controversial theory about the existence of a sub-atomic particle. It took nearly 50 years for his theory about the so-called 'God Particle' to be proven after hugely complex experiments were carried out by CERN, the European Organization for Nuclear Research. Higgs was awarded the Noble Prize for Physics in 2013.

Stockbridge also has a strong connection with sporting history. The first international rugby match took place here on 27 March 1871, when Scotland played England at the Edinburgh

Academy sports ground (a few hundred yards to the west of here off Raeburn Place – not visited on the walk).

The Edinburgh Academical Football Club, the oldest rugby club in Scotland, is still based at the site today. It is one of the best amateur rugby teams in Scotland, and has produced dozens of international players. The club's name refers to football because when it was founded in 1857, the split between rugby football and association football (i.e. soccer) was yet to take place.

Next door is The Grange Club, the main home of the Scottish cricket team. While Scotland is not commonly associated with cricket, the game has a small but dedicated following, in Edinburgh in particular. The Grange has hosted numerous international matches including legends such as Shane Warne and WG Grace.

You should now be standing by the Stockbridge bridge. The first stone crossing over the Water of Leith was built in 1786 and the current structure dates from 1801. On the west side look down to see one of Antony Gormley's statues standing in the Water of Lieth. Just beside the bridge is a **26 clock tower** which was originally part of the Edinburgh Savings Bank building that was constructed in around 1840. In the mid-19th century the north-east side of the bridge was dominated by the Stockbridge flour mill and Stockbridge Market.

Go down the small flight of stairs on the left-hand side of the bridge and return to the **27 Water of Leith pathway**. Continue on, and after a few hundred yards the path leads you up to a bridge. Cross the bridge and bear right through Bridge Place to reach Glenogle Road.

Continue along Glenogle Road, passing the **28** **Stockbridge Colonies**. These parallel terraces were built between 1861 and 1911 by the Edinburgh Co-operative Building Company, although they were mainly completed by the 1870s. A number were named after the company's founders including the stonemason, geologist and journalist Hugh Miller (1802-56), David Bell (joiner), James Collins (stonemason), and James Colville (stonemason).

If you walk along the south side of the terraces you can see (facing Glenogle Road) stone plaques depicting the tools of various trades, such as plumber, joiner and plasterer. The development began after a group of stonemasons decided to build affordable accommodation for artisan and skilled workers. Look out for the plaque dated 1861 that recalls the original name of the development – Glenogle Park. The company also founded similar residential developments in other parts of Edinburgh.

When finished at the Colonies, take a look at the **29** **Glenogle Baths**. These date from c.1900 and are a fine example of swimming baths from the late-Victorian era. The name Glenogle may be named for the Haig family, who ran a distillery nearby and had property in Glenogle in Perthshire.

Walk past the baths and on the corner take the ascending steps on your left. You are now in Saxe-Coburg Place, dating from the early 1820s and designed by James Milne. It was not fully completed and the baths fill a section that was left empty, having originally been meant for housing. It was named after Prince Leopold of Saxe-Coburg, the widowed husband of George IV's daughter Charlotte. Charlotte, who was the only daughter of George IV and Caroline of Brunswick, died at the age of 21.

This is one of the most attractive parts of Stockbridge. Carry along Saxe-Coburg Street, looking out on the left for **30** **Stockbridge Parish Church** (originally called St Bernard's Church), also by Milne, which dates from the early 1820s.

Milne (c.1778-c.1850s) is not one of the best-known architects in Edinburgh's history but was responsible for a number of buildings and streets in Stockbridge including Ann Street, Danube Street and where you are now. He worked in Edinburgh between 1809 and 1834 and later moved to Newcastle.

From the church, retrace your steps and follow the map along Dean Bank Lane to join Hamilton Place. Just here is **31** **Stockbridge Library**, which dates from 1898. Beside it is a plain yet attractive former Salvation Army Hall that once served as the organisation's divisional headquarters in Scotland. Hamilton Place is named after a Mrs Hamilton who moved here in 1813. Numbers 10-11 are the site of Hamilton Place Academy, where Alexander Graham Bell (1847-1922) studied.

Bear right and shortly on the left is a small entrance into **32** **St Stephen Place** (originally Market Place) which leads into the former site of Stockbridge Market. The market was built where a farm once stood, and operated between 1825 and 1906. As

you walk through, look back to see the old entrance arch which refers to what was sold here – 'Butcher Meat Fruits Fish & Poultry'.

Continue ahead to reach St Stephen Street. This smart thoroughfare contains some of the most charming shops in Stockbridge. According to Edinburgh lore, the Velvet Underground singer Nico lived on the street in the 1980s. Sadly this has never been proven.

Turn left and walk up a hundred yards or so to see the curious little **33 red-brick building** on the right (beside number 104). Now a hall used by a dance company, this was originally attached to nearby St Vincent's Church and dates from the early 1860s. Next door is the former **34 St Stephen's School** building, dating from the 1830s. The school was once connected to St Stephen's Church (designed by Playfair), which stands a short walk along St Stephen Street.

Continue along a bit further. Number 97 was used for external shots of DI John Rebus's flat in the television adaptation of Ian Rankin's novels, which starred Ken Stott as Rebus.

Just on the west side of St Stephen's is the former site of Tiffany's (number 99). This began as the Grand Cinema in the 1920s, and later became a nightclub. Many famous acts played

here including Iron Maiden, Iggy Pop, and The Police.

From here walk westwards, back down St Stephen Street to reach Kerr Street. You pass on the right-hand side Bells Diner – an Edinburgh institution that makes the tastiest burgers in Scotland.

At Kerr Street turn right, crossing over the street to reach Jubilee Gardens opposite. The excellent **35 Stockbridge Farmers' Market** is held here every Sunday between 10am and 5pm. Opposite the Gardens is Baker's Place, named in connection with the flour mill and associated baking trade that historically were located in this part of Stockbridge.

From Jubilee Gardens walk up Gloucester Street. This was once called Church Street and was the route local people walked along to reach central Edinburgh in order to attend services at St Cuthbert's Church (off Lothian Road). The building of Stockbridge Parish Church in the 1820s meant this long journey was no longer necessary.

A little way up on the left is a shop with a sign above it that reads 'Fear God Onlye 1605 IR'. The IR refers to Iacobus Rex – then King James VI of Scotland, who had become James I of England and Ireland in 1603. This was known as **36** **Duncan's Land** and is where the painter David Roberts (1796-1864) was born. He became well known during the Victorian age for his theatrical design work and lithograph prints made from sketches of places such as Egypt and Jerusalem. The building dates from the 1790s and incorporates stones (including the sign from 1605) that came from demolished buildings in the Old Town.

This is the end of the walk – you can return to the bustling streets of Stockbridge, where there are plenty of bus stops. Alternatively, if you continue up Gloucester Street northwards you will reach Queen Street, just a short walk from Princes Street and the heart of the New Town. ●

## VISIT...

**Scottish National Gallery
of Modern Art**
73 Belford Rd, EH4 3DR
*www.nationalgalleries.org*

**Patriothall Gallery**
1 Patriothall, EH3 5AY
*www.patriothallgallery.co.uk*

## SHOP...

Stockbridge Farmers' Market
Saunders Street, EH3 6TQ
*www.stockbridgemarket.com*

## EAT, DRINK...

**Söderberg**
3 Deanhaugh St, EH4 1LU

**Bells Diner**
7 St Stephen St, EH3 5AN
*www.bellsdineredinburgh.com*

**Stockbridge Tap**
2-6 Raeburn Pl, EH4 1HN

# 9 Canonmills, Warriston & Silvermills Walk

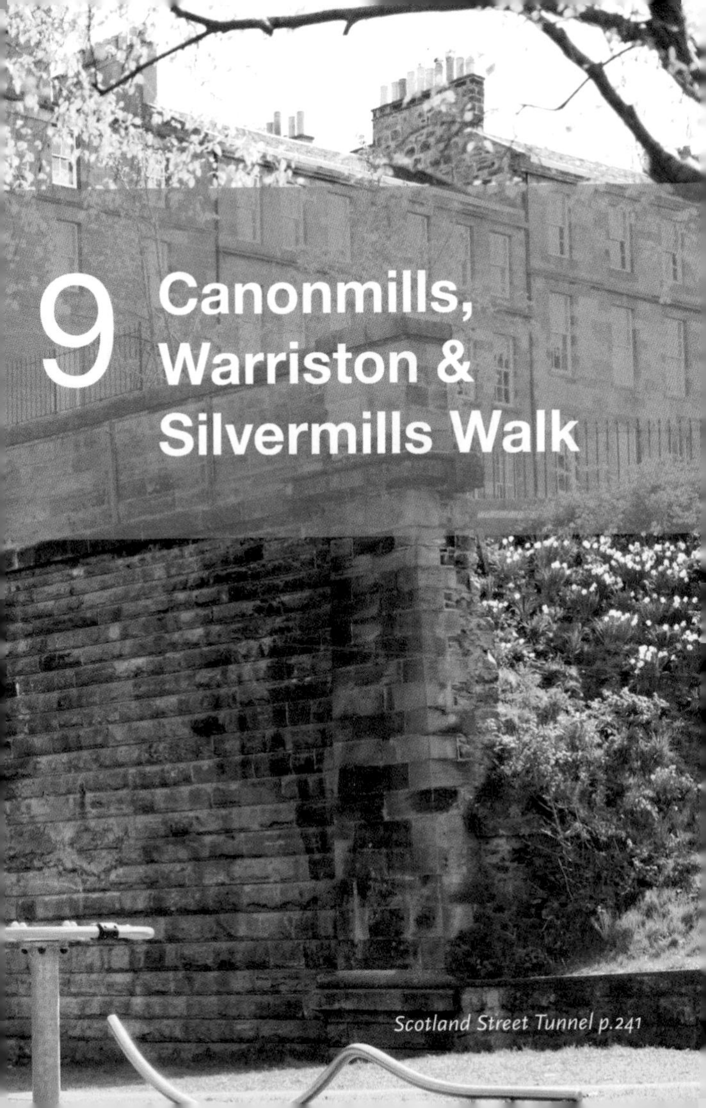

*Scotland Street Tunnel p.241*

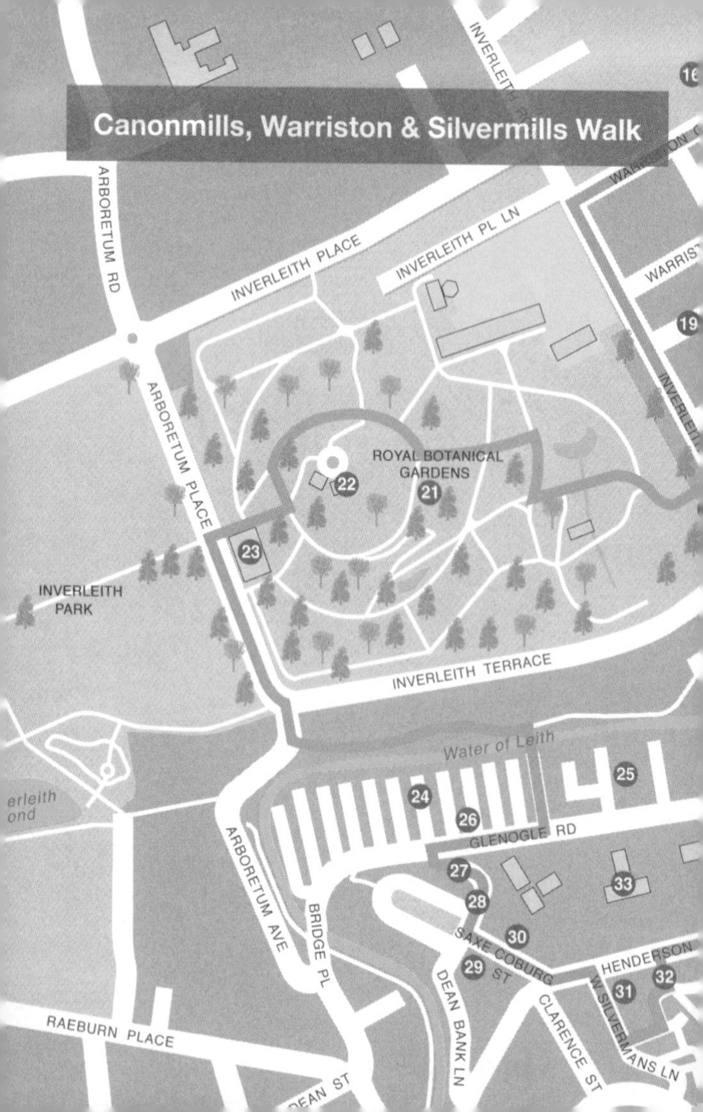

# Canonmills, Warriston & Silvermills Walk

**INVERLEITH**

16

**ARBORETUM RD**

**ARBORETUM PLACE**

**INVERLEITH PLACE**

**INVERLEITH PL LN**

**WARRISTON C**

**WARRIS**

19

**INVERLEITH**

**ROYAL BOTANICAL GARDENS**

21

22

23

**INVERLEITH PARK**

**erleith ond**

**INVERLEITH TERRACE**

**Water of Leith**

24

26

25

**GLENOGLE RD**

**ARBORETUM AVE**

**BRIDGE PL**

27

28

30

33

**SAXE COBURG ST**

29

**DEAN BANK LN**

**HENDERSON**

31

32

**W SILVERMANS LN**

**CLARENCE ST**

**RAEBURN PLACE**

**DEAN ST**

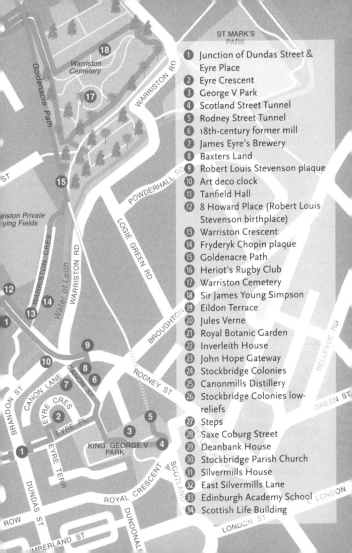

ST MARK'S PARK

Warriston Cemetery

Goldenacre Path

WARRISTON RD

POWDERHALL RD

LOGIE GREEN RD

riston Private ying Fields

WARRISTON CRES

WARRISTON RD

Water of Leith

BROUGHTON

BELLEVUE RD

GREEN ST

BRANDON ST

CANON LANE

CANON ST

EYRE CRES

EYRE PL

RODNEY ST

EYRE TERR

KING GEORGE V PARK

SCOTLAND

E LONDON

DUNDAS ST

ROW

ROYAL CRESCENT

DUNDONALD

CUMBERLAND ST

LONDON ST

# Canonmills, Warriston & Silvermills Walk

Start: Junction of Dundas Street and Eyre Place
Finish: Junction of Henderson Row and Dundas Street
Distance: 3.92 miles

This walk begins at the ❶ **junction of Dundas Street and Eyre Place**. It explores two 'lost' villages of old Edinburgh – Canonmills and Silvermills. During the walk you also have an opportunity to explore the crumbling grandeur of Warriston Cemetery and the Royal Botanic Garden.

You are standing now on the site of the old village of Canonmills. It was named after flour mills which once stood here by the Water of Leith and were controlled by the canons of Holyrood Abbey. The abbey was gifted the land by King David I in 1128 and the mills were first formally recorded in 1423. For many years, the Baxters – an important trade incorporation or guild of the bakers of Edinburgh – were obliged to obtain their flour from the mills. This provided the abbey with a lucrative source of income.

Follow the map into ❷ **Eyre Crescent**, named after James Eyre. He was a brewer who in the early 19th century built a large property named Canonmills House, which stood in the middle of today's Eyre Crescent. He died in 1832 and his grand house was demolished in 1879; a church then stood on the spot for several decades. Eyre also owned a substantial brewery just to the north-east, at the top end of today's Canon Street.

A number of industries that required access to a good water supply were located in Canonmills, and at various times during the 19th century you would have found a tannery, distillery, brewery and paper-making factory. Like the flour mills, many of these businesses used water brought here through a man-made channel known as a 'lade' or 'lead' that was connected to the Water of Leith.

The original medieval mills, powered by water wheels were located on the south side of the Water of Leith. Over time farms and cottages were built around them to form a small village. With the Reformation, the influence of the abbey on Canonmills ended. While new industries moved here to take advantage of the water supply, the flour mills along this part of the Water of Leith began to decline during the 19th century. This was largely because they were unable to compete with larger, steam-powered mills in Leith.

Follow the map into **❸ George V Park**. This is located on the former site of Canonmills Loch, which was formed in the hollow of the Canonmills area, possibly by an overflow of water from the Water of Leith that became trapped. The loch was only a few feet deep and was drained in a number of phases from the 18th century until finally being emptied in 1847.

One of the country's oldest curling clubs was based by the loch and many matches were held on the frozen water during winter. Local people also skated and fished here. In the late 18th century Canonmills was well known for its orchards and strawberry fields – a rural idyll that was soon swept away when the Industrial Age arrived.

In the 1860s, after the loch had been drained, the Royal Patent Gymnasium was built on this site. It lay beside the Scotland Street railway station (which was on the north-east side of today's park). The Gymnasium was the creation of a philanthropist and businessman named John Cox who wanted to create novel entertainments that also encouraged visitors to take part in physical exercise. The Cox family was based in Gorgie and made their fortune out of the production of gelatine.

Cox thought on a big scale, with his site resembling an outdoor 'Gym of the Gods'. A major feature was the 'Great Sea Serpent' – a massive circular structure located on a pool of water that allowed up to 600 people to sit and row, turning the structure around. There was also a huge see-saw that could hold 100 people, raising them up 50 feet in the air. In the 1870s a skating rink and curling pond were added.

There had been nothing like it in Edinburgh before and it was initially successful. Special events such as athletics meetings were also held here. At its peak, a single day would see around 15,000 visitors. By the late 19th century, however, the Gymnasium's popularity had declined – perhaps because of the weather and changing fashions in entertainment, particularly the increase in theatres and music halls. The site was then taken over by the 'Saints' – St Bernard's Football Club.

This 'lost' Edinburgh football club began life in 1874 when a team was formed by men serving in the Third Edinburgh Rifle Volunteers. Games were originally played on The Meadows (alongside the early Hibs and Hearts teams). The team later split from the regiment and was renamed after St Bernard's Well by the Water of Leith (see p.223-226). The club moved in 1880 here to play on the grounds of the Royal Patent Gymnasium – affectionately known as the 'Gymmie'.

The team initially played in the first division, and in 1895 won the Scottish Cup (beating Hearts in the semi-final). Thousands of people greeted the victorious team on their arrival back in Edinburgh at Waverley Station. However, after this promising start, the club struggled to attract the kind of support given to their Edinburgh rivals Hearts and Hibs, and at the start of the 20th century St Bernard's were demoted to the second division where they were to stay. They continued to be based here and struggled financially until eventually being dissolved in 1943.

The abandoned site was then converted into a public park – one of many public amenities around the country dedicated to

George V (1865-1936). WWII caused many such projects to be delayed, helping to explain why a park dedicated to George V only opened in 1950.

Follow the map into George V Park to see the entrance to the **④ Scotland Street Tunnel**.

Scotland Street Railway station once stood near here and work on the tunnel was completed in 1847. It created a link from Canal Street Station (near today's Waverley Station) to Scotland Street and then to Granton and beyond. The tunnel went under St Andrew Square, Dublin Street and Scotland Street. It cost over £100,000 – a huge sum in the mid-19th century, which reflected the difficulties of overcoming the steep gradient between here and central Edinburgh.

In the 1860s, an alternative railway line to Leith via Abbeyhill was opened and though the line here was used for a while for goods traffic, the station was closed to the public in 1868. The only exception to this was in August 1963 when a one-off train service arrived at the station carrying railway enthusiasts.

Scotland Street Station became a goods terminus for

241

5

6

9

many years. The tunnel was later used for a variety of purposes, including as a coal depot and then as a mushroom farm. During WWII the tunnel became a bomb shelter and emergency control centre, and up to 3,000 people could stay down here. In the late 1940s radiation experiments were carried out in the tunnel and in the 1960s cars were stored inside. Today the tunnel and the former station are empty and closed to the public.

On the north side you can see the ❺ **Rodney Street Tunnel**, which is open to the public, and is part of the cycle-path network. It is a much shorter tunnel that opened in 1842 as part of the same railway line as the Scotland Street Tunnel.

Robert Louis Stevenson (1850-94), who was brought up around here, later recalled Scotland Street Station and 'The sight of the train shooting out of its dark maw with the two guards upon the brake, the thought of its length and the many ponderous edifices and thoroughfares above, were certainly things of paramount impressiveness to a young mind.'

Retrace your steps and walk up Canon Street. On the corner here is an ❻ **18th-century former mill**, the last surviving mill building in the area. In the 1870s the Canonmills flour mills stretched all the way up to the right-hand side of Canon Street – where the petrol station is today. By the 1890s maps indicate the site as 'disused' – an indication of the declining fortunes of the local milling industry.

The north-west side of Canon Street was the site of ❼ **James Eyre's Brewery** in the early 19th century.

Continue up Canon Street and stop by the **petrol station**. On the wall by the entrance (on the north side) look out for an old sign referring to the ❽ '**Baxters Land**' dating from 1686. The Baxters were the trade guild of bakers mentioned earlier, who had their flour milled in Canonmills. This sign was discovered in the 1960s during building construction.

Irvine Welsh, the author of *Trainspotting*, was born approximately where the garage is today at 13 Canonmills (now demolished) in 1957. His family soon moved to Leith.

The small church in front of Canon Court was originally a school (before being enlarged), and was the first school attended by ❾ **Robert Louis Stevenson** in about 1857. There is a small plaque to this effect on the corner of the building.

Head north over Canonmills Bridge, looking out for the ❿ **art deco four-sided clock** on the left. This dates from the mid-1940s and is a local landmark that featured briefly in the film *Trainspotting 2*.

The area to the left of the north side of the bridge is now a modern building complex, but in the mid-19th century this was the approximate site of ⓫ **Tanfield Hall** (there is a memorial stone facing the pavement). This was the scene of one of the most dramatic events in Scottish history when on 18 May 1843 hundreds of ministers and elders split from the Church of Scotland.

They stood up *en masse* and walked out of the Church of Scotland General Assembly being held at the church of St Andrew on George Street (see p.171). From there, in a pre-arranged move, they walked down Hanover Street and through Canonmills before crossing the bridge and reaching Tanfield Hall. It was a calculated publicity stunt, and no doubt caused this part of Edinburgh to come to a standstill. The ministers and their supporters then held the first meeting of the Free Church of Scotland inside the hall.

Hundreds more ministers would join this break-away movement, a split that would take many decades to heal. Many were driven by an unhappiness with the way the Church of Scotland allowed wealthy landowners to decide who the minister of a kirk should be – the Free Church wanted this decision to lie with the congregation.

The north side of Canonmills Bridge was also the location for a sedan-chair station in the 18th century, from which four men would carry passengers up the steep hill into central Edinburgh.

Continue up what is now Inverleith Row. Just on the right is **12 8 Howard Place**. This is where Robert Louis Stevenson was born in 1850. He suffered from poor health all his life – dying aged just 44. He is best known today for *Treasure Island*, *Kidnapped* and *The Strange Case of Dr Jekyll and Mr Hyde*.

His family soon moved away from this address, perhaps worried about the effect of damp and pollution from the Water of Leith nearby. However, it is known that as a child Stevenson loved playing in the Water of Leith and skating on Canonmills Loch – and he would have been familiar with many of the places you visit today.

Retrace your steps and walk up ⓭ **Warriston Crescent**. This elegant street is today one of the most expensive in Scotland. It was part of a development of the Warriston area in the early 19th century that was largely designed by James Gillespie Graham (1776-1855). The street was completed by 1820 and was due to be extended but the building of the railway to the north-east of here ended those plans.

Before these streets were laid out, this area was still largely open fields dominated by two large houses – Warriston West house (built in the 1780s) and Warriston East house (built in the early 1800s). The former was demolished in the 1960s and the latter was incorporated into Warriston Crematorium. This area was first recorded as being called Warriston from the 15th century and the name is thought to be derived from the Norse name 'Warin' combined with the Norse 'tun' or Scots 'toun'.

In 1848, the great Polish pianist and composer ⓮ **Fryderyk Chopin** (1810-49) stayed at number

10 as the guest of Polish émigré doctor Dr Adam Lyszczyñski. He became increasingly ill during his tour of Scotland, and was not happy for much of the time, writing, 'I am cross and depressed, and people bore me with their excessive attentions. I can't breathe, I can't work; I feel alone, alone, alone, although I am surrounded.' Chopin became so ill that he had to be carried up the staircase by his servant. He died the following year. In 1948, the Polish community placed a commemorative plaque here to mark the centenary of the visit.

The next section of the walk takes you into Warriston Cemetery. There are not many access points you need to take a ten-minute walk along the ⓫ **Goldenacre Path**, which lies on the old railway line that ran between Granton and Scotland Street Station. (If you do not wish to visit the cemetery then I suggest you skip the next section and return to Inverleith Row to proceed to the Royal Botanic Garden.)

At the end of Warriston Crescent, bear right up some steps to reach public footpaths. Take the left-hand path, signposted as the Goldenacre Path – and continue north. This takes you on a route passing the western edge of the cemetery.

After a few minutes you pass under a bridge and then should take the exit immediately on your left, which brings you out onto a

road named Warriston Gardens. To your right is the Goldenacre sports complex, home to the ⓰ **Heriot's Rugby Club** – one of the top amateur teams in Scotland. The grounds and main stand feature in some of the scenes from the film *Chariots of Fire* (1981).

Bear left on Warriston Gardens and continue around the bend to reach ⓱ **Warriston Cemetery**. This was built by the Edinburgh Cemetery Company, and occupies around 14 acres. It was part of a general commercialisation of the burial process which saw private companies invest in cemeteries, largely because the older graveyards associated with the churches of central Edinburgh had become overcrowded.

Warriston opened in 1843 and was designed by the architect David Cousin (1809-78). He was also responsible for a number of other cemeteries in Edinburgh such as those at Dalry and Rosebank. (Dean Cemetery is another fine example which also opened in the 1840s – see walk 12, p.316).

Warriston contains many thousands of graves, and a large number of fine gothic Victorian tombs. Perhaps the most notable person buried here is the physician ⑱ **Sir James Young Simpson** (1811-70) who pioneered the use of chloroform as an anaesthetic. He is buried by the Simpson family obelisk (located just to the east of the vaults that line the wall dominating the middle of the cemetery). Near to here is the burial place of Captain John Orr (1790-1879) – the inscription on his triangular headstone records that he fought at the Battle of Waterloo.

Shortly after it was built, the cemetery was divided by the Edinburgh Leith and Newhaven Railway and a tunnel was built to link the north and south sections. The line was closed in the 1950s and has now been converted into a public path.

The cemetery remained in private ownership until the 1990s when it was taken over by the City of Edinburgh Council. Sadly, much of the site had become overgrown and many of the finest tombs had been vandalised.

In recent years, however, some excellent restoration work has begun, particularly through the efforts of the Friends of Warriston Cemetery.

This atmospheric place features in Ian Rankin's crime novel *The Hanging Garden*: 'A cemetery should have been about death, but Warriston didn't feel that way to Rebus. Much of it resembled a rambling park into which some statuary had been dropped... there were obelisks and Celtic crosses... people who'd died in India, and some who'd died in infancy.'

The walk around Warriston Cemetery depends on how much time you have. However, I would suggest that you bear left as you enter and walk in a clockwise direction around the edge, passing through the arch into the southern section of the cemetery as you move further down. When you return from here, walk through the central part of the cemetery before heading back up to the north-west corner and leaving along the path you arrived on.

When back on Warriston Gardens, follow the map down Warriston Avenue then turn right on Warriston Drive. This leads you back to Inverleith Row.

Head south, looking out for ⑲ **Eildon Terrace** on the left. This lies on the old entrance road to Warriston West house, which even in the 1880s is shown on maps as standing largely alone in open grounds. The site of the Goldenacre sports ground was then a large garden nursery and this was also a fairly rural area, despite the industrialisation of Canonmills to the south.

Cross over to reach the entrance to the Royal Botanic Garden, Just past the entrance on the right is number 6 Inverleith Row. The French author ⑳ **Jules Verne** (1828-1905) came to Edinburgh in 1859, and visited the Bain family who lived here. Mr Bain was the manager of a bank in Edinburgh, and his wife was a relation of Verne's travelling companion.

At this time Verne had still to have a novel published, and the events on his trip became the basis of his book *Backwards to Britain*. However, the draft was rejected by his publisher and *Backwards to Britain* was not issued until 1989. In the years following his visit to Edinburgh, Verne would become world famous for novels such as *Twenty Thousand Leagues Under the Sea* and *Journey to the Centre of the Earth*.

After arriving at number 6, Verne was taken by Mrs Bain on a walk, first going through the Botanic Garden and then over to Warriston Cemetery. Verne was particularly impressed by the cemetery, comparing it favourably to the burial grounds he was used to in France. After the walk Verne had dinner with the Bains at and was much taken by their 18-year-old daughter Margaret.

Enter the ㉑ **Royal Botanic Garden** (entrance is free, see p.257). Edinburgh's original botanic garden was founded in 1670 near Holyrood Palace. Its plants and herbs were used for medicinal purposes as well as for scientific research. The garden later moved to a site near today's North Bridge and Waverley Station and then near to Leith Walk before coming here in the 1820s. It contains a vast number of plant varieties and specialist gardens, and other attractions include the Palm House (there is an entrance fee for the glasshouses).

21  Royal Botanic Garden

As with Warriston Cemetery, you can spend as much time as you wish here before continuing on the walk. However, I suggest you follow the signs for Inverleith House – situated in the centre. From here you can continue westwards and exit the Garden on the opposite side before picking up the walk directions again. If you have time, try to visit the vast 19th-century glasshouses, filled with tropical plants and with a climate that will make you forget you are in Scotland! At the rear of the glasshouses look out for a hidden treasure, the Linnaeus Monument (c.1778) by the famous architect Robert Adam. It was commissioned by the great Edinburgh botanist John Hope, who was instrumental in turning the Botanic Garden into one of the world's leading centres for the study and cultivation of plants in the 18th century.

**㉒ Inverleith House** was built in 1774 and designed by David Henderson for the Rocheid family – once the main landowner here. For many years the house served as the official residence of the directors of the Royal Botanic Garden, and from the 1960s was the Scottish National Gallery of Modern Art before it re-located in 1984. It continues to host excellent contemporary art exhibitions and there is a pleasant café if you need to refuel.

When finished at the Garden, head out of the exit on the west side by the **㉓ John Hope Gateway** – a modern award-winning biodiversity and information centre that contains a café and gift shop. It features a number of renewable energy systems including a wind turbine on the roof. From

here walk down Aboretum Place. Then continue south on Aboretum Avenue before joining the Water of Leith Walkway (signposted for the Rocheid Path). Continue eastwards along the north bank of the Water of Leith. The source of the Water of Leith is in the Pentland Hills and it flows through Edinburgh before emptying into the Firth of Forth by Leith.

Water of Leith

On your right you can see the **24** **Stockbridge Colonies** – a series of parallel terraces originally called Glenogle Park that were built from 1861 by the Edinburgh Co-operative Building Company. The company was founded by a group of stonemasons and their supporters who decided to build affordable accommodation for artisans and skilled workers.

The company was also responsible for other similar developments elsewhere in Edinburgh. A number of the streets in the Colonies were named after the company's founders, including the stonemason, geologist and journalist Hugh Miller (1802-56).

After a few minutes, turn right over the first footbridge you see, which leads into Glenogle Place. Walk up the narrow street and at the end turn right into Glenogle Road.

The area to the east of here is approximately where the **25** **Canonmills Distillery** was once located. This operated between 1780 and the 1840s and was founded by James Haig (1755-1833), the leading member of a great whisky dynasty whose origins go back to the 17th century. The distillery was owned from about 1790 by

John Stein – a member of another prominent whisky family from this era who owned several distilleries in Scotland. A map of 1805 shows 'Mr Stein's Distillery' standing alone among fields.

For a while the Canonmills Distillery was the largest of its kind. The Haig family bought it back from the Steins in 1825 and it continued to operate as a distillery until the 1840s. After it closed, the malting houses were used by a brewery and the main buildings were demolished in the 1970s. Haig Whisky is still a popular brand, although the Haig family sold out their interest many decades ago. It is now owned by the global drinks company Diageo and in 2014 it was heavily marketed in a campaign featuring David Beckham.

In 1784, many poorer residents of Edinburgh were suffering due to the high food prices that were the result of a widespread agricultural famine. An angry mob tried to storm the distillery as they believed its owners were hoarding stores of oats and potatoes. Soldiers were required to protect the premises and one of the protestors was shot dead. The ringleaders were subsequently caught, whipped in public and transported to the Colonies.

Continue west along Glenogle Road, passing the Colonies now on your right-hand side. Look out for small **26** **low-reliefs** representing different professions at the end of some of the terraces. There is also a stone plaque from 1861 recalling the development's original name of Glenogle Park. Today this is a very desirable place to live and is probably well out of reach of the types of workers the houses were originally built for.

Take the **27** **steps** on the left-hand side (marked Gabriel's Road). These follow a small section of the much longer Gabriel's Road that was first recorded in 1717. Before the New Town was built, the road ran across largely open fields towards the Old Town, passing through what later became St Andrew Square and finishing near Calton Hill. At that time Gabriel's Road was known as 'lovers' lane', with courting couples walking along it from the Old Town into what was still mostly

countryside. It is said they would stop for strawberries and cream at a small cottage named 'Peace and Plenty' that once stood on the east side of St Andrew Square.

At the top of the steps you enter **28 Saxe Coburg Street** – named after Prince Leopold of Saxe-Coburg, the widowed husband of Princess Charlotte of Wales. Charlotte, who was the only daughter of George IV and Caroline of Brunswick, died aged 21. Her death was widely mourned by the public, many of whom were not very keen on her father and had hoped Charlotte might become queen one day.

These streets were designed by James Milne (c.1778-c.1850s), responsible for a number of buildings in the Stockbridge area, including Ann Street – often described as the most attractive street in Edinburgh (see p.227).

Follow the map bearing left, passing **29 Deanbank House** on your right, a pretty building dating from the 18th century.

Shortly on your left is **30 Stockbridge Parish Church**. This was originally known as St Bernard's Church and its origins go back to the early 1820s when the church authorities of St Cuthbert's (by Lothian Road) commissioned James Milne to design a church to serve the growing population of Stockbridge. The opening of a church here saved the congregation from having to walk uphill into central Edinburgh to attend St Cuthbert's.

Walk down Saxe Coburg Street to reach Henderson Row. Cross over Henderson Row into West Silvermills Lane (which also follows the route of Gabriel's Road). You are

standing now where the Silvermills Village was once located. It is named after a mill or mills that were built here in the late-medieval period to smelt and refine silver ore. The village was identified by this name on a map of 1560.

It is known that in the early 17th century a supply of silver ore was discovered in West Lothian. James VI of Scotland (who was James I of England) may have invested in these silver mines, and also may have built the mill here to reduce the cost of transporting the silver ore down to London.

However, the history of the original Silvermills Village is not entirely clear and there is nothing left of that era to see today. The oldest surviving building is the three-storey **31** **Silvermills House** (on the left), which dates from 1760. Nearly everything else was swept away in the modern housing development that stands on all sides.

Follow the map and head left on Silvermills and then up **32** **East Silvermills Lane** to rejoin Henderson Row. Straight ahead on the north side is the **33** **Edinburgh Academy School**, which opened in 1824 and still occupies its original Greek Revival-styled building. It

was founded by a group of influential Edinburgh men who felt that the Royal High School, founded in the 12th century, was not providing a sufficiently rigorous classical syllabus. Key early supporters included the prominent lawyer Henry, Lord Cockburn, and Sir Walter Scott – both themselves once pupils at the Royal High.

A book on Edinburgh dating from 1829 suggests these men also wanted to found a new school because they desired 'to have their children separated from those of a more plebeian extraction'.

The building on the west side of the Academy was originally Donaldson's School for deaf children. It was used to depict the fictional Marcia Blaine School for Girls in the 1969 film adaptation of Muriel Spark's book *The Prime of Miss Jean Brodie*.

The Academy has long been one of the best schools in Scotland and past pupils include physicist James Clerk Maxwell, physician (and inspiration for Sherlock Holmes) Dr Joseph Bell, writer Robert Louis Stevenson, and more recently television presenter Magnus Magnusson.

Continue eastwards along Henderson Row. This lies on an old lane called Silver Mills that was still indicated on maps of the 1820s. At that time this area was largely open fields with a few scattered buildings and a tannery just to the south. This tannery became significant as it helped stop the northwards expansion of the New Town (called the

'Northern' or 'Second' New Town) that began in the early years of the 1800s.

By 1850 the area had been developed considerably. A church (St Bernard's Free Church) stood on the south side of Henderson Row opposite Edinburgh Academy, and nearby there was a school and timber yard. Silvermills was clearly no longer a rural village and it would become increasingly incorporated into the sprawl of Edinburgh.

Shortly on the right you will see the **34 Scottish Life Building**, which retains the façade of an old tramway depot that was built here in the 1880s by the Edinburgh Northern Tramways Company. The memorial stone on the wall recalls that cable tram cars ran from here to Princes Street, Goldenacre and Stockbridge until 1920. It was later used as a police garage and public wash house for many years before being redeveloped into the current office block.

Continue along until you reach the junction with Dundas Street and the end of this walk. ●

## VISIT...

**Royal Botanic Garden**
Arboretum Place, EH3 5NZ
*www.rbge.org.uk*

**Water of Leith Walkway**
*www.waterofleith.org.uk*

## SHOP...

**Stockbridge Farmers' Market**
*www.stockbridgemarket.com*
Open Sun from 10am-5pm

## EAT/DRINK...

**The Terrace Café**
Royal Botanic Garden,
Inverleith Row, EH3 5LR
*www.rbge.org.uk*

**Gateway Restaurant**
Royal Botanic Garden,
Arboretum Place, EH3 5NZ

*Cramond Island, see p.271*

# 10 Cramond to Barnton Walk

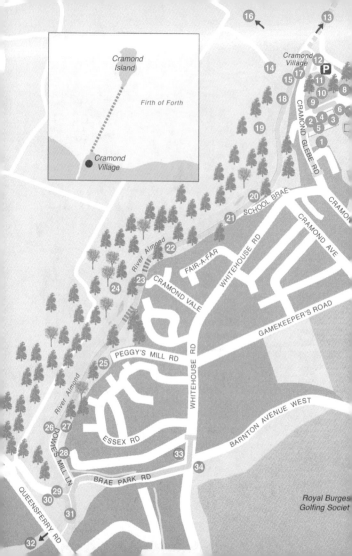

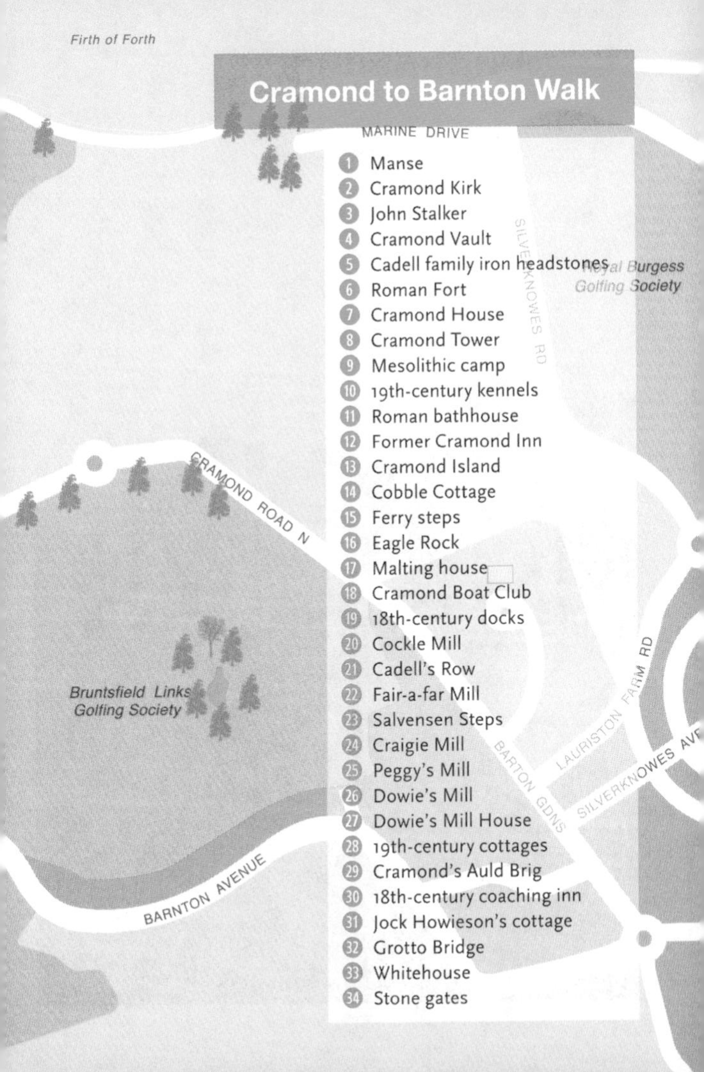

*Firth of Forth*

# Cramond to Barnton Walk

MARINE DRIVE

SILVERKNOWES RD

...al Burgess
Golfing Society

CRAMOND ROAD N

LAURISTON FARM RD

BARTON GDNS

SILVERKNOWES AVE

Bruntsfield Links
Golfing Society

BARNTON AVENUE

1. Manse
2. Cramond Kirk
3. John Stalker
4. Cramond Vault
5. Cadell family iron headstones
6. Roman Fort
7. Cramond House
8. Cramond Tower
9. Mesolithic camp
10. 19th-century kennels
11. Roman bathhouse
12. Former Cramond Inn
13. Cramond Island
14. Cobble Cottage
15. Ferry steps
16. Eagle Rock
17. Malting house
18. Cramond Boat Club
19. 18th-century docks
20. Cockle Mill
21. Cadell's Row
22. Fair-a-far Mill
23. Salvensen Steps
24. Craigie Mill
25. Peggy's Mill
26. Dowie's Mill
27. Dowie's Mill House
28. 19th-century cottages
29. Cramond's Auld Brig
30. 18th-century coaching inn
31. Jock Howieson's cottage
32. Grotto Bridge
33. Whitehouse
34. Stone gates

# Cramond to Barnton Walk
Start: Cramond Glebe Road
Finish: Whitehouse Road
Distance: 1.94 miles

**2** *Cramond Kirk*

This walk starts in Cramond at the southern end of Cramond Glebe Road (near the bus stop). Alternatively, you can park in the car park further along that road and return to walk past Cramond Kirk.

The first stopping place is the ❶ **Manse** – the home for the minister of the kirk. 'Manse' is a traditional Scottish term for a clergyman's residence, derived from the Latin 'mansus' (or dwelling). This elegant house dates from the mid-17th century, although it was substantially rebuilt in 1745. Opposite the Manse is the former school building which dates from 1875 and was important in its day as a reflection of the development of the village in the late 19th century.

From here walk towards ❷ **Cramond Kirk** itself, entering through a gate in the wall. The kirk stands on the site of a major Roman fort, and Christian worship here may date back to the 6th century. The gatehouse by the entrance to the kirk is today home to the city's smallest art gallery, restored by the renowned architect Sir Basil Spence in 1932. It was originally used as a watch house to deter body snatchers.

Situated by the River Almond and Firth of Forth, Cramond was an attractive location for the Romans as it offered a site for a large fort which could be easily supplied by sea and river. It also allowed troops easy access to the nearby Antonine Wall, which attempted to regulate the troublesome Caledonian tribes that the Romans never fully subjugated.

The Romans occupied Cramond on two occasions – the first time in around 140 CE during the reign of Antoninus Pius (86-161), the Emperor responsible for the Antonine Wall that once stretched between the Clyde and Forth estuaries. The fort in Cramond was occupied only until around 165, and together with the Antonine Wall was abandoned as the Romans retreated behind Hadrian's Wall to the south.

The Romans later invaded Scotland again in around 208, led by the Emperor Septimius Severus (145-211). This was most likely

Memento mori

to punish troublesome tribes, and the fort in Cramond was re-occupied and served as a supply depot for the Roman army heading further north. However, the impetus for the campaign ebbed away after Severus died in York in 211. The fort at Cramond was abandoned, but its structure served as the early focal point for what would become a village, and the site of the kirk. The village's name itself reflects this period of Roman occupation, derived from 'Caer Amon' – or 'fortified place by the river'.

Walk around the kirkyard itself, full of fascinating headstones and family tombs. The earliest one (dating from 1608) remembers ③ **John Stalker** (east wall). You will also see plenty of evidence of *memento mori* – embellishments that were popular in the 17th and 18th centuries to remind visitors of the temporary nature of life. The most common are carved skulls and crossbones and hourglasses – visual statements whose meaning would have been obvious even to those who were illiterate. There are also three examples of 'Green Man' masks, their origins dating back to Roman times when pagan leaf masks were used. They symbolise life springing out of death.

On the east side of the kirk is the 17th-century ④ **Cramond Vault** which contains the memorials of the Craigie Halkett Inglis family who until a few decades ago owned the neighbouring Cramond House and surrounding estate. They were descendants of the Inglis family that purchased Cramond Tower and estate in the 1620s (seen shortly).

There are also headstones and tombs for a number of prominent families who owned houses and estates in the parish (then much larger than it is now). Examples include, just south of the Cramond Vault, the burial place of the Howieson-Craufurd family of Braehead House, descended from Jock Howieson who saved James V from robbers at Cramond Brig (seen later in the walk).

On the north-east wall is a headstone for the MacKay family who occupied the Whitehouse – a major house in the area that we will visit shortly (and later the home of JK Rowling). The headstone remembers the death of Hamish MacKay in 1916 whilst fighting in WWI.

For several centuries the major local estate owners – known as Heritors – were responsible for contributing funds towards the maintenance of the kirk. In return they had significant influence over its running, including the selection of its minister. A number of these Heritors were important enough to have their own seating gallery inside the kirk, including the owners of the large estates centred around Barnton House, Cramond House and Dalmeny House.

Look out for the unusual **5** **iron headstones of the Cadell family** (examples on the extreme south-east and south-west corners of the kirkyard). During the age of the Industrial Revolution the Cadell family owned a number of the ironworking mills along the River Almond, the locations of which are seen later in the walk. The Cadells even tried to promote the use of metal headstones, but it was never a popular product. In the south-west corner by the back wall is the iron gravestone remembering Anne Wilson, wife  of Alex Cadell. She died in 1851, drowning in the Almond while returning home from a New Year's Eve party. Later in the walk you will go past the site of this tragedy.

While people may have worshipped in the ruins of the Roman buildings as far back as the 6th century – evidence of a kirk (and a mill) here dates from the 12th century. The kirk was probably connected to the abbey on Inchcolm Island in the Firth of Forth and dedicated to St Columba. By the 16th century Cramond had the status of a burgh under the Bishop of Dunkeld, who was the feudal lord, and the small village would have been mainly occupied by peasants and fishermen. The area was then known as Cramond Episcopi – or Bishop's Cramond; it was later known as Kirk Cramond.

The tower you see is all that remains from the 15th-century kirk, and much of the rest dates from 1656, when the structure – then in ruins – was rebuilt. The following centuries saw many modifications, most notably during a restoration c.1911. The walls of the kirk continue to bear a Roman influence to this day, with old bricks from the ancient fort having been re-used in their construction.

One of the ministers of the kirk was Robert Walker (1755-1808) – the famous *Skating Minister* painted by Henry Raeburn (1756-1823). The painting, which captures Walker elegantly ice-skating on Duddingston Loch, can be found in the Scottish National Gallery in Edinburgh (see p.185). Raeburn was one of Scotland's greatest portrait painters and also found time to develop Stockbridge from a rural village into a prime residential area. While *The Skating Minister* is one of his most famous works, there has been some speculation in recent years that he may not have painted it after all and it could be the work of a French artist, Henri-Pierre Danloux.

In 1651, Oliver Cromwell's army occupied Edinburgh and the surrounding districts, and the soldiers of General Monk stole the kirk's records and its bell, which had been cast in Holland. The parishioners managed to have the bell returned after pleading their case to Monk. By this time the kirk had fallen into disrepair before being largely rebuilt in 1656.

Cramond bore the impact of the 'Disruption' of 1843 when hundreds of ministers broke away from the Church of Scotland over the issue of patronage – essentially an objection to the right of wealthy landowners (rather than the congregation) to determine the selection of a kirk's minister. George Muirhead was the minister of Cramond Kirk in 1843 and, aged 79, he was the oldest minister to sign the original deed setting up the Free Church. He was one of many who walked away from a secure living within the Church of Scotland, and he helped to found a 'free church' in nearby Davidson's Mains.

With many of the congregation following him, life in the village would have been hugely disrupted by the split, with neighbour pitted against neighbour and friend against friend.

Until the split, the elders of the kirk, members of a body called the Kirk Session, had wielded enormous influence on daily life in Cramond. They influenced not just the running of the kirk, but schooling, poor relief and the enforcement of moral behaviour. Those who contravened the code – by plucking a chicken on a Sunday or playing a game – could face the humiliation of having to sit on a high seat in front of the congregation during a three-hour Sunday service. Sadly the kirk is not usually open to visitors so if you want to go inside it is best to pre-arrange this with the kirk office.

Walk out of the other side of the kirkyard. Almost immediately in front of you are remains of the **6 Roman Fort**, with modern bricks helping to show the outlines of where the barracks and granary lay. Hundreds of Roman soldiers lived here at the peak of the occupation, drawn from countries throughout the Empire. There are some useful information boards providing more details about the Roman period.

After the Romans left, new invaders came in the shape of the Angles from North Germany, who settled first in Northumberland. They introduced the word 'kirk' – from 'kirche' – the German word for church.

Follow the map away from the kirk. Ahead is **7 Cramond House**, with the modern kirk hall to the right.

On the left of Cramond House is ⑧ **Cramond Tower**. Neither the tower nor Cramond House are open to the public – so please respect the privacy of those who live and work there.

The tower may have been founded as early as the 12th century and was used as a summer residence by the Bishops of Dunkeld – possibly after King David I granted them lands here. After the Reformation the tower had a succession of new owners. It finally came into the hands of the Inglis family in 1622 (whose family tomb was mentioned earlier in the walk).

Reflecting social changes taking place in Scotland, in 1680 the family moved out of what was originally meant to be a defensive tower, and instead lived in the more opulent Cramond House. The Inglis family continued to own the lands around here – known as the Cramond Estate – until the 19th century. The estate then passed to various relatives until the Craigie Halketts took over – this family occupied Cramond House until the 1950s.

Sir John Inglis of Cramond sat on the jury that considered the case of John Porteous, one of the most notorious figures in Edinburgh's history, who ordered the Town Guard to fire on an Edinburgh mob in 1736. When the London government reprieved the convicted man, the Edinburgh mob rebelled, and Porteous was lynched in front of a huge crowd in the Grassmarket (see p.114).

The tower lay derelict from 1680 until the 1970s when a new owner converted it into the charming private residence it remains to this day.

Walk back to look at Cramond House – more substantial than it may appear at first sight. As mentioned earlier, it was built in

1680 and was enlarged over later years. It is a fine example of a Scottish country house. The Inglis family who occupied the house was hugely influential on the development of Cramond. They helped to introduce reforms in agriculture that affected the way land in the area was farmed, and also changed the lay-out of the village.

The village green that lay outside their house, and the road that ran between the house and the kirk, were central to day-to-day life. However, in the late 18th century the Inglis family decided they wanted more privacy, closing the road and having what is now Cramond Glebe Road built instead. The village green was incorporated into the grounds of Cramond House and a number of villagers saw their houses demolished and were forced to move further westwards. The entrance of Cramond House was moved to the west side, and it has been said that the occupants were literally turning their backs on the village.

Perhaps Cramond House's most famous occupant was the Duchess of Kent – mother of Queen Victoria – who lived here in 1860. The Queen, after visiting her mother here on the way to Balmoral, wrote (in a letter to King Leopold) about a 'charming residence at Cramond, quite near the sea, with beautiful trees, and very cheerful'. Victoria also attended a service at the kirk, sitting up in the gallery.

The house and tower are cited as the inspiration for the 'House of Shaws' in Robert Louis Stevenson's book *Kidnapped* (1886). In the book, the central character, David Balfour, is sent to Cramond to meet his evil uncle, who inhabits a ramshackle mansion. The uncle tries to cause David's death by making him walk up a dangerous, unfinished tower in the darkness. It is known that Stevenson stayed at the Manse and perhaps he walked up the decrepit Cramond Tower one dark winter's night himself.

The modern kirk hall was built on the site of Cramond House's horse stables and if you have time, walk around the back of the kirk hall to see (past the car park) the old garden wall of Cramond House – now surrounding a children's park.

During WWI the house was used as a hospital for soldiers wounded in France. Today Cramond House is occupied by a nursery and other commercial enterprises.

Follow the map north from the kirk down a small and often muddy path into a wooded area (there is an information board to aim for). This recalls that in recent years evidence of a **⑨ Mesolithic camp** dating back to 8,500 BCE has been discovered, making this one of the earliest-known sites for human habitation in Scotland. When the Romans arrived thousands of years later they found a Pictish tribe here that they called the Votadini (their descendants known as Gododdin). It was the Votadini who are thought to have given the village its name, derived from 'Caer Amon' or 'fort on the river'. Given this ancient history, Cramond is thought to be the oldest occupied village in Scotland.

Bear right from the information board to see some **⑩ ruins** – these are the **19th-century kennels** once attached to Cramond House. In around 1760 Sir John Inglis of Cramond House moved residents of the village away from this general area towards the site of the cottages you will see shortly, his purpose to give the house more privacy.

Continue northwards and very soon you reach the main Cramond car park. You get a good view of Cramond Tower from here. Turn left and walk along the south side of the car park, stopping

at another information board (before the car park exit). Just in front of the information board lies a huge **⑪ Roman bathhouse** that was discovered on this site in the 1970s and would have served the soldiers in the fort. Sadly, this has now been covered over again. There is evidence that victims of the plague were buried in the bathhouse latrine in the 14th century. Skeletons found here in 1975 have been dated back to the 6th century, and were possibly members of a royal family. Several had suffered violent deaths.

Walk through the car park entrance and turn right down the hill, flanked by the picturesque cottages that make this such an attractive place. Until recently you could have enjoyed a pint at the ⑫ **Cramond Inn** on the right – which was one of the most atmospheric pubs in Edinburgh. The building remains, with parts of it dating back to the 17th century. When pints were still pulled there were reports of a poltergeist with a penchant for smashing glasses, but the ghostly apparition and the reasonably priced Samuel Smith's beers are now sadly part of Cramond's history.

Continue down the road to reach the shoreline, with the Firth of Forth stretching out ahead of you. On your left is the River Almond, making it easy to understand why the Romans liked this spot with its natural harbour and local supplies of fresh fish.

Bear right past the flagpole to see ⑬ **Cramond Island**, just under a mile away to the north. Depending on the tide, you may be able to walk out to the island but be very careful – around 100 people

⑬ *View from Cramond Island towards the mainland*

each year have to be rescued so always check the timetable on the information board and give yourself at least 20 minutes to walk back. The island, which covers around 19 acres, features a number of old army fortifications and the ruins of a farmhouse.

There is an incredible diversity of wildlife visible on the mudflats when the tide is out, particularly in early summer. Species include waders, gulls, finches, king-fishers, mute swans, cormorants, grey wagtails, oystercatchers, curlews and grey herons. In 2013, a pilot whale died after becoming stranded just to the east of Cramond Island – despite strenuous attempts to save it.

You are now standing in the footsteps of Robert Louis Stevenson. He would have known this view very well, and described it in one of his books called *St Ives*, when one of the characters arrives in Cramond, described as 'a little hamlet on a little river, embowered in woods, and looking forth over a great flat of quicksand'.

The island is connected to Cramond by a concrete barrier, flanked by huge 'teeth', that was erected during WWII as a defence against enemy ships. Over the centuries the island has been used for oyster fishing, farming, holiday cottages and even in the 17th century as a haven for 'unfortunate females requiring temporary retirement'. Today it is uninhabited and contains a number of WWII-era fortifications in various states of repair. Peter Hogg – the last person to farm on the island – died in 1904; you can see his headstone in the kirkyard.

Look out towards the east. Until the advent of cheap foreign package holidays, Cramond was a popular beach resort. On a summer's day the beach would have been thronged with hundreds of people enjoying the sun. While it remains a popular spot today for dog walkers, kite fliers, joggers and tourists, the beach has never regained this level of mass popularity.

If you wish to visit Cramond Island (assuming the tide is in your favour), there is a tide timetable at the start of the walkway, or alternatively you can text 'cramond' to the RNLI at 81400 and get details of the safe crossing times. If not visiting the island, follow the map to walk away from the Firth of Forth past the pretty white-washed cottages to your left and the River Almond to your right.

In recent years the island has been the site of a punk festival – described by STV as a 'secretive institution of the punk music calendar, celebrating the very nature of the movement, a cultural phenomenon which emphasises individuality over conformity'. With perhaps the exception of Morningside, Cramond is probably the last place in Edinburgh where you might expect to see hordes of kids with brightly coloured mohawks carrying amps and armfuls of alcohol, the DIY nature of the event a refreshing change from the overly commercialised festivals.

On the other side of the river is the Dalmeny Estate, which has been in the ownership of the Earls of Rosebery since the 18th century, with Dalmeny House as its focal point. The pretty ⑭ **Cobble Cottage** stands marooned on the other side of the river, once occupied by the ferryman who took people across the water. It is probably named after the 'coble' – a type of fishing boat.

Cramond Causeway

A ferry operated here from at least 1662 until 2001, when it was closed because of health concerns after an outbreak of foot-and-mouth disease. This was believed to have been the shortest ferry crossing in Britain when it was operational, and in recent years discussions have taken place about its re-opening.

The ferry made national news in the mid-1990s when the ferryman, Robert Graham, spotted something in the silt beside the ⑮ **ferry steps**. It turned out to be a spectacular Roman carved lioness eating an unfortunate victim. Known as the 'Cramond Lioness', it can now been seen in the National Museum of Scotland (see p.99). Graham was reported to have received £50,000 under the government's treasure-trove rules.

Further around the coastline you should be able to see ⑯ **Eagle Rock** in the Dalmeny Estate. This contains the figure of an eagle – now sadly greatly eroded – that accordingly to local legend was carved by the Romans.

Cramond has another literary connection as this is where in Muriel Spark's book *The Prime of Miss Jean Brodie* (1961), Mr Lowther lives, and Miss Brodie is a frequent visitor. The 1969 film of the book, starring Maggie Smith, also includes scenes shot near here (using Barnbougle Castle just around the coast – visible if you walk up to the site of the flagpole and look towards Eagle Rock).

Continue along the side of the river with the cottages, the majority of which date from around 1780, on your left. Cramond has a peaceful, slightly sleepy feel to it, but in the 18th and 19th centuries the village would have been much busier and less gentrified. Hundreds of people were crammed into these cottages, often living in slum conditions. They worked on local farms and estates, in the riverside mills (seen shortly), and in the fishing and kelp industries. In those days the parish of Cramond was considerably larger

Cramond Beach

than it is today, covering 12 square miles and including areas such as Blackhall, which today are substantial suburbs in their own right. This area was also then known as the 'toun' of Nether Cramond, with Upper Cramond located further along the River Almond by Cramond Brig (seen later on).

There is a pleasant café in the middle of the row of cottages which is worth a stop at. It also sells local art works and contains a large wall painting that depicts how the Roman fort might once have looked.

In the 19th century a sandy beach stretched from the river right up to a rough path outside these cottages, long before the current tarmac road and shore wall were built.

Until the 1970s, the Royal Oak Inn stood near here and included a brewery and malting house. It was probably the inspiration for the 'University of Cramond' inn that was visited by a group of drunken men in Robert Louis Stevenson's book *St Ives*. Today the **⑰ malting house** survives (just beside the café) and contains an excellent museum dedicated to local history (see p.285). It is open from April to September, 2pm to 5pm (Sat & Sun only) and daily during the Edinburgh Festival.

While today the cottages are well maintained, in the early 1960s the village had become very dilapidated and was even scheduled for demolition until the estate was bought by Edinburgh city council. A major redevelopment took place, and many long-resident families moved away, changing the village's character forever. The renovated cottages became increasingly popular with retirees and those seeking a second home.

This quiet village was in the headlines for the wrong reasons in 1831 when a man named John Howison committed murder 'in a very brutal and barbarous manner, on the person of a very innocent and industrious old woman, at Cramond, within five miles of Edinburgh, by cutting her face, with a garden spade, down and across her face, which laid it fully open, in a shocking manner, even in broad day-light.' Known as the 'Cramond Murderer', Howison was hanged shortly after and his body dissected at the University's medical school. You can see the Cramond Murderer's skeleton on display in the Edinburgh University Anatomical Museum (see p.99).

Continue along what becomes a river path, passing the **18 Cramond Boat Club**, which was founded in 1932. The River Almond

begins at Hirst Hill in Lanarkshire before emptying 28 miles later into the Firth of Forth. The name Almond comes from an old Celtic word for river.

After you pass the last part of the boat club, on the right-hand side of the bank can be seen the remains of three **19 18th-century docks** that served the Craigie Quarry on the Dalmeny Estate (the site of the quarry is seen later). Stones cut in the quarry were brought by cart along a track by the river's edge before being shipped by barge down to Leith docks.

Continue along the peaceful river path, looking out for the herons that are often seen here. Shortly you will reach a substantial old building on the left, today housing a pleasant café and B&B (see p.285). This was once a store and office building within the ⑳ **Cockle Mill**. Cockle Mill was possibly the earliest of a number of grain mills founded along this stretch of the River Almond in the 12th century, close to farms that could supply the raw product to be milled, a powerful river whose current could turn the water wheels,

and with easy access to the rest of Scotland via the Firth of Forth.

In 1752, Cockle Mill felt the direct impact of the Industrial Revolution, switching from milling grain to the more profitable enterprise of ironworking – the first of four mills on this stretch of the river to be converted in this way. The river continued to supply power to the mill until the mid-19th century, when the steam engine took over. However, the mill's name continued to reflect its original purpose – the cockle being a type of weed found in corn crops.

By 1800, competition from larger ironworking centres meant most of the mills along the river began to decline, and after 1860 nearly all had been converted for other uses such as the production of paper, gelatine and furniture. In its heyday, Cockle Mill would have been an extremely busy place with dozens of workers, horses and carts moving around in all directions. The main mill stood where the open grass area lies today (located between the café and the river). The old mill manager's house of 1778 also stands up high on the hill above the café, no doubt intended to emphasise the status of its occupant, who could look down on the workers below.

The River Almond became fairly toxic during this period of industrialisation, at one point being described as the most polluted river of its size anywhere in Britain. In 1884, angling on the river stopped completely because of the appalling quality of the water which was said to flow 'nearly black at times and oil and particles of coal dust had been seen'. In the last few decades things have

improved considerably and the Cramond Angling Club (formed in the 1960s) has re-established the sport of fishing here. As you walk along, you should also look out for grey herons, kingfishers and dippers.

The Cadell family, whose iron headstones you may have seen earlier in the kirkyard, bought a number of mills along the river in the late 18th century, and were responsible for converting them for ironworking. The family would control much of the industrial output along this stretch of the river for nearly 100 years and was one of the biggest employers.

Continue along the edge of the river by the path – you shortly pass **㉑ Cadell's Row** (named after the family), which contains cottages that were originally inhabited by the ironworkers.

After a few minutes you reach the ruins of **㉒ Fair-a-far Mill** – standing by a huge weir that was constructed in around 1790. The ruins are largely from the mill that stood here in the 17th century, which was originally a grain and waulk mill, 'waulk' being a Scottish term for a cleansing and softening process for making woollen cloth. The work led to a genre of Scottish folk songs known as 'waulking songs' – the workers would sing them as they rhythmically beat newly woven wool to soften it. Perhaps if you had walked here long ago you would have heard the singing above the noise of the river.

In 1773, the mill was converted to manufacture industrial goods and a horse-drawn tram connected it to Cockle Mill. Ironworking stopped here in the 1860s and – along with Cockle Mill – Fair-a-far-Mill was sold to the Inglis family of Cramond House. The ruined building that remains originally contained the forge used to shape metal goods. By the huge weir next to the ruins, you can see a fish ladder and, also on the west side, indentations in the wall. These were used to hold up a track that connected the nearby Craigie Quarry to the docks seen earlier near the Cramond Boat Club.

Continue along the river path and up **㉓ Salvensen Steps**. These were built in the 1960s on land gifted to the public by

*Fair-a-far Mill-weir*

*River walk view from steps*

Captain Keith Salvesen, a member of the Salvesen family whose firm (based in Leith) ran the largest whaling fleet in the world until the mid-20th century. Captain Salvesen lived nearby in Inveralmond House, long since demolished but remembered in some local street names and a surviving coach house.

Before the steps were built, it was a fairly difficult climb from the Cramond Village side to continue along by the river. It was here that Anne Wilson – who married into the Cadell family and whose iron gravestone in Cramond Kirk was mentioned earlier – fell to her death returning home after a New Year's Eve party in 1851. A newspaper reported on the 'late melancholy drowning at Cramond' describing how Mrs Cadell 'fell into a mill-lade on the river Almond and was supposed to be carried out to sea, [but her body] had been found by some fisher-men on the neighbouring coast'.

Parallel with the steps on the other side of the river bank are the approximate locations of **24 Craigie Mill** (a grain and waulk mill originally) and Craigie Quarry – owned in the late 18th century by the Dalmeny Estate. (It is very hard to see the remains of the mill and quarry from this side of the river, particularly before winter thins the tree line.) Stone from the quarry was taken down by cart on a track along the west side of the river to the docks seen earlier by the Cramond Boat Club. The stone was used in the construction of the New Town in Edinburgh.

As you come down the stairs, you pass by (near the bottom of the adjoining lane) the site of **25 Peggy's Mill**. It was bought by the Cadell family in the 1780s and from about 1815 this became a paper mill. However, the increasing pollution of the river meant the quality of the paper was poor. The Cadell family closed their business in the 1860s, and the mill was later used for gelatine production before closing in the 1960s. The mill was completely demolished and the only remains are a few stones from the mill lade that stand on either side of the path (about 20 yards after you pass the entrance to Peggy's Mill Road).

Continue on, and look out for some ruins by the river edge just before you reach a pretty cottage on the left. The ruins are of 26 **Dowie's Mill** and the cottage is the early 19th-century 27 **Dowie's Mill House**, once the mill manager's house. A recent occupant of the cottage claims to have encountered a ghost here – an old woman dressed in blue. The main part of the mill complex stood between the cottage and the river. The riverside ruins of the mill (opposite the cottage, down by the riverside) are an approved location for members of the Sikh and Hindu faiths to scatter the ashes of the deceased.

As you continue along the main river path you reach Dowie's Mill Lane. This contains a charming row of early 28 **19th-century cottages** once occupied by mill workers. Opposite these cottages and down by the river's edge is a weir and more remains of the old mill complex. Dowie's Mill was first recorded back in 1697 and later bought by the Cadell family, who converted it from a grain mill. It was later used to make spades and other metal implements.

If you stand overlooking the weir, you are standing near the site of the two water wheels that once stood here. You can still see

a man-made channel that continues to force water down a narrow path at high velocity, giving a sense of the natural power that was once so important to the hundreds of workers whose livelihoods depended on the mills. Dowie's Mill is said to be named after David ('Dowie') Strachan, owner of the Whitehouse (seen shortly) in the mid-18th century.

Continue along and after a few hundred yards you reach a small road where you should bear right. You soon reach **㉙ Cramond's Auld Brig** – or old bridge. A wooden bridge was built here in the late-medieval period, and the later stone bridge was substantially rebuilt in 1619. At the centre of the bridge on the south side you can see inscribed on the wall the dates of subsequent major repairs that were carried out until 1854.

This historic bridge was where a local man named Jock Howieson is said to have saved King James V (1512-42) from robbers. James, in disguise at the time, asked Howieson to come to Holyrood Palace, where the King revealed his identity to Jock and also rewarded him with a grant of land. A condition was placed that Jock, or his descendants, would attend to the reigning monarch whenever he or she crossed the bridge. A ceremony at the bridge involving George

29

IV meeting one of Howieson's descendants took place in 1822, organised by Sir Walter Scott. As mentioned earlier, descendants of Jock are buried in Cramond kirkyard.

On the other side of the old bridge is a restaurant which occupies what was originally an **30** **18th-century coaching inn**.

To see the supposed remains of **31** **Jock Howieson's cottage**, follow the map just past the bridge on the east side (there is a plaque).

The old bridge was part of the route linking Edinburgh to Queensferry. As road traffic increased in the late 18th century, the need for a modern bridge was identified. This was designed by the great civil engineer John Rennie (1761-1821), who designed a large number of canals, bridges and docks throughout Britain. It was completed in 1823, but also fell victim to increasing levels of traffic and was demolished in 1962, making way for the undistinguished new structure you see today on the south side.

If you have the time and energy, it is possible to continue along from this point beside the River Almond for a couple of miles or so – a rewarding 'there and back' detour that is very peaceful, even though it goes as far as Edinburgh airport. After about a mile you cross over the small, charming **32** **Grotto Bridge**. Below the bridge is a small gap in the rock formation that the River Almond is violently forced through. The ornamental Grotto Bridge dates from 1757, and was accompanied by a bathhouse. Both structures were commissioned by a local landowner named Charles Hope-Weir and the architects

are believed to have been members of the famous 18th-century Adam family. The ruins of the bathhouse can just be seen south-west of the Grotto Bridge.

If you do not want to follow this detour by the River Almond, retrace your steps, and follow the map away from the river and up the gentle incline of the road. You pass the pleasant suburban homes for which this area is well known.

You are now in Barnton, a prosperous suburban area that adjoins Cramond. Though its housing stock dates largely from the 20th century, Barnton was first recorded in around 1400 (known as Bernetoun, Berntoun or Barntoun). The origin of the name may lie in an old name for a barn where crops were stored.

Continue to follow the map to reach Whitehouse Road. On your left, behind the tall trees, is the ㉝ **Whitehouse**. It dates from 1615 and was originally fortified – the towers are still visible. The Whitehouse would have once stood alone among acres of open fields but is now surrounded by modern suburban houses and flats. In recent years the author JK Rowling lived here and her efforts to build a large tree-house, as well as the impact on local traffic when (in 2015) the tall hedges surrounding her property were trimmed, attracted a great deal of press coverage.

Cross over to the ㉞ **stone gates** on the other side of Whitehouse Road. These date from 1810 and once formed part of a grand entrance to the Barnton Estate and House.

In around 1800, William Ramsay, a director of the Royal Bank of Scotland, rebuilt the original 17th-century estate house of King's Cramond and this became known as Barnton House. He also built a wall around the Barnton Estate, covering about 50 acres, much of which still exists today.

The estate originally stretched across 400 acres. By the late 19th century, however, the property began to be sold off. Some of the finest (and largest) houses in Edinburgh can be found on the site of the former estate, particularly along Barnton Avenue, where a number have sold for several million pounds.

A large part of the estate was also sold to the Bruntsfield Links Golfing Society (founded 1761) and the Royal Burgess Golfing Society (founded 1735). Two of the oldest golf clubs in the world, they were both founded on Bruntsfield Links near the Meadows (see p.337). The Links became increasingly crowded for golfers so both clubs moved first to Musselburgh and then to this part of Edinburgh in the late 19th century. Barnton House itself was eventually demolished in the 1920s

This is the end of the walk. If you parked back near Cramond Kirk you can wait for a 41 bus to take you along Whitehouse Road, or alternatively walk back along the pavement. If you want to rejoin the river path, you can either retrace your steps, or walk some of the way back on the pavement and after a few minutes take a left down Peggy's Mill Road to rejoin the river path at the foot of the wooden steps encountered earlier on.

If you are getting the 41 bus back into Edinburgh, you can get on at the bus stop on the south side of the road (just opposite the Whitehouse). 

## VISIT...

**Cramond Island**
*www.britishbeaches.info* (for tide & weather information) or text 'cramond' to the RNLI at 81400

**The Maltings Museum**
*www.cramondassociation.org.uk*
Open 2-5pm Sat & Sun (April-Sept) & daily during Edinburgh Festival

## EAT/DRINK...

**Cramond Bistro**
4-5 Riverside, Cramond Village
EH4 6NY

# 11 Fountainbridge, Tollcross & Lothian Road Walk

*Fountainbridge Library, see p.292*

# Fountainbridge, Tollcross & Lothian Road Walk

1. Caledonian Whiskey Distillery
2. Scotia Cinema
3. Dalry House
4. Dalry Swim Centre
5. Dalry Road Station
6. Western Approach Road
7. Fountainbridge Library
8. Fountainbridge brewery
9. North British Rubber Works
10. Union Canal
11. Lochrin Basin
12. Palais de Danse
13. St Cuthbert's Co-operative Association
14. Edinburgh Meat Market
15. Edinburgh Industrial Brigade Home

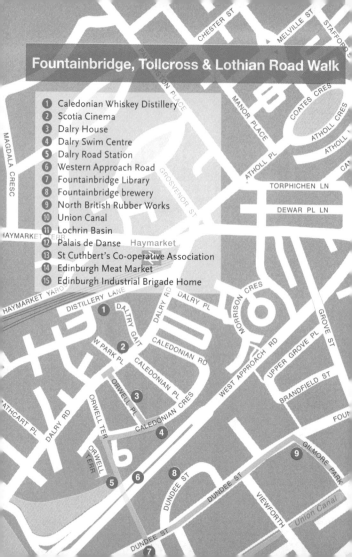

16 Municipal slaughterhouses
17 Cav nightclub
18 Central Hall
19 Tollcross
20 King's Theatre
21 Bennets Bar
22 Lochrin House
23 Cameo Cinema
24 Lothian House
25 Former Trustee Savings Bank
26 Odeon Cinema
27 Spittal Street
28 Festival Square
29 Usher Hall
30 Royal Lyceum Theatre
31 Poor house of St Cuthbert's Church
32 Picture House
33 King's Stables Road
34 St Cuthbert's Church
35 Watchtower
36 St John's Church
37 Waldorf Astoria Caledonian Hotel
38 Princes Street Station gates

# Fountainbridge, Tollcross & Lothian Road Walk

Start: Dalry Road
Finish: Rutland Street
Distance: 3.6 miles

This walk begins on Dalry Road, opposite the entrance to Orwell Place. While it is hard to believe it now, just a few decades ago Edinburgh was still a thriving industrial centre, and its breweries, distilleries and factories supplied products that were sold throughout the world. In the 19th century, the creation of new railways and a canal revolutionised transport links and changed the geography of the city forever. During this walk you will see some remnants of this industrial heyday.

The first evidence is apparent if you look north to see a tall chimney. This was once part of the ❶ **Caledonian Whisky Distillery** that operated here from the mid-19th century until closing in the late 1980s. It was built by Graham Menzies and was, for a while, the biggest distillery in Scotland. It used to draw water from the canal – seen later – until the canal closed and the water became stagnant. Sadly, nearly all the former distillery buildings have gone.

During the 18th and 19th centuries Edinburgh was at the heart of the Scottish drinks industry on account of its good water supply and transport links. The water wells in Holyrood, Canongate, the Cowgate, the Grassmarket and Fountainbridge have even been described as the 'charmed circle'.

By the 1870s, around 40 breweries were operating in Edinburgh, employing thousands of people. Sadly, just one from that golden era remains today – the Caledonian Brewery (or the 'Caly'), which has been located on the Slateford Road since 1869. The rest closed down over the years, hit by escalating alcohol duties that reduced profits and a major consolidation among brewery owners both nationally and internationally.

As you stand on Dalry Road, look towards number 90. This was once the foyer of the ❷ **Scotia Cinema**, which opened in 1912 and – before it was largely demolished – was believed to have been the second-oldest cinema building in Scotland. It began life as the Haymarket Cinema, became the Scotia in 1946, and continued to show films until 1964. It was once owned by John Maxwell, an influential figure in the early years of British cinema. He owned Elstree Studios, and employed a young Alfred Hitchcock as a

director. Until fairly recently, the former auditorium was used by a garage, but it was sadly demolished and only the former entrance survives today.

Walk down Orwell Place. This street dates from the 1870s and is typical of the tenement housing common in Dalry. Shortly on the left you will find the historic ❸ **Dalry House**. This was built in 1661, though an earlier building stood on the site from the early 1600s. It was owned for many years by the Chiesley family, who owned the surrounding estate, and it is said that the ghost of John Chiesley still haunts the house.

John divorced his wife in 1688, and then killed a local magistrate who had ordered him to pay his ex-wife a financial settlement. Found guilty of murder, John was tortured, his arm cut off, and then hanged. His one-armed spectre is said to have haunted his old home thereafter, and in 1965 a one-armed skeleton was found beneath the building.

The house was bought by the Walker family in 1812, and in the 1860s it was still surrounded largely by fields and farm land. The Walker family then moved and the surrounding area was quickly developed with the housing you see today. The house is now converted into residential flats.

Follow the map and bear left into Caledonian Crescent. Dalry itself is first recorded as a name in around 1328 and most likely is derived from a Celtic word for 'heathery dale'.

Walk along and stop outside the ❹ **Dalry Swim Centre**. Dating from the 1890s, the baths were founded in an era when many local working people would not have had a bath at home, and so coming here meant more than just a chance to have a leisurely swim. In recent years a hard-fought campaign prevented the baths from being demolished.

Retrace your steps slightly along Caledonian Crescent and follow the map to pass through the Telfer Subway. Just before you pass under the busy Western Approach Road, look up at the side entrance on the right and walk through it. The modern walkway occupies the site of ❺ **Dalry Road Station**, which operated from the 19th century until its closure in the 1960s. The station was demolished, but the ghostly remains of the old platform can still be seen.

Return to the subway and cross under the ❻ **Western Approach Road**. On the other side, stop to look back at the road.

The road, built in the early 1970s, follows the old route of the Caledonian Railway line. The Caledonian Railway was formed in the 1830s and its main line to Edinburgh opened in 1848. At one time you could have hopped on a train at Carlisle or Barnton Junction and stopped at Dalry Road before ending the trip at Princes Street Station (for passengers) or Lothian Road Station (for goods).

All the Edinburgh stations just mentioned were closed down long ago. After the railways were nationalised in 1948, many routes disappeared and this section of the railway line became obsolete when Princes Street Station was closed in the mid-1960s.

You come out onto Dundee Street. Look across the road to see the art deco ❼ **Fountainbridge Library**. This dates from the late 1930s and was designed by John AW Grant. The exterior bronze reliefs depict various educational activities, as knowledge is dispensed to adults and children. Inside, there is a particularly attractive art deco staircase that is worth a look if you have time.

Follow the map, with the Fountainbridge entertainment complex on your left. The origin of the name Fountainbridge is not entirely clear. It may be derived from a well known as Foullbridge Well or Foulbriggs, which stood nearby not far from the entrance to Gilmore Park. Developers building on fields in the district in the late 18th century may have decided 'Foul' was not a very attractive term for potential residents and so coined the current name instead.

The entertainment complex lies on top of another historic industrial site, in this case the ❽ **Fountain Brewery** that was for around 150 years the home of the world-famous McEwan's beer. The original brewery was founded by William McEwan (1827-1913), who started his own business in 1856. He made a great deal of money over the following decades and one of his finest philanthropic efforts was to fund the grand McEwan Hall at the University of Edinburgh. As with Usher Hall seen later, many of the best buildings in Edinburgh owe their foundation to profits made from the whisky and beer sold in the city's pubs. The business merged with another to form Scottish Brewers Ltd in 1931 and it was this era that the famous Cavalier figure that features on McEwan's beer cans was adopted.

In 1960, Scottish Brewers merged with Newcastle Breweries to form Scottish & Newcastle. This was then the largest brewing company in the UK and it expanded south of Dundee Road to take over the site of the old North British Rubber Works.

The brewery dominated this immediate area and was a major local employer. However, in later years, as beer sales fell, the Fountain Brewery came under increasing financial pressure and the northern site was closed – to be replaced in due course by the entertainment complex. Finally in 2004, the southern site also closed, ending McEwan's historic link with the area. Some beer production was shifted to the Caledonian Brewery on Slateford Road – the last of the 19th-century breweries still in operation.

Continue along Fountainbridge and cross over to the south side. The whole area on the south side was for many years dominated by the North British Rubber Works, and after it closed, by the extension of the Fountain Brewery. Successive generations of local families worked in these businesses and the eventual closure of the site in recent years has hit the community particularly hard.

Continue as far as the junction with Gilmour Park on the right-hand side. Look back at this point to the north side. This is approximately where the Scottish actor Sean Connery was born, in a tenement in 1930. It was later demolished and built over by Scottish & Newcastle – a complex which is also long gone.

Turn right up Gilmour Park. The buildings on the right-hand side are some of the only remaining evidence of the **❾ North British Rubber Works** that once dominated the land between here and the canal.

The rubber works was founded in the 1850s by a wealthy American named Henry Lee Norris. It stood on the site of an earlier silk mill that had opened in the 1830s to cash in on the demand for imitation Kashmir shawls, but which was forced to close in the following decade because it could not compete with rival mills in Paisley.

The products of the rubber works included the original

Wellington boots, hot water bottles and pneumatic tyres. The company won a lucrative order to make trench boots during WWI, providing over 1.2 million pairs. During WWII the factory concentrated on gas masks and materials for barrage balloons, and in the 1950s on motorway traffic cones. However, after being taken over by a US company, the factory closed in 1959. In the early 1970s Scottish & Newcastle bought the site as an extension of the Fountain Brewery, which covered around 22 acres.

Continue up the hill. In medieval times this area was covered by royal orchards that produced vegetables and fruit and housed livestock for consumption by the King and his courtiers. Shortly you reach a bridge over the Union Canal: walk through the opening to access the towpath of the canal itself, then continue eastwards. Look for the swing-bridge over the canal – this was originally situated further along and you would have crossed it when travelling over the canal before it was truncated.

The ❿ **Union Canal** runs from Falkirk to Edinburgh and was completed in 1822. It originally stretched for 32 miles, ending at the Port Hopetoun Basin in Edinburgh. However, the last mile was filled in after the canal closed and today ends at Lochrin Basin. The original purpose of the canal was to create a route to transport coal and other minerals from Lanarkshire to Edinburgh.

A separate canal, the Forth and Clyde Canal, was completed in 1790 and runs from Glasgow to the Firth of Forth, connected via the River Carron near Grangemouth. The Union Canal closed in the 1930s, as did the Forth and Clyde Canal in the 1960s, both unable to compete with rail and road transport. Today the two canal systems are connected at Falkirk, where the famous Falkirk Wheel allows boats to be moved between them. It is possible to cycle or walk between Glasgow and Edinburgh by sticking to the towpaths alongside both canal systems.

Continue along the towpath. Just a few years ago, this area was very run down following the closures of the canal and local businesses. However, in recent years new developments have sprung up that have improved the surroundings considerably.

10 *Union Canal*

Shortly you will reach ⑪ **Lochrin Basin**, the current end of the Union Canal.

To follow the path of the original canal before it was truncated at Lochrin Basin, continue along to rejoin Fountainbridge Road. When the canal was operational and stretched its original length, you could have walked under the bridge seen earlier and continued along the towpath.

Directly ahead is Gardiner's Crescent. In the early 1990s, JK Rowling lived in a flat at number 28. She later recalled writing ideas for her Harry Potter novels on any bits of paper she found in her flat, including her housing benefit application form!

Turn right and walk for a couple of minutes to reach on the right-hand side the former site of what was once one of Edinburgh's finest entertainment spots, the ⑫ **Palais de Danse**. It was opened in 1911 as a cinema (then the largest in the city) and ballroom, and became the Palais in 1921. In late 2016 the historic building was demolished to make way for student accommodation for 250 students.

Sean Connery, known as 'Big Tam', worked as a bouncer on the doors and was often seen dancing at the Palais with many female admirers on his nights off. Bands who played here included Manfred Mann. The venue closed in 1967 and for many years was used as a bingo hall before being abandoned.

Directly opposite are the former headquarters of ⑬ **St Cuthbert's Co-operative Association**. Founded in 1859 and at one time the largest co-operative in Scotland, it

provided many services, including a dairy with daily horse-drawn milk deliveries that were a familiar site in Edinburgh until 1985. It later merged with another organisation and continues today as Scotmid. Local lad Thomas Sean Connery first worked for St Cuthbert's when he was just 14 as a barrow pusher, later returning after time in the navy to be a 'horseman'. He left in 1950, and 12 years later found global fame in the James Bond film *Dr. No*. St Cuthbert's was almost bankrupted by the cost of building its headquarters here in 1880, and – as Scotmid – left 130 years later. If you look up above the main door, you can see the words, 'he that would reap must sow'.

Continue along until you reach (on your left) the old entrance

archway of the ⑭ **Edinburgh Meat Market**, which opened in 1884. The meat market stood beside the canal (before it was filled in) and remained here until 1921, when it moved out to Chesser. This followed the move of the city slaughterhouses out to Chesser in 1909.

Before the late 19th century, the selling of livestock, and butchered meat, as well as slaughtering, took place in a variety of places, mainly in the Old Town. There then was a move to centralise the trade in this part of Edinburgh, and so a cattle market opened in Lauriston Place nearby and a municipal slaughterhouse in Tollcross (seen shortly).

After it closed, the old market building was used as a nightclub in the 1960s before becoming the site of a burger restaurant. The main market building was demolished in 2007 and only the arch survives. If you walk behind the arch and bear right, you can find information boards that tell you more about the area's connections to the meat trade, and about the canal that originally extended all the way along here.

Passing the arch, on the right on the corner with Ponton Street stands the former ⑮ **Edinburgh Industrial Brigade Home**. Built in 1897, it provided accommodation and education for homeless boys. The location of the home in what was then the industrial heart of the city provided the boys with apprenticeships in the local tanneries, breweries and slaughterhouses. In its heyday, 85 boys were in residence, the largest provision of its kind in Scotland. The home moved out in 1962.

Follow the map down Ponton Street. On the right, Tollcross Primary School now stands at the centre of what was once a substantial complex of **16** **municipal slaughterhouses**. The slaughterhouses operated from the mid-19th century until WWI, when they were demolished and replaced by the school. The only remaining feature of the slaughterhouses is known as the Janitor's House.

Walk up West Tollcross and look out on the right-hand side for a nightclub called **17** **Cav**. In the 1940s it was a dancehall, and during its heyday in the late 1960s to mid-1980s many great bands performed here including Pink Floyd, The Jam, The Clash, The Ramones, The Stranglers, U2, Depeche Mode and The Smiths, to name, but a few. In the late 1970s, the club, known as Clouds, was one of the key venues in the Northern Soul movement and also featured a roller-disco. The Cav features heavily in the 2017 film *Trainspotting 2*, when Renton encounters Begbie in a nightclub toilet and flees for his life.

Continue along West Tollcross and stop outside **18** **Central Hall** on the corner. This is one of the most impressive buildings in Tollcross and was built by the Methodist Church in 1901. Before the first cinemas were founded in Edinburgh, cinematograph exhibitions were held here. Today it is owned by the Morningside Baptist Church.

You are now standing in ⑲ **Tollcross**, a junction of five roads. The name was first recorded in the 15th century, although it has been hard to prove there was actually a toll operating here so the real origin of the name remains obscure. Look out for the distinctive clock in the middle of the junction, which dates from 1901 and is a well known Edinburgh landmark.

Follow the map south to the ⑳ **King's Theatre**. This was founded in 1906 and famous names who have performed here include Noël Coward, Maggie Smith, Sean Connery, Led Zeppelin and Monty Python. It stands on the site of Drumdryan Brewery, another of Edinburgh's many lost breweries. The brewery operated during most of the 19th century and old photos show it had a chimney that would have been as prominent as the one you saw at the very start of the walk. The brewery stood near to a mansion named Drumdryan House, which was built in the 1730s. It was later incorporated into the brewery site and both were demolished before the construction of the King's Theatre.

Beside the theatre, and frequented by many a fine actor, is ㉑ **Bennets Bar** (see p.311). The current building dates mainly from 1891, and contains one of the city's finest interiors from the golden age of Victorian public house design. If you look down the side of Bennets, you can see some old signage for 'Marshall – Wine – Spirits'. This refers to the pub's original name – Marshall's Bar.

Marshall's Brewery opened the first pub on this site in 1839. The Bennet family took

8 BENNETS BAR 8

A. USHER & CO

BERNARL'S
MILD & PALE ALES

21 *Bennets Bar*

over in around 1910 and continued to run the pub until the 1970s. Bennets also contains a bar counter that was taken from the warship *HMS Belfast*.

Almost directly opposite the King's Theatre was the former site of **㉒ Lochrin House** – a substantial property built in the early 19th century which stood until the 1890s. This immediate area was also dominated from the 1730s by a brewery, and then by the Lochrin Whisky Distillery. This was founded in around 1780 by James Haig and became one of the largest in Scotland before closing in 1848. Today the brand Haig is owned by Diageo – recently advertised by David Beckham.

In a map of 1804, Haig's steam engine is marked as a noteworthy feature, a reminder of the impact the Industrial Revolution was having on the geography of Edinburgh. The excellent **㉓ Cameo Cinema** (see p.313) – once run by the Poole family (more of which later in the walk) – stands on the eastern edge of the former distillery complex. Part of the old distillery complex was incorporated into the Lochrin Iron Works business that was founded in 1859. This produced iron fences and gates for big estates in Scotland. This business left Edinburgh many years later and survives today as Lochrin Bain, a company producing fences which is now based in Cumbernauld but whose name still recalls its earliest days over 150 years ago.

This immediate area is known as Lochrin, named after an old 'rin' or burn that ran from the old South Loch (where the Meadows is today) through this area before emptying into the Water of Leith. It still runs underground and would have been used by the local breweries and distilleries that once operated here.

Retrace your steps and walk northwards to Tollcross, passing Central Hall on your left. Continue until you reach the junction of East Fountainbridge and Lothian Road. One of the busiest roads in the city, Lothian Road was completed in 1785 and was planned to link the west side of the New Town to the junction at Tollcross.

Looking north, all the buildings on the block on your left stand on what was originally the water-filled Port Hopetoun Basin, which stood at the very end of the canal you walked beside earlier. The art deco  **Lothian House** with its distinctive rural relief decorations dates from 1936, and dominates the west side of Lothian Road. Inspired by Kodak House in London, it was recently described in an official planning-permission report as 'an iconic and significant presence on Lothian Road and [which] contributes very positively to a streetscape that is in many other respects poor. It is unique in Edinburgh in terms of its scale and design.' Originally a tax office, in the 1980s it was converted into flats and boasts a swimming pool.

Opposite Lothian House is the 19th-century  **former Trustee Savings Bank** building. Now a branch of Lloyds-TSB, it contains a pretty and unusual mosaic above the entrance that reads 'thrift is blessing'. These words are taken from a speech by Shylock in Shakespeare's *The Merchant of Venice*: 'This was a way to thrive, and he was blest: And thrift is blessing, if men steal it not.'

Continue north up Lothian Road and at the next junction on the left is an  **Odeon Cinema**. This began its life as the ABC Regal in 1938, and its heyday was in the 1960s when many famous bands played here. In 1964 alone, The Beatles, The Rolling Stones, The Yardbirds, Gerry & The Pacemakers, The Kinks, Marianne Faithfull, and Davy Jones & The Manish Boys all played here. Davy Jones later changed his surname to Bowie

and achieved slightly more success. Other highlights included Bob Dylan's concert in 1966. When The Beatles played, hundreds of fans camped all night around the block to try to buy tickets.

If you have time, walk down Bread Street until you reach **27 Spittal Street**. This is where George Gibson (1904-2001) was born (at number 6). A trained artist, Gibson left Scotland for Hollywood where he became a well known designer of film sets. He was also responsible for the iconic horizon view of the Emerald City that features in *A Wizard of Oz* (1939). It has been suggested that his design was inspired by the view he would have been familiar with from this part of Edinburgh up to the castle.

Continue down Lothian Road and after a few minutes you will see **28 Festival Square** on your left. For over a century this area was dominated by the Caledonian Railway. The railway track, passing along the route of today's Western Approach Road, reached its original terminus here after the railway line was extended to the city in 1848.

Later the railway track was extended and in 1870 a temporary terminus for passengers – Princes Street Station – was built just further along Lothian Road, facing Princes Street. This temporary

passenger station was replaced by a much grander permanent station in the 1890s. The station buildings, located where Festival Square is now, continued to be used as a goods station. Look out for the Bell Clock Tower, gifted in the 1960s by the Arthur Bell & Sons whisky distillers. It used to stand by the Usher Hall on the other side of the road, but its chimes were a great source of irritation to audiences attending concerts. They were first silenced, and then in 2010 the whole tower was moved over the road to its current site.

㉙ **Usher Hall** opposite has been one of the finest concert venues in Edinburgh since it opened in 1914, made possible by a donation in 1896 of £100,000 by Andrew Usher (1826-98).

The Usher family was heavily involved in the brewing and whisky businesses, and Andrew made his fortune from popularising blended whisky around the world. He became known as the 'Father of Scottish Whisky' and his fellow board members included John Dewar, John 'Johnnie' Walker and Arthur Bell. These men later developed their own whisky brands, and their surnames are still seen on whisky bottles all over the world today. Andrew Usher also helped to found the North British Distillery Company. This continues today in the Gorgie district of Edinburgh and is the city's last remaining grain distillery.

The Usher family's wealth was not just derived from alcohol. They also owned slaves in Jamaica, and, along with dozens of other residents of Edinburgh, put in a claim for compensation from the British government after slavery in the Empire was finally abolished in 1833. The actual claim was asserted by Andrew Usher (c. 1782-1855), father of the Andrew Usher who was responsible for Usher Hall. Sadly, none of the freed slaves received any compensation.

At their most powerful, the Usher family owned considerable land in Scotland and also a substantial house on West Nicholson Street – known as Pear Tree House. Today this is home to a pub and the modern-day Andrew Usher & Co brewing company, who have resurrected old family beer recipes. The shape of the counting-house room in the West Nicholson Street building is said to have inspired the design for the dome of Usher Hall itself.

Usher Hall is usually associated with classical music but over the years great rock and pop bands have played here including Pink Floyd, The Rolling Stones, Johnny Cash, Chuck Berry and Led Zeppelin. Prime Minister HH Asquith gave a speech here on the war effort in 1914, and thousands protested when fascist leader Sir Oswald Mosley came to speak at the hall in 1934. By strange contrast, the Eurovision Song Contest was held here in 1972, hosted by Stockbridge resident Moira Shearer.

This area around the Usher Hall has long been associated with entertainment. The **30** **Royal Lyceum Theatre** next door has been providing first-class drama and opera in Edinburgh since 1883. It is said to be haunted by a mysterious 'blue lady' – possibly the ghost of the famous actress Ellen Terry.

Also close by was the Royal Edinburgh Theatre, which opened in 1875. It was built to meet the growing demand for entertainment from the city's rapidly expanding population but it was not successful, and within a couple of years it was sold to the United Presbyterian Church. They re-opened the venue as their Synod Hall.

In the early 20th century the Poole family began renting out Synod Hall to show moving panoramas (known as myrioramas). They later ran a cinema here, the first in Edinburgh to show 'talkies' in 1926. The Poole family also ran the Roxy Cinema on Gorgie Road and the Cameo (seen earlier) at Tollcross. Sadly, the Synod Hall finally closed in 1965 and the building was demolished. The area lay empty until Saltire Court was built in 1991.

Continue north, stopping at the junction with the Western Approach Road to your left. Just on your left, where the buildings face the south side of the Western Approach Road, once stood the ③ **poor house of St Cuthbert's Church**. Before it was opened in 1758, the poor of the parish were maintained from a tax on beer, as well as from the sale of begging licences. The poor house included a school were children could be taught a trade. It was demolished in 1869 to allow the extension of the railway station.

On your right is the ② **Picture House**. This began life in 1923 as the Caley Picture House and has been used for various entertainment purposes over the years. During the 1960s and 1970s many great bands played here including David Bowie (1969), T-Rex (1970), Queen (supporting Mott the Hoople, 1973), ACDC (1976), as well as R.E.M, Orange Juice, The Smiths and the Psychedelic Furs (1984).

Cross over Castle Terrace, looking out for ③ **King's Stables Road** running down to the right. It was most likely named after the horse stables that were first built here by the English garrison occupying the castle during the reign of Edward III in the 14th century. Later, Scottish kings stabled their horses here before the court moved from the castle to Holyrood Palace.

Pass the watchtower and descend the steps on your right to enter the graveyard of ③ **St Cuthbert's**. Dating back to the 9th century, this is part of the Church of Scotland. The current church is the seventh to be built on this site and dates from 1894.

This has been a place of Christian burial for a thousand years, and many prominent people in Edinburgh's history have been interred here. It is worth a wander through the graveyard if time permits. With the castle looming in the distance, it is atmospheric and a tranquil place in contrast to the noise and traffic of Lothian Road.

You will see many headstones whose inscriptions link the deceased to places throughout the British Empire when it was at its height. Edinburgh provided a large number of doctors, soldiers, administrators and lawyers who were stationed in places such India, Australia, South Africa and the West Indies.

John Napier (1550-1617) is buried here, best known as the inventor of logarithms and after whom Napier University in Edinburgh is named. His memorial plaque is in the church's entrance hall. Thomas De Quincey (1785-1859), the essayist and author of *Confessions of an English Opium-Eater*, is also buried here.

The **35 watchtower** in the graveyard was built in 1827 so that a guard could protect the graves from body snatchers. Edinburgh's most infamous body snatchers were William Burke and William Hare, although they avoided the difficulties of stealing bodies from graveyards by instead murdering around 16 people during

1828 in order to sell the bodies to an anatomist. Burke was executed after being convicted for murder, while Hare escaped justice after giving King's evidence against his accomplice. Both men originally came from Ireland to help dig the Union Canal you walked beside earlier.

Leave St Cuthbert's and continue to **36 St John's** (on the corner of Princes Street), an elegant Episcopalian church designed in the perpendicular gothic style. It was consecrated in 1818.

36 St John's Church

Particularly notable for its fan-vaulted ceiling, St John's contains a memorial to the famous Scottish painter Sir Henry Raeburn (1756-1823). There is also a small plaque inside (north side) that commemorates John Stuart-Forbes, who was born in Edinburgh in 1849 and became the black sheep of his family. After many adventures he ended up in America, and joined the US Cavalry. He died fighting alongside General Custer in 1876 at the Battle of the Little Bighorn. It is worth looking around St John's graveyard, which is full of fascinating memorials and tombs.

On the north-east side of the graveyard is a modest headstone for Malvina Wells: 'Born in Carriacou, West Indies – Died at Edinburgh 22 April 1887 aged 82 years – For upwards of 70 years a faithful servant and friend of Mrs Macrae'. Malvina was born on a plantation – her father was a white planter and her mother almost certainly a black slave. Malvina would have become the property of her mother's owner when she was born (slavery in the Empire was only abolished in 1833). She came to Edinburgh when some of the Macrae family

she served returned to the city from their plantation in Grenada, and she was later listed in the census as a 'lady's maid'. She is the only woman identified in an Edinburgh graveyard who was most likely born a slave.

Leave St John's using the pedestrian crossing to stand in front of the 37 **Waldorf Astoria Caledonian Hotel**. This grand hotel opened in 1903 and was built above Princes Street Railway Station. In 2010, an American woman jumped to her death from the 4th floor of the hotel in front of horrified onlookers.

While it is hard to imagine it now, the bottom third of the building from the Caledonian sign downwards was part of the original façade of Princes Street Station. Every day, hundreds of people would have walked in and out of the station through three large entrances (now filled with windows).

For decades Princes Street Station was a rival to Waverley Station; however, nationalisation of the railways in the mid-20th century saw a wave of consolidation take place and this station closed in 1965. The main structure was demolished over the next few years. Today, only the hotel gives a sense of how big the station was; it would have stretched almost all the way back to Festival Square, which you visited earlier.

Walk around the side of the hotel (on Rutland Street) to see the 38 **old gates** through which traffic passed in and out of the station. The original station clock is still within the hotel. Like many of the Caledonian Railway buildings, the hotel was constructed using red sandstone, which the railway owners could afford to transport cheaply to Edinburgh. This is the end of the walk. From here you can join the throngs of shoppers on Princes Street or alternatively escape to Princes Street Gardens. ●

---

## VISIT...

**Fountainbridge Library**
137 Dundee Street, EH11 1BG

**Cameo Cinema**
38 Home St, EH3 9LZ
www.picturehouses.com

## EAT/DRINK...

**Bennet's Bar**
8 Leven St, Tollcross, EH3 9LG

**Timberyard**
10 Lady Lawson St, EH3 9DS
www.timberyard.co

Pink granite pyramid grave, designed by William Playfair, see p.226

# 12 Dean Cemetery Walk

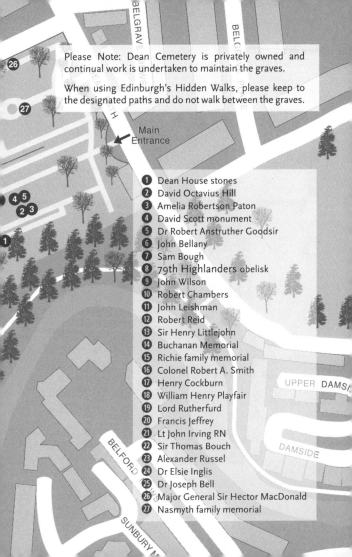

Please Note: Dean Cemetery is privately owned and continual work is undertaken to maintain the graves.

When using Edinburgh's Hidden Walks, please keep to the designated paths and do not walk between the graves.

Main Entrance

1. Dean House stones
2. David Octavius Hill
3. Amelia Robertson Paton
4. David Scott monument
5. Dr Robert Anstruther Goodsir
6. John Bellany
7. Sam Bough
8. 79th Highlanders obelisk
9. John Wilson
10. Robert Chambers
11. John Leishman
12. Robert Reid
13. Sir Henry Littlejohn
14. Buchanan Memorial
15. Richie family memorial
16. Colonel Robert A. Smith
17. Henry Cockburn
18. William Henry Playfair
19. Lord Rutherfurd
20. Francis Jeffrey
21. Lt John Irving RN
22. Sir Thomas Bouch
23. Alexander Russel
24. Dr Elsie Inglis
25. Dr Joseph Bell
26. Major General Sir Hector MacDonald
27. Nasmyth family memorial

# Dean Cemetery Walk

Start: Dean Cemetery entrance
Finish: Dean Cemetery entrance
Distance: 1 mile

This walk begins at the entrance to Dean Cemetery, which is located along Dean Path (accessible either from Queensferry Road to the north or Dean Village to the south).

Walk through the gates. The cemetery stands on the site of Dean House, a grand building erected in 1614 as part of the Dean Estate bought by Sir William Nisbet in 1609. The estate house was totally demolished in preparation for the creation of the cemetery, which was laid out in 1845. The house would have stood almost directly in front of you and slightly to the west of the grass-covered roundabout.

The creation of Dean Cemetery was a commercial venture driven by a private company, and it was not connected to a particular church. This was a major development in the mid-19th century as the graveyards of the older central churches had become overcrowded and could no longer cope with the increased number of burials that were the inevitable result of a growing population.

Dean Cemetery was designed by David Cousin (1809-78). Cousin served for many years as Edinburgh's City Superintendent of Works and was responsible for over a dozen churches as well as other privately owned cemeteries including those at Warriston, Dalry, Rosebank and Newington. He learnt his craft working for one of Edinburgh's great architects – William Henry Playfair. You will see monuments here to both Cousin and Playfair (the latter is buried here).

After you enter through the grand gates, bear left along the south end and walk down some steps to visit a lower terrace. This faces onto Dean Village and the Water of Leith down below. The original Village of Dean was situated almost opposite the entrance to the cemetery but, like Dean House, it was demolished in the mid-19th century. The name was then co-opted by the Water of Leith Village which became known as Dean Village (see walk 8, p.209).

Walk along the terrace and look out for ❶ **stones** set up high on the wall which are rare survivors from the demolished Dean House.

When you have finished, go back up the stairs and then follow the next path up on the south side. Look for the prominent bust of ❷ **David Octavius Hill** (1802-70), an early pioneer of photography. During the 1840s he photographed a wide range of subjects, including some of the most prominent citizens of Edinburgh as well as ordinary people such as the fishwives of Newhaven. Hill worked with his associate Robert Adamson at Rock House on Calton Hill, largely using the sun to illuminate his photographic subjects. Photography had only recently been invented so their photographs were in every sense pioneering.

Hill was originally a painter and remained one throughout his life. His most famous painting depicted the 'Disruption' Assembly of 1843 (see p.171) when hundreds of ministers stormed out of a meeting of the Church of Scotland to found the Free Church of Scotland. Hill photographed those who had attended the meeting in order to make the painting as realistic as possible. One outcome of the 'Disruption' was that people who left the Church of Scotland had no church burial ground available when they died. This helped to spur the growth of the new, commercially run cemeteries.

The bust, in the style of a Roman emperor, was the work of Hill's second wife, ❸ **Amelia Robertson Paton** (1820-1904). Buried beside Hill, she was a prominent sculptor, and today you can see her statue of the explorer David Livingstone near to the Scott Monument by Princes Street.

Nearby is a Celtic-styled ❹ **monument to David Scott** (1806-49), a brilliant but tragic Scottish painter who died young. The stone was designed and erected years later by his brother William and the green bronze head weeps a black tear.

Also near this group is the burial place of ⑤ **Dr Robert Anstruther Goodsir** (1823-99). He took part in two missions in 1849 and 1850 that sought to find out what had happened to the ill-fated Franklin Expedition, which had set out in 1845 under the leadership of Captain Sir John Franklin to find the fabled North-West Passage.

Franklin's expedition was a disaster, particularly after its ships *Terror* and *Erebus* became trapped in ice in September 1846. Over the next couple of years, the crew died one by one, the final tragedy taking place as a group made a desperate attempt to walk back to civilisation in Canada. Out of a crew of 129, there were no survivors.

Goodsir's interest was personal – his brother was a doctor who had accompanied Franklin. Over the next few decades nearly 40 different missions sought to find out what had happened to Franklin and his men, gradually piecing together most of the tragic story. Later on you will see another tomb linked to the expedition.

In 1850 Goodsir published a grim account of his own experiences looking for his brother entitled *Voyage to Baffin's Bay and Lancaster Sound, in Search of Friends with Sir John Franklin*.

SAMUEL BOUGH

**7** R. S. A.

Just further along in this section is the striking modern marble headstone of the artist **6** **John Bellany** (1942-2013), one of the greatest Scottish painters of the modern era. Bellany was born a few miles away in the fishing town of Port Seton and his experiences there greatly influenced his style of painting. Bellany's own health problems over the years also inspired his work, even to the extent of painting self-portraits while in hospital.

Follow the map westwards along the path leading away from the small roundabout. Just on the right is the gravestone of artist **7** **Sam Bough** (1822-78), his likeness forever captured in a bronze portrait by the sculptor William Brodie. Bough was a noted landscape painter, born in England but spending most of his life in Scotland. He was much admired by Robert Louis Stevenson, who wrote a favourable obituary of the artist. You can see some of Bough's paintings in the Scottish National Gallery in Edinburgh (see p.185). You will see another example of Brodie's work shortly.

Continue to a tall **8** **obelisk** that commemorates hundreds of members of the 79th Highlanders who died in far-flung parts of the Empire, including during the Crimean War and in India.

**8**

The rear of the monument recalls their role in the containment of the Indian Mutiny at Lucknow. This is just one of many reminders in Dean Cemetery of the enormous number of Scots who joined the army or navy during the heyday of the British Empire. You will see from the brief biographical details on some of the headstones that many Scots were actually born abroad in places such as India or South Africa, or spent much of their lives overseas as colonial administrators, soldiers, doctors and engineers.

Oddly enough, another group of Scots fought under the 79th name – the 79th New York Volunteer Regiment. Founded in 1859 in New York, it was formed by Scots immigrants and went on to fight for the Union side in almost every big engagement that took place during the American Civil War (1861-65). Another Scots connection with the American Civil War will be seen shortly.

Continue directly ahead then take the path bearing left. Just ahead is a large memorial to ❾ **John Wilson** (1800-49), a once famous Scottish singer. The son of a coach driver, he worked his way from the choir at Duddingston Parish Church to the stages of Drury Lane and Covent Garden in London, even performing for Queen Victoria.

Bear left here, and very shortly on the left is a red sandstone Celtic cross that marks the burial place of ❿ **Robert Chambers** (1832-88). He was a member of the firm W & R Chambers, which became a leading publisher during the 19th century. It was once best known for its encyclopaedia, although its principal legacy today remains the famous dictionary. This Robert was the son of the Robert Chambers who co-founded the firm with his brother William.

Robert Chambers senior (1802-71) was largely self-educated and among his many accomplishments was the authorship of a controversial work titled *Vestiges of the Natural History of Creation* (1844). Its radical theories relating to the evolution of the world made it a literary sensation that influenced Charles Darwin. Chambers published the

work anonymously, worried that it could harm the reputation of the family publishing firm.

Continue southwards and just around the bend stop at the striking and unusual gravestone of **①① John Leishman** (1801-61), shared with his grandson, Brigadier Offley-Shore. Leishman was a 'Writer to the Signet' – a term for solicitors in Scotland dating from medieval times when Writers to the Signet were lawyers authorised to oversee the use of the King's seal. The gravestone is dramatic, with three defending winged lions below three rams' heads and at the top three cranes. The result is one of the most intriguing designs to be found in any Scottish cemetery.

On the south wall (almost opposite Leishman) is a memorial to the architect **①② Robert Reid** (1774-1856). Like Playfair (whose burial place is seen shortly), Reid was responsible for many of Edinburgh's finest buildings and streets, particularly in the so-called Northern New Town built in the early 19th century (see p.191). He is best known for the exterior of Parliament Square, and West Register House in Charlotte Square (originally St George's Church).

Near to Reid is the modest gravestone of ⓭ **Sir Henry Littlejohn** (1826-1914), surgeon and public health pioneer. He served as the city's first Medical Officer of Health and did much to improve sanitation in Edinburgh. He also co-founded the Royal Hospital for Sick Children, which is still open to this day.

Continue westwards. Very shortly on the right you will see the vast ⓮ **Buchanan Memorial**. This classical mausoleum is one of the finest monuments in the cemetery. It commemorates James Buchanan (1785-1857), a wealthy Glasgow merchant and philanthropist whose legacy funded the Buchanan Institution in Glasgow. The monument was designed by the sculptor William Brodie – best known for his statue of Greyfriars Bobby (see p.128) – who is also buried in Dean Cemetery.

Now walk along the top path that runs along the western edge of the cemetery. This is known as 'Lords Row' because of the many titled people buried here.

Just here on the west wall is a ⓯ **family memorial** to a Scottish newspaper dynasty. John Ritchie (1778-1870) helped his brother William to found the *Scotsman* newspaper. John later became sole proprietor, and employed his great-nephew John Ritchie Findlay (1824-98). John Ritchie Findlay became the new owner when John Ritchie died, and was also a prominent philanthropist in Edinburgh. His many projects include Well Court in nearby Dean Village (see p.215), designed to help less well-off workers, and the funding of the Scottish National Portrait Gallery (see p.185). Both men are buried here.

16

Continue along Lords Row and shortly on the right is a memorial stone for Edinburgh-born ⓰ **Colonel Robert A. Smith**. Smith's father was an industrialist from Paisley who had a property at 65 George Street. As a teenager, Robert emigrated to join his older brother in Jackson, Mississippi. His brother was already friendly with Jefferson Davis, the man who would become President of the Confederacy when the American Civil War broke out. Robert, in his early twenties, joined the Confederate Army, and at one point acted as bodyguard to Davis. He was by all accounts a superb solider, and already a colonel when – aged 26 – he died leading a Confederate attack in 1862 during the Battle of Munfordville in Kentucky. The following year the Scottish press reported on the obelisk being placed here by Smith's brother, and how as Smith lay dying, 'he was attended up to the last by his faithful negro, whom no persuasion on the part of the Yankees could induce to "come with him and be free".'

A few years after the Civil War ended, ex-President Jefferson Davis visited Scotland. The world's best-known White Supremacist, he stayed with the prominent Edinburgh publisher John Blackwood (also buried in Dean Cemetery), and was seemingly fêted wherever he went. In Edinburgh he stayed at the Royal Hotel (which stood beside the site of Jenners on Princes Street) and in Glasgow he stayed with Colonel Smith's older brother. It seems almost certain that Davis would have come here to visit the memorial his friend had placed in memory of his younger brother, and Davis's former bodyguard.

There are usually Confederate flags left on the memorial, evidence that Colonel Smith remains something of a folk hero among those who continue to remember the Confederate cause. Perhaps ironically, there is a grand statute of Davis's great foe Abraham Lincoln in Old Calton Cemetery on the other side of the city (see p.163).

Continue along this path (walking northwards). Shortly on the left by the wall is the burial place of ⑰ **Henry Cockburn** (1779-1854), an influential lawyer, judge and literary figure. Lord Cockburn wrote extensively for the influential *Edinburgh Review* and was a member of the Speculative Society during its great era when members included figures such as Sir Walter Scott and Francis Jeffrey (see later). He also co-founded the Edinburgh Academy – one the city's best-known public schools. Cockburn made great efforts during his lifetime to protect the historic buildings of Edinburgh and this legacy continues today in the Cockburn Association.

The neighbouring white altar is part of the burial plot of the architect ⑱ **William Henry Playfair** (1790-1857). Playfair designed some of Edinburgh's greatest buildings, including Old College (begun by Robert Adam), the Royal Scottish Academy and Scottish National Gallery, the (unfinished) National Monument on Calton Hill and the Surgeons' Hall. He contributed greatly to the image of Edinburgh as the 'Athens of the North'.

Cockburn and Playfair were great friends who regularly met up with some of Edinburgh's most prominent figures in the 'Friday Club' – one of several Edinburgh societies that existed during the 18th and early 19th centuries to allow like-minded men to socialise and exchange ideas. This helped to create an openness to progress that made the city world famous for being at the heart of an intellectual movement that became known as the Scottish Enlightenment.

Just ahead is perhaps the most ostentatious burial spot in Dean Cemetery, a pink granite pyramid, designed by Playfair, that commemorates the lawyer and **19 Lord Rutherfurd** MP (1791-1852) and his wife **Francesca**. The styling is evidence of the influence that archaeological finds in Egypt were having on cultural tastes in Europe.

Just next to the Rutherfurd tomb is a metal door that leads directly to the Scottish National Gallery of Modern Art (see p.331) which has an excellent café.

Next to this is a table-altar to **20 Francis Jeffrey** (1773-1850). Lord Jeffrey was a judge and literary critic, and another member of the Speculative Society mentioned earlier. He helped to found the influential publication, the *Edinburgh Review* in 1802, which he edited for around 26 years. The publication leant towards political and social reform and was often involved in controversial debates. Jeffrey also became a prominent lawyer and MP, typically of a number of high-achieving Edinburgh residents of his era who managed to succeed in a number of different fields.

Just ahead is the monument to **21 Lt John Irving RN** (1815-c.1847/8). He died on Franklin's doomed expedition to find the North-West Passage mentioned earlier. A US expedition of 1878-80 discovered Irving's remains and he was later identified because of a silver medal found on his body. Irving had won the medal in 1830 after doing well in a maths exam at school and kept it with him thereafter. Only three other bodies from Franklin's expedition have ever been identified.

Irving's remains were buried here in November 1881, the funeral party led by his surviving relatives. The Franklin expedition exerted a morbid grip on the imagination of the public in Britain for several decades, with rescue parties returning with tales of the doomed men resorting to cannibalism. The expedition still makes the news even today – in 2014 the Canadian Prime Minister Stephen Harper announced the wreck of the *Erebus* had been found after years of searching by the Canadian authorities. *Erebus* was located only after the search team looked again at previously discounted clues contained within the oral histories of the Inuit Indians. Amazingly just two years later the discovery of *Terror* was announced, almost perfectly preserved. Hopefully historians will be able finally to piece together the full story of what really happened so many years ago.

Irving's funeral procession – led by pipers – drew huge crowds. Irving was born at his family home at 106 Princes Street and his father was a childhood friend of Sir Walter Scott. Irving himself was a fairly undistinguished naval officer, but during his short life he typified the globe-travelling nature of many Scots in the heyday of the British Empire, spending time in Malta, Naples and Australia before dying on Franklin's expedition.

From here you walk eastwards back along the path towards the roundabout just inside the entrance.

About 20 yards before reaching the roundabout, look out on the left-hand side for the grave of ㉒ **Sir Thomas Bouch** (1822-80). He was

a prominent Victorian engineer who helped the spread of the railways throughout Britain and was knighted for his efforts. However, his career was ruined because of the Tay Bridge Disaster of 1879. Bouch had designed the bridge, which collapsed during a storm as a train was crossing it. Around 70 people on the train were killed and Bouch bore much of the blame for the bridge's inadequate design. His health was broken by the stress of the subsequent investigation and within a year he was dead.

23 Alexander Russel

Continue to the roundabout (with the entrance ahead of you) and then move to the next path to the north (running by a wall) and walk westwards again. Shortly on the right is an opening in the wall. Go through this to reach the northern section of the cemetery.

Walk towards the middle of this section, aiming for the huge granite obelisk dedicated to ❷❸ **Alexander Russel** (1814-76). He served as an influential editor of the *Scotsman* for nearly 30 years. By the time of his death, the daily circulation had risen to 50,000, the largest of any newspaper outside of London. It is difficult today to understand how much influence a relatively small number of newspapers had on public issues in the 19th century, and Russel helped to drive the political and social agenda in Scottish life for a considerable period. He first came to the *Scotsman* after being noticed by John Ritchie – the newspaper's owner, whose headstone you saw earlier.

Russel was a famously difficult man. When it was suggested that he might want to congratulate a staff member on an excellent article, he responded, 'Man... I can't. I can't praise anybody; I never could.'

Walk past the obelisk, heading west, and shortly on the right you should find the modest headstone of ❷❹ **Dr Elsie Inglis** (1864-1917): it is before you reach a small grass roundabout. So far, few women have been mentioned on this walk, perhaps a result of how stratified Scottish society was in the 19th century. However, Inglis represented a new age for women.

A noted suffragette, surgeon and reformer, she was – like many high-achieving Scots – actually born in India. There her parents, away from the stricter social mores of Edinburgh, were able to provide Elsie with a first-rate private education. She entered the medical profession when it was still largely closed to women and founded a maternity hospital in Edinburgh in 1902. She came to prominence during WWI, when she set up the Scottish Women's Hospitals for Foreign Service Committee, which provided female-

24

staffed hospitals in Serbia, Russia, France, the Ukraine and Romania. She was awarded Serbia's highest national award, but sadly died of cancer before the Great War ended.

From here, walk north to reach the north wall, then turn right (heading eastwards). Continue walking until you are nearly parallel with Russel's obelisk and look to the north wall. Here you will see a white marble cross above the burial spot of ㉕ **Dr Joseph Bell** (1837-1911). This prominent Edinburgh physician served as Queen Victoria's personal doctor when she was in Scotland. However, today Bell is best known because he served as the inspiration for the creation of Arthur Conan Doyle's Sherlock Holmes.

The author studied under Bell as a medical student at Edinburgh University, and for a while served as Bell's clerk. Doyle later wrote to Bell, stating, 'It is most certainly to you that I owe Sherlock Holmes'. It is also thought that Sir Henry Littlejohn (mentioned earlier) – whom Doyle also knew – may have contributed in a minor way to the creation of the great detective.

Continue along the path by the north wall and shortly you will see on the right-hand side the green obelisk that commemorates ㉖ **Major General Sir Hector MacDonald** (1853-1903), one of the most controversial figures to have served in the British army. Known as 'Fighting Mac', he was born into a crofting family and became a private in the Gordon Highlanders. He excelled as a soldier during the Afghan campaigns and by 1891 had become a Major. His tactics during the Battle of Omdurman (1898) helped to save the British army and made him a household name. He continued his meteoric rise during the Boer War, where he led the Highland Brigade and was knighted. Disaster struck after allegations arose that he was conducting affairs with young men while stationed in Ceylon. He shot himself before the court martial and many believed he had been framed. His funeral was attended by a crowd of around 30,000 people.

Years later a story arose (probably through German propaganda) that he had not died but had assumed the identity of a General in the German army – August von Mackensen. Mackensen did bear an uncanny resemblance to MacDonald, serving with distinction as a Field Marshall during WWI and sitting beside Hitler during the 1936 Olympic Games in Berlin. Mackensen – or perhaps the Fighting Mac – died in 1945.

Walk south from this spot to reach the large Celtic cross that marks the burial place of the **㉗ Nasmyth family**. James and Patrick Nasmyth are buried here, both sons of the painter Alexander Nasmyth (1758-1840). Alexander's portrait of Robert Burns can be found in the Scottish National Portrait Gallery (see p.185), and he also designed St Bernard's Well by the Water of Leith (see p.223). Patrick also became a painter, though it is James (1808-90) who is today best known. He was a prolific inventor, best known for creating the steam-hammer, which played an important part in the Industrial Revolution. There is a relief on one side depicting his steam-hammer.

This is the end of the walk – you can leave the cemetery by the entrance gates. ●

## VISIT/EAT/DRINK...

**Dean Cemetery**
63 Dean Path, EH4 3AT
www.deancemetery.org.uk
Open: Mon-Sun, 9am-dusk,
Winter (Oct-Mar)
Mon-Sun, 9am-5pm, Summer
(April-Sept)

**Scottish National Gallery of Modern Art One**
73 Belford Rd, EH4 3DR
www.nationalgalleries.org

**Scottish National Gallery of Modern Art Two**
73 Belford Rd, EH4 3DS
www.nationalgalleries.org

Bruntsfield Links and Barclay Viewforth Church

# 13 Brunstfield Links, The Grange & Marchmont Walk

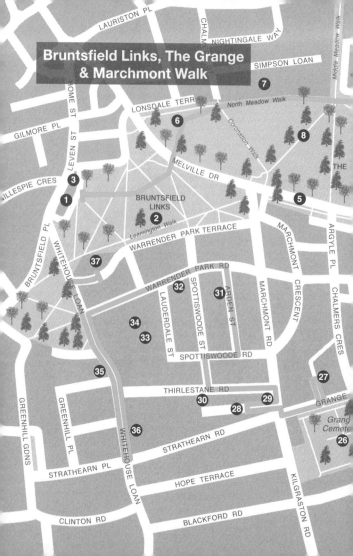

# Bruntsfield Links, The Grange & Marchmont Walk

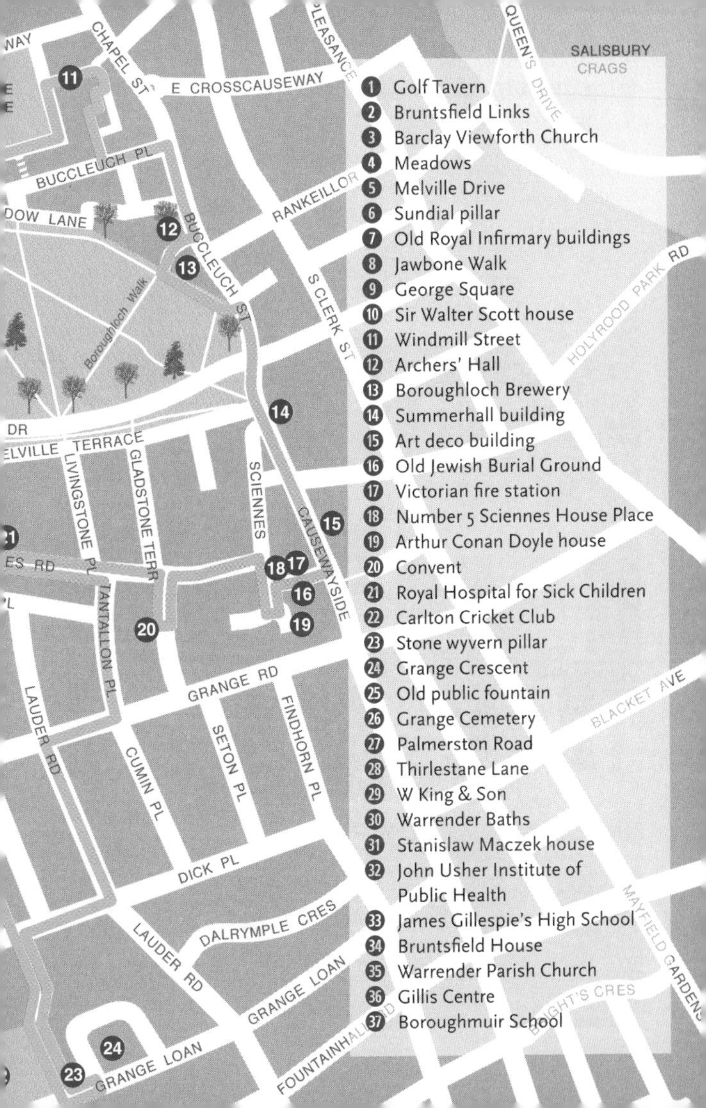

1 Golf Tavern
2 Bruntsfield Links
3 Barclay Viewforth Church
4 Meadows
5 Melville Drive
6 Sundial pillar
7 Old Royal Infirmary buildings
8 Jawbone Walk
9 George Square
10 Sir Walter Scott house
11 Windmill Street
12 Archers' Hall
13 Boroughloch Brewery
14 Summerhall building
15 Art deco building
16 Old Jewish Burial Ground
17 Victorian fire station
18 Number 5 Sciennes House Place
19 Arthur Conan Doyle house
20 Convent
21 Royal Hospital for Sick Children
22 Carlton Cricket Club
23 Stone wyvern pillar
24 Grange Crescent
25 Old public fountain
26 Grange Cemetery
27 Palmerston Road
28 Thirlestane Lane
29 W King & Son
30 Warrender Baths
31 Stanislaw Maczek house
32 John Usher Institute of Public Health
33 James Gillespie's High School
34 Bruntsfield House
35 Warrender Parish Church
36 Gillis Centre
37 Boroughmuir School
SALISBURY CRAGS
CHAPEL ST
E CROSSCAUSEWAY
PLEASANCE
QUEEN'S DRIVE
BUCCLEUCH PL
RANKEILLOR
BUCCLEUCH ST
S CLERK ST
HOLYROOD PARK RD
Boroughloch Walk
MELVILLE TERRACE
LIVINGSTONE PL
GLADSTONE TERR
SCIENNES
CAUSEWAYSIDE
TANTALLON PL
GRANGE RD
FINDHORN PL
SETON PL
CUMIN PL
LAUDER RD
DICK PL
DALRYMPLE CRES
GRANGE LOAN
BLACKET AVE
MAYFIELD GARDENS
FOUNTAINHALL RD

# Bruntsfield Links, The Grange & Marchmont Walk

Start: Wright's Houses
Finish: Leamington Walk
Distance: 4.45 miles

This walk begins on a small road named **Wright's Houses** on the east side of Bruntsfield Links, with the ❶ **Golf Tavern** to your rear. The open space in front of you is ❷ **Bruntsfield Links**, covering around 36 acres and the only remaining part of the Burgh Muir that once dominated this part of south Edinburgh.

The Burgh Muir was originally part of the great Drumselch Forest, and was gifted to the city by King David I in the 12th century. The Burgh Muir once covered many hundreds of acres and for centuries this was where people hunted, where robbers and outcasts sought refuge and where plague victims were quarantined and buried. It was also where on half a dozen occasions the Kings of Scotland mustered their armies. A number of quarries were also located here.

In 1508, a Royal Charter issued by James IV allowed development to take place on the Burgh Muir and it was gradually de-forested. Residents of the Old Town were even allowed to extend the front of their houses if they came to collect the felled timber. As Edinburgh's suburbs spread southwards, the Burgh Muir reduced in size, and it was during the 19th century that much of the residential building you will see along this walk was constructed.

Look back at the Golf Tavern. Said to date from 1456, it recalls the glorious years when Bruntsfield Links was one of the most popular places to play golf in Edinburgh. Golf was recorded as being played here in 1695 and was no doubt taking place prior to then.

Beside the Tavern is the ❸ **Barclay Viewforth Church**, whose 250-foot steeple is a local landmark. It was built as the Barclay Free Church in the 1860s and is named after Miss Mary Barclay, who left over £10,000 for its construction upon her death in 1858.

The association of the game of golf with Bruntsfield Links was probably at its closest during the 18th century. Two of the oldest golf clubs in the world began here – the Royal Burgess Golfing Society (founded 1735) and the Bruntsfield Links Golfing Society (founded 1761). During the 19th century the Links became too busy for the golfers to play in peace, and both clubs moved away to Musselburgh in the 1870s before moving on once again to north-west Edinburgh (where they remain today, see p.205).

For many decades it was the golfers using the Links who led the resistance against the quarry owners and property developers who were encroaching on the land. The town council then took matters in hand to protect this last remnant of the old Burgh Muir. This was achieved principally by the Edinburgh Improvement Act of 1827, which protected both the Links and the Meadows (seen shortly) from redevelopment. Today you can still play golf on the Links – there is a short-hole course that claims to be the oldest in the world and visitors can rent clubs from the Golf Tavern.

Sir Walter Scott, before he became a famous author, served as quartermaster of a volunteer cavalry regiment in Edinburgh. In 1798, he sought permission to train his men on the Links; however, the strong objections of the golfers forced Scott and his men to go elsewhere.

'Bruntsfield' is possibly derived both from the name of the Broune family that owned land here in medieval times, and from the early Scots word 'feld' meaning 'open country'. 'Links' comes from the golf term for sandy ground near the sea shore, later used more generally for a golf course.

Cross over the Links, heading in a north-easterly direction towards Melville Drive – named after Sir John Melville, who served as Lord Provost in the 1850s.

As mentioned earlier, royal armies were mustered on the Burgh Muir. The most famous occasion was in 1513 when James IV commanded 'all able bodied men between the ages of sixteen and sixty to muster on Edinburgh's Burrow Muir'. Many of those men died on the fields of Flodden a short while later, a pivotal moment in Scottish history.

As you reach Melville Drive, the park to the north is the **④ Meadows**, one of Edinburgh's most popular public spaces. However, the area covered by the Meadows was once a loch, known as Burgh Loch or the South Loch. The southern bank of the loch marked the northern edge of the Burgh Muir.

**⑤ Melville Drive** was opened in the late 1850s and became very popular with members of fashionable society, who liked to parade up and down in their carriages while taking in the sights of the Meadows.

Cross over Melville Drive and on the west side of the Meadows look out for a **⑥ sundial pillar**. This is a rare survivor from the Edinburgh International Exhibition of Industry, Science & Art of 1886. This exhibition was held from May to October that year, and was opened by Queen Victoria's grandson, Prince Albert Victor. Around half the area of the Meadows was occupied by the main hall, which featured 20,000 exhibits from around the world. These included a full size reconstruction of a 17th-century Edinburgh street featuring a number of 'lost' buildings such as the Netherbow Port.

Very little else survives of the exhibition, mainly because the law prohibited permanent structures being built on the Meadows. From the sundial, the next key destination is George Square. You can explore the Meadows at your leisure before getting to George Square, but a direct route from here is to continue ahead to join the path on the north side and continue eastwards.

1 old Royal Infirmary buildings

For many centuries the Burgh Loch was a source of drinking water for the residents of Edinburgh. Later, from the 17th century, a number of breweries were allowed to set up in the area, using water from the loch in the beer-making process. Remnants of the local brewing industry will be seen shortly.

The loch covered around 63 acres and was the city's primary source of drinking water until a piped water supply from Comiston arrived in the 17th century. This new supply was needed particularly as local breweries were consuming vast amounts of water from the loch, and it was also becoming polluted by a variety of other local industries.

In the 1650s, the town council decided to start draining the loch, but this was not fully successful. The real change began after 1722, when an 'agricultural improver' and politician named Sir Thomas Hope (c.1681-1771) obtained a long lease of the area and was tasked with completing the drainage and setting out a public garden. He did more than anyone to create the Meadows as you see them today, and a number of local streets are named after him, including Hope Park Crescent. The poet Robert Burns's father worked for a while as a gardener here, helping to transform Hope's plans into reality. The area became officially known as Hope Park, but this name never caught on.

To the north of the Meadows you will see the ❼ **old Royal Infirmary buildings**. The original hospital, founded in 1729, was located near today's Infirmary Street. It moved to Lauriston Place in 1879 and stayed here until the site was sold in 2001. The Royal Infirmary, the oldest hospital in Scotland, moved to Little France (to the south-east of here) and the buildings you can see have been converted into residential flats.

Follow the map eastwards and just by the old Royal Infirmary buildings you will see (on the right) a sign for ❽ **Jawbone Walk**, named after huge whale jawbones that were left here after the 1880 exhibition.

Continue on the north side of the Meadows and very shortly after Jawbone Walk follow the map north into the south-west corner of ❾ **George Square**.

George Square was laid out in 1766 and was the first new Georgian-era square to be built in Edinburgh. However, it was quickly overshadowed by the construction of the first New Town to the north from the late 1760s. It was built by James Brown and named for his brother George (it was originally known as George's Square). ❿ **Sir Walter Scott** lived at **Number 25** as a young man (his father bought the house) and Arthur Conan Doyle lived at No 23 in the late 1870s when he was a student at the University. A resident in the early 1930s was Eric Liddell, the Scottish rugby player and Olympic sprinter immortalised in the 1981 film *Chariots of Fire*.

A number of sections of the original Square have been lost over the years, and the buildings are today owned by the University, whose campus you are now at the heart of. Walk along the south side, passing the main library. This was designed by Sir Basil Spence (1907-76), a prominent Scottish architect best known for Coventry Cathedral.

On the north-east side of the Square is a plaque recalling Benjamin Rush (1746-1813). He was born in America and travelled to Edinburgh in the 1760s to study medicine at the University. He later returned to America and played an important role in the events that led up to the American Revolutionary War.

In 1776, Rush became one of the signatories of the United States Declaration

of Independence. He later recalled: 'The two years I spent in Edinburgh, I consider as the most important in their influence upon my character and conduct of any period in my life... perhaps there is at present no spot upon the earth where religion, science, and literature combine more to produce moral and intellectual pleasures than in the metropolis of Scotland.'

From the east side of the Square, enter ⑪ **Windmill Street**. This is named for a windmill that once stood here, whose purpose was to draw water from the loch for local breweries. Walk down the street, and directly ahead of you is the back of Buccleuch Parish Church, now owned by the University. It was built in the mid-18th century and was originally a Chapel of Ease under the control of St Cuthbert's (near Princes Street, see p.307).

The parish of St Cuthbert's covered a large geographical area, much of it originally rural in nature. As the fields were ripped up and new suburban streets laid out, the population of the parish became simply too large to comfortably attend St Cuthbert's Church and so new buildings such as the one here were required.

You can visit the old church cemetery here during normal office hours, and the old windmill was probably located here. The most famous (or infamous) person buried here is Deacon William Brodie (1741-88). Deacon Brodie was a respectable figure in Edinburgh society, but led a secret life as a thief. He was eventually caught and hanged, his sordid life of deception inspiring Robert Louis Stevenson to write *The Strange Case of Dr Jekyll and Mr Hyde*.

Charles Darwin (1758-78) is also buried here. He was a gifted medical student at the University who died tragically young. He may have possibly gone on to achieve as much as his nephew Charles Darwin, the famous author of *The Origin of the Species*. The dead student's father was a friend of James Hutton, known as the 'Father of Modern Geology' (see p.51), and Hutton helped his friend to organise the carving of the epithet on the gravestone.

There is a modern building on the right in Windmill Street – immediately at the end, turn right and head southwards, passing through the modern University complex. Take a left on Buccleuch Place and then a right onto Buccleuch Street.

Follow the map to find ⓬ **Archers' Hall**. This is the home of the Ancient Royal Company of Archers, an exclusive body whose history goes back to 1676, when a private club was founded to practise archery. Practice butts were set out on the Meadows after the loch was drained. In the early 18th century the club became a Royal Company, and from 1822 it was given an official role as the monarch's ceremonial bodyguard in Scotland.

Among many important events, the Company attended the famous landing of George IV in Leith in 1822 – the beginning of the King's tour of Scotland organised by Sir Walter Scott. Both Scott, and the famous Scottish portrait painter Henry Raeburn (1756-1823), served as members of the Company.

The hall dates from the 1770s and behind it is a bowling-green. It is used mainly as a venue for various dinners and meetings of the Archers. The Company is today made up of around 400 members, many of whom are members of the Scottish nobility.

Continue on past the hall and take the next right down a street named Boroughloch. Continue down and on the left look for the stone signage for the old ⓭ **Boroughloch Brewery**. The original brewery here was built before 1805; it was later acquired by Alexander Melvin in around 1850. It became known as Alexander Melvin & Co, and was said to be the fifth-biggest brewery in Scotland, with products sold internationally. After a fire in the 1890s, the complex was rebuilt – the buildings you see today are from that era. Alexander Melvin was succeeded by his son

13  *Boroughloch Brewery*

and the brewery closed in 1907. This may have been due to a general demise of the brewery industry in the city. During the 19th century around 40 breweries operated in Edinburgh, attracted by the good water supply from a number of wells and the excellent transport links. However, there was a gradual decline in the fortunes of the breweries, largely because of increasing taxes on beer that reduced profits and also increased competition, forcing many businesses to close or consolidate with rivals.

Continue past the old brewery to reach the Meadows again, and then turn left. In the 1870s, the Meadows was used by a number of football teams for matches, including the early Hearts and Hibs teams. Those two rivals played their first Edinburgh derby match very near to here on 25 December 1875.

Continue along the north side of the Meadows and shortly you reach Hope Park Crescent. Head south down to the junction and cross over. On the left after the junction is the ⑭ **Summerhall building** – home for many years to the Royal School of Veterinary Studies. It was generally known as Dick Vet after William Dick, who

14

founded the original veterinary school in 1823. Donald Sinclair graduated from Dick Vet in 1933, later working with another vet named Alf Wright. Wright later wrote a hugely successful series of books based on his life as a vet, using the pen name James Herriot, with the figure of Siegfried Farnon based on Sinclair. The BBC turned Wright's stories into the even more successful television series *All Creatures Great and Small*. The building occupies the site of an earlier brewery which was built in the early 18th century and would have used water from the Burgh Loch. Today it is home to a thriving arts centre and creative hub. It has a great café and if you need something a little stronger, The Royal Dick features ales from Summerhall's very own resident craft brewery – Barney's Beer. The brewery occupies the oldest part of the campus where the original 18th-century Summerhall Brewery once stood.

Continue on, reaching Causewayside – a corruption of 'Causey Side'. This was once part of a raised road that crossed the boggy Burgh Muir. The Scots 'causey' is derived from an old term for a paved or metalled road.

On the left look out for a striking **⑮ art deco building** that was originally called the South Side Garage (today a wine store). It dates from the 1930s and the architect Sir Basil Spence, as a young man, contributed to the design by providing drawings. In the 1920s, Spence attended both George Watson's College in the city, and the Edinburgh College of Art.

Much further along Causewayside, at number 183, is the site of a tenement block destroyed by a bomb dropped from a German Zeppelin in 1916 (not visited on this walk).

Turn right into Sciennes House Place and stop on the left-hand side by a gated cemetery. This is the **⑯ old Jewish Burial Ground** that operated from c.1816-70, and in its early years was the only Jewish cemetery in Scotland. During the 19th century, Jews from Germany and the Low Countries came to Edinburgh as traders, typically dealing in

furs, clothing and jewellery. Many settled in this part of the city, setting up shops to cater for the Jewish community. However, in recent decades the Jewish presence in the area has faded, and this burial ground is a rare reminder of its former influence.

On the other side of the road is a ⑰ **Victorian fire station** built in the 1880s and now converted for commercial use.

Cross over and stop outside ⑱ **number 5 Sciennes House Place**. A plaque on the exterior recalls that this was where two of Scotland's greatest writers – Robert Burns and Sir Walter Scott – met for the only time. Scott was just a teenager when the encounter took place, during the winter of 1786-87. The house was then occupied by Professor Adam Ferguson (1723-1816), a philosopher and historian who was a key member of the Scottish Enlightenment. He hosted many 'literary dinners' here that drew some of the most prominent people in the city. Burns was apparently impressed by Scott, who was the only person present at the dinner who could identify the author of some lines of poetry Burns was considering. 'You'll be a man yet, sir', Burns told the future author. Sciennes Hill House was built in 1741, and incorporated into a larger building in the 1860s.

Follow the map into nearby Sciennes Hill Place. The last building on the left, number 3, is where ⑲ **Arthur Conan Doyle** lived from 1867 to 1874 with his many siblings. During this time, his father Charles, originally an architect, became increasingly unstable and suffered from chronic alcoholism. This was a difficult period in Arthur's life, and within a few years his father ended up in an asylum.

This district of Edinburgh is named Sciennes (pronounced 'sheens'). The reason for this connection goes back to the days when parts of Burgh Muir woods were the haunt of robbers and outcasts. In around 1512, a chapel dedicated to St John the Baptist was established by Sir John Craufurd, a canon at St Giles' Kirk – probably on the site of today's Sciennes Hill House. The chapel shone a light to help guide those travellers tentatively making their way through the often dangerous woods.

Just a few years later a group of aristocratic ladies, most of whom had been widowed after the battle of Flodden in 1513, obtained permission from the Pope to establish a Dominican convent here. Craufurd allowed them to take over the chapel he had just built. The convent was dedicated to the 14th-century St Catherine of Sienna – hence the district's name today, as Sciennes is derived from the French word for Sienna, French being the language used by the Royal Court during most of the 16th century.

This was the last convent to be founded in Scotland before the Reformation. It was badly damaged during an English attack in the 1540s and then destroyed during the Reformation in 1559. Later on, you will see the remains of the first convent to be founded after the Reformation.

Walk down Sciennes Road and on the left-hand side stop at St Catherine's Place. The site of the old ❷⓪ **convent** mentioned earlier is approximately where number 16 stands today (there is a plaque just visible in the front garden). Maps from the 19th century show visible ruins but sadly these were cleared away as the area was developed for housing.

Continue along Sciennes Road to find on the right-hand side the **㉑ Royal Hospital for Sick Children** or 'Sick Kid's Hospital', as it is fondly known. This was originally founded in 1860 in Lauriston Lane and moved to this location in 1895. Dr Joseph Bell (1837-1911), who taught Arthur Conan Doyle when he studied medicine at the University, was the first surgeon here. Doyle acknowledged that Bell was the key inspiration for the famous literary detective Sherlock Holmes.

The hospital stands on the site of an earlier Trades Maidens Hospital – a charitable foundation set up by the Incorporated Trades of Edinburgh. The Incorporated Trades is a body comprising a number of individual trade guilds whose origins date back to the 15th century. Each guild controlled a particular trade or profession in Edinburgh and for many years had rights of representation on the town council.

In 1704, the Incorporated Trades body founded a boarding school for 'the daughters and granddaughters of decayed craftsmen'. It was helped by a donation from a wealthy philanthropist and businesswoman named Mary Erskine. The school came here in the 1850s before selling the site to the hospital in the 1890s. Today the

Incorporated Trades body no longer operates a school but provides charitable assistance to young women in need. It is based on Melville Street and you can visit their museum (see *www.edinburghtrade.org* for more details).

From here retrace your steps and head south down Tantallon Place to reach Grange Road. Cross over and continue down Lauder Road and then turn right onto Dick Place. Walk down Dick Place and on the left-hand side look out for a path (almost opposite a red postbox).

Path south to Grange Loan

Walk down the narrow path southwards. On your right, you pass **㉒ Carlton Cricket Club**. This was founded in 1863 and is one of the best cricket clubs in Scotland. It is named after the Conservative Carlton Club in London, and moved to this site in 1904. In 1936 a cricket match against members of Hearts football club was held here, and though Hearts lost, it was closer than expected.

At the end of the path you reach Grange Loan. You also see by the entrance to the path a **㉓ stone pillar** surmounted by a mythical creature named 'the wyvern'. This is one of the few visible reminders of Grange House, which gave this area its name. Another matching pillar is found just further east of here along Grange Loan – both are believed to date from the early 1700s. As a boy, Sir Walter Scott climbed up to see if the tongue of the creature was of 'veritable paint or veritable fire'.

Walk a few yards up Grange Loan and stop by **㉔ Grange Crescent**, where Grange House once stood. This is the central part of the Grange area and was once part of

the Burgh Muir. In 1150, King David I's son Henry founded the Cistercian monastery of Holm Cultram in Cumbria, then part of Scotland. The monks were given charge of Edinburgh's parish church of St Giles, and a building was erected here for use as a farmhouse by the monks. 'Grange' is derived from an old French word and was often used in the context of a farmhouse detached from the owner's main estate.

The monks of Holm Cultram lost control of their house and estate here – then known as St Giles' Grange – in the 1320s. In the 16th century the manor was given by James IV to John Cant, a prominent Edinburgh burgess. Cant and later generations of his family built Grange House upon the site of the monks' original dwelling. The estate was bought from the Cant family (during a game of golf) in the 1630s by Sir William Dick – one of the wealthiest merchants of his era.

One of his descendants, also named William Dick, and his wife Lady Anne Seton, entertained Bonnie Prince Charlie at Grange House in 1745. In the early 19th century the eminent architect William Henry Playfair was commissioned to extend and renovate the 16th-century Grange House.

In 1731, Isabel Dick married Sir Andrew Lauder and the Dick-Lauder family continued to own the Grange (and Grange House) for many years. This family oversaw the development of the surrounding fields for residential housing from the mid-19th century, and this

explains why so many streets were named after them. The Dick-Lauders stopped living in Grange House in the mid-19th century, although they still owned it. By the early 20th century the house had begun to fall into disrepair and it was eventually demolished in 1936, despite much local opposition.

Though it is hard to imagine it now, maps of the 1830s show that this area still consisted largely of open fields, except for Grange House and – also nearby – Grange Farm House and a stone quarry.

25

You will have noticed the grand houses along these roads. In recent years, Dick Place and Grange Loan have been regularly included in lists of the top ten most expensive residential streets in Scotland. Many of the grandest villas along here date from the 1850s onwards. 'Loan' is an old Scots word for a lane or path, often leading to a meadow where cows were milked.

From here you need to retrace your steps back up the path and past the cricket club. When you reach Dick Place, again cross over and continue on the equally narrow path on the other side (the entrance is just by the red postbox). After a few minutes, when you reach Beaufort Road, look out for the ㉕ **old public fountain** on the wall, dating from 1889. Turn left to reach ㉖ **Grange Cemetery**. Enter by the main gate, or the side gate near the fountain if it is open.

The cemetery was laid out in 1847 and designed by the architect David Bryce. It was built during an era when a number of new cemeteries, such as Dean Cemetery, were being built away from the older, overcrowded burial grounds of central Edinburgh.

Notable people buried here include (on the north wall) Dr Thomas Chalmers (1780–1847), who was heavily involved in the 'Disruption' of 1843 that saw hundreds of ministers leave the Church of Scotland to found the Free Church. Near to him on the

*Stuart family tomb, Grange Cemetery*

26

north side is the last resting place of the geologist, writer and religious leader Hugh Miller (1802-56). Miller suffered severe depression for much of his life, and died after shooting himself at his house in Portobello. The north side also contains the striking Stuart family tomb.

Andrew Usher (1826-1898), of the whisky and beer dynasty, is buried in the south-west corner. His donation funded the construction of the famous Usher Hall off Lothian Road (see p.305). You will see another example of the Usher family's philanthropy later in the walk.

It is worth spending a while walking around the cemetery. In the middle are steps leading up to an elevated terrace from which you can get a great view of the surrounding area.

When you leave the cemetery, look out for ㉗ **Palmerston Road** on the north side. Number 10 on this road was where St Trinnean's girls' school was based between 1922 and 1925. It later moved away from Edinburgh and closed in 1946. The school was immortalised after a chance meeting between the cartoonist Ronald Searle (1920-2011) and two girls from the school during WWII. He modified the school's name for his famous stories about the chaotic St Trinian's, where the girls run amok.

Numerous films have been based on the stories, perhaps the best being *The Belles of St Trinians* (1954), which starred Alastair Sim. By coincidence, Sim was educated near to here – both at Bruntsfield Primary School and James Gillespie's High School.

From here walk up Marchmont Road. Marchmont is the name of another district of Edinburgh, centred on the surrounding streets and also standing on the former Burgh Muir. It contains a number of tenements built originally for the middle classes and remains a popular location for professionals and students in particular, given its proximity to the Meadows, the University and the centre of Edinburgh.

Look out for the charming and narrow **28 Thirlestane Lane** immediately on the left – full of small workshops and garages. There is also a nearby pharmacy named **29 W King & Son** which was founded in 1879 and is one of the oldest businesses in Marchmont.

The history of Marchmont as a residential district really begins in 1695 when the estate here was sold to George Warrender, later Lord Provost of Edinburgh. The Warrender family lived in Bruntsfield House (seen shortly), which remained in their ownership until 1935.

From the late 19th century Sir George Warrender (1825-1901) began the development of new residential housing on the estate. Originally Marchmont consisted only of Marchmont Street, Road and Crescent, but the name was gradually used for an extended area. It was common for landowning families to ensure their legacy by naming new residential developments after family estates and titles. In this case, 'Marchmont' was selected by Warrender because his wife was the daughter of the 5th Earl of Marchmont. Other examples include Thirlestane Road and Lauderdale Street – both named after a relative of George Warrender who was the Earl of Lauderdale and Baron of Thirlestane.

Between 1878 and 1900 Warrender Park Road, Marchmont Road and the streets to the north and east were completed, followed shortly by Spottiswoode Street and Road, Arden Street and Lauderdale Street. After Sir George died in 1901 his estate was held on trust and then sold to the council in 1935. Unlike Grange House, Bruntsfield House escaped plans to demolish it and it became part of James Gillespie's High School in the 1960s.

Turn left into Thirlestane Road and stop by the grand façade of the ❸⓿ **Warrender Baths,** home to Scotland's oldest and most prestigious swimming club. The baths were opened in 1887 by a private club which bought the land from Sir George Warrender. A number of Scotland's top swimmers have trained here including David Wilkie, winner of a gold medal at the 1976 Montreal Olympics. Wilkie later recalled his time here: 'Warrender is where I fell in love with swimming'.

Walk north up Spottiswoode Street to reach the junction with Spottiswoode Road. Turn right and then left to go up Arden Street. This is where Ian Rankin's famous detective John Rebus lives. The author waited until he had written nearly 19 books before revealing a clue that suggested the actual address was a flat at number 17. As a

post-graduate student at Edinburgh University, Rankin also lived on this street (at number 24) while working on his thesis, which related to the works of Muriel Spark. He later wrote that he first came up with the idea of Rebus while sitting in his flat in Arden Street in 1985.

There is another literary connection with this area, as Pat MacGregor, a key character in the *44 Scotland Street* series written by Alexander McCall Smith, lives in Spottiswoode Street for a while in *Love Over Scotland*.

Number 16 Arden Street (on the left-hand side) was once occupied by a Polish General named **㉛ Stanislaw Maczek** (1892-1994). He fought in WWI before becoming a tank commander in WWII, fighting valiantly against the Germans when they invaded Poland. Escaping capture, he ended up in Scotland where he led the newly created 1st Polish Armoured Division. Maczek led the division in France after D-Day and it took part in a number of important battles.

After WWII, Maczek fell foul of the Communist regime in Poland and was stripped of his citizenship. He had to remain in Edinburgh with no pension, working as a waiter at one point. Eventually he received an apology from the Polish government and was awarded the Order of the White Eagle – Poland's highest state decoration. He died here aged 102 and his obituary appeared in the *New York Times* under the title 'General who led the Poles in WWII'. Continue down to the bottom of Arden Street and turn left onto Warrender Park Road. Continue west along this road.

Very shortly on the left look out for a large building dating from 1902 which was originally founded as the **㉜ John Usher Institute of Public Health**. Funded by a gift of over £10,000 from Sir John Usher, this was in its day a very advanced centre

for medical research into public health matters and its work continues within the current medical department of Edinburgh University. The University was the first in Britain to have a department devoted to public health matters, and today has a John Usher Professor of Public Health.

Sir John Usher (1828-1904) was a leading member of the Usher family, whose main interest was in the production of blended whisky and beer – not something generally seen as helping to promote public health!

Continue along Warrender Park Road and on the left you will see ㉝ **James Gillespie's High School**. Its history goes back to 1803, when a wealthy manufacturer of snuff and tobacco named James Gillespie (1726-97) left a legacy for the foundation of a hospital and school. Much of Gillespie's fortune came from the tobacco harvested by slaves in the plantations of Virginia in the United States, which was imported by Gillespie at Leith docks. The current school opened here in the 1960s.

The author Muriel Spark (1918-2006) was born not far from here (at 160 Bruntsfield Place on the west side of the Links) and attended the school from 1922 (when it was situated on another site). Her most famous novel is *The Prime of Miss Jean Brodie* (1961), and Gillespie's was the model for the fictional Marcia Blaine School for girls. The character of Miss Brodie was drawn from one of Spark's teachers named Christina Kay.

34

Within the modern school building complex you will see – at a distance – the historic **㉞ Bruntsfield House**. This was constructed on the site of an earlier castle and estate which may have been built by the Broune family mentioned earlier. These lands were later granted to the Lauder family in the 14th century and they rebuilt the house in the 16th century.

As mentioned earlier, the estate and Bruntsfield House were sold to the Warrender family in 1695 and Sir George Warrender initiated the 19th-century residential development which became known as Marchmont. After he died, Bruntsfield House was held on trust and then sold to the council in 1935.

It is said that Sir George realised that, based on the number of windows in the house, there must be a hidden room. The caretaker was forced to reveal it, and inside was discovered blood on the floor and a skeleton buried by the window. This became known as the Ghost Room and the house is said to be haunted by an apparition named the Green Lady.

Follow the map south down Whitehouse Loan. This is named after another large house that stood near here – probably white-washed, hence the name. On the right is the former **㉟ Warrender Parish Church**. Built in an Italian Renaissance style using red Dumfries ashlar sandstone, this impressive building dates from 1891 and in recent years has been coverted into flats.

Continue down Whitehouse Loan and on the left you will see a substantial building that is today part of the **㊱ Gillis Centre**. This is used as a conference and residential centre by the Archdiocese of St Andrews and Edinburgh. Originally the late-medieval Whitehouse stood just here, and the area was recorded as being named Whitehouse in 1505.

In 1585, there was an outbreak of the plague in Edinburgh and the town council sought to have some of the victims 'enclosed with keepers' in the Whitehouse. However, the then owner, Lady Cliftonhall, strongly objected and her appeal to the town council was successful. Just a few years later she was convicted of witchcraft and burnt alive at the stake. In 1596, the then tenant of the Whitehouse saw five of his children die of the plague.

The Whitehouse and its estate were owned by a number of different families until 1834 when everything was sold to the Catholic church. The estate originally covered an area that lies within the modern-day streets Whitehouse Loan, Whitehouse Terrace, Thirlestane Road and Kilgraston Road.

The main house dating from c.1670 was incorporated into St Margaret's Convent, which was built here in 1835 – the first convent to be built in Scotland since the Reformation. The design of the chapel was by James Gillespie Graham (1776-1855), one of the most prominent Scottish architects of his day and best known for laying out the Moray Estate (see p. 187). The convent was founded by

Bishop James Gillis and for the next 150 years was run as St Margaret's Convent and School under the ministry of the Ursulines.

For many years, a relic (provided by Gillis) of St Margaret of Scotland was also housed here. The Ursulines left in 1986 and after a spell as a training centre for the priesthood, the site became the Gillis Centre.

From here, retrace your steps up Whitehouse Loan and after a few minutes you will reach Bruntsfield Links again. On the north side is a substantial building facing the Links, which opened in 1905 as ❸ **Boroughmuir School** (just past Warrender Park Crescent, which is off Whitehouse Loan). It was occupied by James Gillespie's High School from 1914 and it was this building that Muriel Spark would have known. The school stayed here until it moved to the site you saw earlier. If you look up, you can just about see the Gillespie name on the frontage facing the Links. Today the building is owned by the University.

The walk ends here and you can walk across the Links to reach the starting point. ●

## VISIT...

**Summerhall**
1 Summerhal, EH9 1PL
*www.summerhall.co.uk*
Arts centre, bar & café

## PLAY...

**Bruntsfield Links**
Melville Drive, EH9 1DY
Play golf on the world's oldest short-hole golf course for free. Open daily – you can hire clubs & balls from the Golf Tavern nearby

## EAT/DRINK...

**Golf Tavern**
30-31 Wright's Houses, EH10 4HR
*hwww.golftavern.co.uk*

**The Royal Dick (bar)**
1 Summerhall, EH9 1PL
*www.summerhall.co.uk*

**Birchwood (café)**
146 Marchmont Road, EH9 1AQ
*www.thebirchwood.co.uk*

Commercial Quay, see p.391

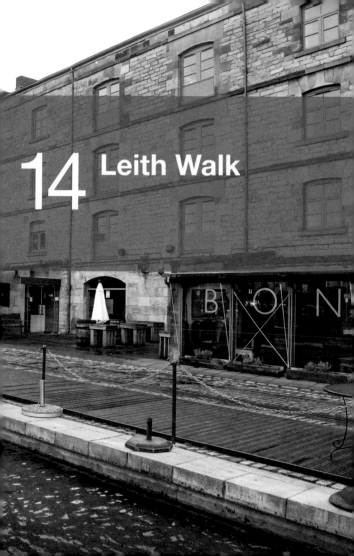

# 14 Leith Walk

MELROSE DRIVE

OCEAN DRI

LINDSAY RD

PORTLA

PRINCE REGENT ST

COMMERCIAL QU

COMMERCIAL ST

JUNCTIO

DUDLEY AVE

NORTH FORT ST

MADEIRA ST

SUMMER

SUMMERSIDE S

MADEIRA PL

FERRY RD

Water of Leith

LE

MILL LAN

PITT ST

SOUTH FORT ST

EWHAVEN RD

GREAT JU

BANGOR

BURLINGTON ST

RD

TENNANT ST

JANE

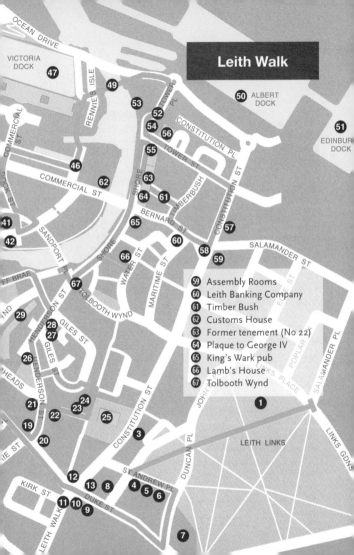

# Leith Walk

59 Assembly Rooms
60 Leith Banking Company
61 Timber Bush
62 Customs House
63 Former tenement (No 22)
64 Plaque to George IV
65 King's Wark pub
66 Lamb's House
67 Tolbooth Wynd

# Leith Walk

Start: Leith Links
Finish: Tolbooth Wynd
Distance: 4.36 miles

This walk starts beside ❶ **Leith Links** in Links Gardens. The Links, covering just over 45 acres, has long been a popular open space used by locals. It is also famous for being where the first rules of golf were drawn up in 1744 by the Honourable Company of Edinburgh Golfers. The 13 rules they wrote down became the basis for the modern game. The company moved away in the 1830s to Musselburgh as the Links were becoming too crowded for the golfers.

Golf has even earlier origins in Leith – in 1457 King James II tried to ban it from the Links as it was interfering with the archery practice that took place here (see p.344). Another popular pastime in 18th-century Leith was cockfighting – the cockpit was situated on the Links.

Links Gardens is where the first American Consul to Scotland was based. President John Adams appointed Harry Grant from South Carolina as Consul in 1798 – not long after America had won its independence from British rule.

The name 'Leith' is derived from 'Inverleith' – meaning the 'mouth of the Leith'. The use of 'Leith' as a name for a river was most likely taken from an old Gaelic term for 'water', and the Water of Leith originates as a river in the Pentland Hills to the south. It runs for 22 miles and passes through Edinburgh before emptying into the Firth of Forth by Leith.

For many centuries the river split Leith into two distinct villages – North Leith and South Leith. These villages, facing each other across the water, developed quite independently for many centuries. They were under the control of different landowners, and also had their own parish churches.

Follow the map across the Links. Between 1548 and 1560, thousands of French troops were based in Leith, originally to help the Scots in an alliance against the English. The French army constructed fortifications around the town and towards the end of their stay here were protecting Mary of Guise (1515-60), then acting as regent for her young daughter Mary, Queen of Scots. In 1560, an English army lay siege to Leith and the bitter fighting only ended when Mary of Guise – based in Edinburgh Castle – died of natural

causes. A treaty was signed and the French army sailed away. It has been suggested that the English artillery batteries were located on the ❷ mounds still visible on the south side of the Links.

Soon you will enter Duncan Place, with Wellington Place opposite. The western edge of the Links where you are now follows the line of the fortified wall built by the French. Leith itself, until the late 18th century, was contained on the other side of this defensive wall and no building was allowed outside the fortifications.

As the Links lay outside Leith, the land was used for mass burials during a terrible outbreak of the plague in 1645. Trenches full of bodies were uncovered when the foundations of Wellington Place were being dug many years later. Leith was devastated by the plague – around 2,400 people died out of an estimated population in South Leith of 4,000.

Look over to Wellington Place. It was named after the Duke of Wellington in around 1813, so actually predated his most famous battle at Waterloo in 1815. A flat on the second floor of number 2 was once the home of the author ❸ Irvine Welsh, best known for *Trainspotting* (1993). The central characters of the book, which in 1996 was made into an influential film directed by Danny Boyle and starring Ewan McGregor, were young

Leithers struggling with drug addiction. Welsh was born in 1957 in Canonmills, and spent part of his childhood living in Leith, where his father worked on the docks. Welsh later played in a punk band, obtained an MBA from Heriot-Watt University and worked as a training officer for the local council. He has most recently come to public attention with the 2017 release of the film *Trainspotting 2*, in which he has a cameo role.

Continue along Duncan Place and then turn left into St Andrew Place.

On the corner is ❹ **Leith Victoria Boxing Club** – the oldest active boxing club in Scotland, founded in 1919, just after the end of WWI. This was a time of high unemployment and the club was formed by workers from the Ramage and Ferguson shipyard in order to help young jobless men to find discipline and maintain their fitness. The club has produced two world champions and many other members have become national champions and boxed at the Olympic and Commonwealth Games. It also has a small museum which has a collection of artefacts and trophies (see p.401).

Stop outside the classical columns of the building right beside the boxing club. This elegant building is currently used by the Hindu community, but was founded as ❺ **St Andrew's Church** in 1827. The original congregation split from the Church of Scotland in the 1730s, and it was later used by various Christian organisations until the 1980s. You will see how other religious faiths have breathed life into Leith's old churches.

Continue on, passing on your right an austere-looking ❻ **primary school** dating from the 1890s. This was the site of Leith Academy – one of Scotland's oldest schools, dating from 1560, though it may be even older. It was originally under the control of South Leith Parish Church and may have met in Trinity House (both seen later). It moved to the site where the primary school is now in 1806 and then moved around the corner to Duke Street in the early 1930s.

Turn right up Duncan Place to reach Duke Street. The impressive building on your left is the ❼ **former Leith Academy building** that was occupied by the school from the 1930s to the early 1990s. It has since moved to new purpose built premises just to the south of here. JK Rowling spent some time teaching French at the Academy before she became a full-time writer.

The former school building stands on the site of the Links golf clubhouse where the first rules of golf, mentioned earlier, may have been drawn up. The clubhouse continued to be used until the 1830s, when the building was sold to help pay off the club's debts. After that the site was used by the John Watt Hospital, which opened in 1862 to help old people and was named after the local merchant who funded it. Today the building is being converted into flats.

As you look south from Duke Street, Easter Road is just to your left. This has long been the main road to Leith on the east side of Edinburgh – its name derives from its location rather than the Christian festival. Further down Easter Road is the home of Leith's most famous football team – Hibernian. Better known as Hibs, the club originated in 1875 and was founded by Irish immigrants based in the Cowgate. The club moved to Leith in the 1890s.

Turn right onto Duke Street and head west. On your right you pass Academy Street, where the ❽ **Leith Dockers Club** is situated (at number 17). It opened in 1956 with assistance from the Forth Ports Authority, and its original purpose was to provide a social club for dockers and their families and friends. Today there are very few dockers left in Leith, but the club continues to flourish. It is portrayed in the film *Sunshine on Leith* (2014), featuring the songs of the Proclaimers. Craig and Charlie Reid of the band were born in Leith in 1962.

Stop at the junction ahead. On your left is the former site of ❾ **Leith Central Station**, which operated between 1903 and 1952 as a terminus of a branch line from Edinburgh Waverley. Between 1952 and 1972 it was closed to passengers but still used as a train depot. After 1972 it was derelict for many years, and became a haunt of drug users. The title of Welsh's book *Trainspotting* came from a scene he set here. The main characters visit the deserted station and a drunken old man, who turns out to be Begbie's father, asks 'What yis up tae lads? Trainspotting, eh?' The novel was set in the 1980s when the deserted station site had yet to be redeveloped. Today it is covered by a supermarket and leisure complex, though you can still see the original clock tower and some of the old offices.

The ❿ **Central Bar** (just around the corner) is also a remnant from the old station. It was built in 1899 and is worth a visit just to see the stunning interior, notable for the Staffordshire tiles depicting various sporting scenes. In *Trainspotting* this is one of Begbie's haunts and it also features in the sequel.

Continue on and stop at the junction. To your left is ⑪ **Leith Walk** – a bustling, vibrant street that connects Leith to the heart of Edinburgh.

Locals have always regarded the port town of Leith as being very different to Edinburgh. Historically Leith was governed by the town council of Edinburgh; however, in 1833 Leith became a separate municipal burgh with its own provost and council. This lasted until 1920 when it became part of Edinburgh again, even though in a plebiscite the vast majority of local people voted against the merger.

For many centuries the road from this part of Leith to Edinburgh was a bare path. In the 1650s, it was built up as a defensive fortification by the Scottish army under David Leslie against the threat of Oliver Cromwell's troops, and later this fortification became the basis of a pedestrian walkway – hence Leith 'Walk'.

At this time the main roads into Leith were Easter Road and a Western Road (most likely the route of today's Bonnington Road). By 1800, Leith Walk had replaced them as the main thoroughfare between the port and Edinburgh.

At the foot of Leith Walk look for a statue of ⑫ **Queen Victoria**, which was unveiled to the public with great ceremony in 1907. The side panels commemorate the monarch's fleeting visit to Leith in 1842.

Look over to a pub named the ⑬ **Foot of the Walk**, facing the junction. The building was originally the Palace Cinema, which opened in 1913 and showed films right up to 1966 before becoming a bingo club. If you go inside, you can still get a sense of the old cinema – the screen would have been on the far wall (with the bar to your right).

To the north of here runs Constitution Street, which dates from around 1800. When it was built, it cut right through the medieval heart of Leith, but greatly simplified transport between Edinburgh and the docks to the north.

Head westwards at the junction, down Great Junction Street. You are continuing to follow the route of the fortified wall that surrounded the town in the 16th century.

Great Junction Street was laid out in 1818 and over later decades became one of the main shopping streets in Leith. In the 19th century it was also notable for its many tenement buildings, factories, timber yards and warehouses.

Continue along and stop at Junction Place on the left. On the corner is a ⓮ **former school** dating from 1839 that was run under Dr Andrew Bell's Madras System. Bell was born in 1753 and after some time working at a chapel in Leith he entered the army as a chaplain. He went to India and ran a school in Madras employing the then novel technique of using older children to teach the younger ones. He brought this system back with him to Leith, where he lived until 1787.

By the time he died in 1832, around 12,000 schools in Britain are believed to have adopted the Madras System. Bell was buried in Westminster Abbey.

Continue down Junction Place. On the left you will see a 19th-century fire station – known as ⑮ **Fire Engine House**. Horse-drawn fire engines were once housed here and you can still see an old sign indicating where the master's office could be found.

Slightly further along is the ⑯ **Leith Victoria Swimming Centre**, named after Queen Victoria, which opened in 1899. The memorial outside records it was sponsored by the Baths sub-committee of the town council. Many towns in late-Victorian and Edwardian Britain had organisations to promote the use of baths to aid cleanliness and better health, mainly in impoverished areas where residents lived in slums with no running water. Known as 'Vickies', these baths originally offered a public bath, as is still the case today, but also individual enamel baths and a laundry. The individual baths were still being used in the 1970s.

Retrace your steps slightly to Great Junction Street and look for a ⑰ **former church** (beside the Bell school) which dates from 1825. It was the first building constructed on this street, and is today used by the local Muslim community – another indication of how Leith has changed demographically over the last few decades.

Cross over the street to see the former ⑱ **Crabbie's Warehouse**, the earliest part of which dates from the 1820s. A large

warehouse and distillery was based here, and for many decades from the mid-19th century John Crabbie & Co made Crabbie's Green Ginger Wine at the site. This famous Scottish beverage was first produced by John Crabbie in 1801, and is still made today (but no longer in Leith). The brand recently sponsored the Grand National race. The Crabbie's building has now been converted into flats.

Crabbie's is a reminder that it was not just the docks and shipbuilding that were once crucial to Leith's economy. For many centuries wine was imported into the docks by merchants and stored in Leith in large warehouses before being moved into Edinburgh and beyond. By the late 19th century whisky had replaced wine as the main beverage being stored in Leith. A major reason for this was the collapse of the grape harvest in Europe in the 1880s. In the mid-20th century there were still around 85 bonded warehouses here, in which approximately 90% of all Scotch whisky was matured. Sadly, the last bonded warehouse closed in the 1990s.

The scale of commerce that once existed in Leith can be difficult to grasp in the modern post-industrial era. For example, a publication of the 1880s describes how the town contained 7 shipbuilding yards, 9 saw mills, 5 flour and meal mills (one of which was the largest in Scotland), 2 sugar refineries, 17 engineering works, 3 breweries, 6 distilleries, 8 chemical works and a rope works that alone employed 1,000 people. And this was just a snap-shot – other industries mentioned as having been based in Leith include sail-making, tanning, glassmaking, coopering and lime-juice making.

Cross over and follow the map up Henderson Street. Stop on the corner to look at ⑲ **Wilkies Bar** – an atmospheric old Leith pub with a distinctive clock outside. It is worth a visit and gives you a sense of what life was like when the docks still dominated the town. In 2013, Mary Martin, aged 81, celebrated 50 years of service here – the longest-serving barmaid in Edinburgh. Sadly, in recent years many of these old Leith pubs have closed, and been converted into flats or restaurants.

On the opposite corner (above the Greggs) look out for the **❷⓿ memorial stone** recording that this building was the first one constructed as part of the Leith Improvement Scheme in 1885. The scheme, designed to help to eradicate the slums in this part of Leith, saw dozens of older houses and closes demolished.

The memorial stone also depicts the coat of arms of Leith, with the figure of the Virgin Mary carrying the baby Jesus on a boat, with the date 1563 below it. It was Mary, Queen of Scots, who decided to alter Leith's coat of arms by implanting this date at the bottom of the waves.

The exact meaning of the coat of arms has generated some debate. Some have speculated that the figures are actually meant to be Mary Magdalene fleeing with her child to France after its father, Jesus, was crucified. This is part of a wider theory (made popular by Dan Brown's 2003 novel *The Da Vinci Code*) that the cult of Mary Magdalene was central to the Knights Templar, and the Holy Grail is really the bloodline of Jesus.

It has also been suggested that the Knights Templar came to Leith after their Order was suppressed by the Pope in the early 14th century, and had connections with the Logan family of Leith, the St Clair family of nearby Roslin (whose Rosslyn chapel features in *The Da Vinci Code*), and the monks of St Anthony's (the site of which is seen later). Some have also traced connections between the Knights Templar and the Masonic movement.

After 1920, when Leith was officially absorbed into Edinburgh, it was no longer allowed officially to use its traditional coat of arms. This was not popular with many Leithers. In 2012, some progress was made when a ceremony was held at Leith library during which the heraldic authority for Scotland officially gave the Leith Neighbourhood Partnership the right to use the coat of arms.

Continue down Henderson Street. It is named after Dr John Henderson (1819-1901), who served as Provost of Leith for several years and who helped to sponsor the Leith Improvement Scheme. By the 1890s, the new residences on this street were occupied by people whose professions reflected the times: seamen and master mariners,

artisans, labourers and school teachers. The street contains a number of listed buildings, many designed by James Simpson (1832-94), Town Architect of Leith, and his successor George Craig. In 2007, Irvine Welsh's television drama *Wedding Belles* was partly filmed here.

Walk up Henderson Street to see another memorial above **㉑ Anderson's Bar** that dates from 1885 and commemorates the first artisan dwellings on the street. It refers to James Simpson as the architect.

Retrace your steps slightly and follow the map down St

Anthony Place. Almost immediately on your right, and before you reach the car park, look out for the **22 Freemasons' Lodge Trafalgar Hall**. The Masonic building was opened in 1888 and is named for the Leith seamen who fought at the famous battle. The lodge was founded in the early 19th century and was based in several locations before arriving here.

This curious building was designed by George Craig (1852-1928) – a Freemason – and is still in use. Look out for the Masonic symbols that can be seen on the exterior. The basement contains some remnants of St Anthony's Priory, which once stood here and after which the street is named.

Much of the history of the priory remains obscure, but it is likely to have been founded in the early 1400s by James I on land granted by Sir Robert Logan of Restalrig for canons of the Augustinian order of St Anthony of Vienne. It was suppressed during the Scottish Reformation of the late 16th century. Continue ahead through the supermarket car park. The supermarket lies on top of St Anthony's Graveyard.

On the left-hand side look out for a **23 Latin inscription** on a wall that forms part of the rear of Trinity House. This inscription dates from 1555 – the year when, allegedly, a charitable house was founded here. Walk past then turn left up the Kirkgate. You will now see the splendid façade of Trinity House – the building dates from c.1816 and sits on the site of a 16th-century almshouse. Just to the south of here is the site of St Anthony's Priory, and to the east is South Leith Parish Church.

24

Though it is hard to imagine it now, the Kirkgate – the street running north to south here – was once a vibrant place full of shops and entertainments, and formed the heart of South Leith. Sadly, many of the old buildings were demolished in the 1960s. Older residents of Leith can remember the days when sailors from all around the world would come here after landing at the docks to buy provisions, enjoy a drink or take in a show at the Gaiety Theatre.

Stand outside the entrance of **24** **Trinity House**. Its origins can be traced back to 1380 when it was established by local ship-owners and shipmasters to provide charitable relief to destitute sailors and their families. The Fraternity of Masters and Mariners of Leith was a maritime trade guild that used its right to tax ships entering Leith (known as the 'Prime Gilt') to help fund its charitable aims. Later on boys were educated here, following a curriculum designed to prepare them for a life at sea. Leith Academy may also have had its origins here though it is not entirely clear. The Masters and Mariners also invested in land near Newhaven, the site today forming the Edinburgh suburb known as Trinity. Trinity House now accommodates a maritime museum (see p.401).

Opposite Trinity House is **㉕ South Leith Parish Church**. In the 15th century this area was part of the parish of Restalrig, which had a parish church of its own. However, locals, particularly artisans who were members of trade incorporations, wanted their own place of worship and so founded a church here in the 1480s dedicated to St Mary. It was an early indication of Leithers' independence of spirit.

By the 17th century the church had become the parish church for South Leith (after Restalrig's church had been demolished). The church is particularly notable for its hammer-beam ceiling, although it is not usually open to visitors. If you do want to visit, it is best to check with the church office, as tours can be arranged (see p.401). The medieval church was battered in later centuries, particularly by English artillery fire during the Siege of Leith in 1560. The front porch contains the arms of Mary of Guise (see p.367) and Mary, Queen of Scots, taken from the old church. The current structure dates largely from the 1840s.

If you have time, walk around the graveyard. There are a number of headstones that bear the symbols of the trades carried out by those buried here. The playwright John Home (1722-1808) is also buried here. His play *Douglas* was put on at the Canongate Playhouse in 1756, despite facing severe opposition from the church authorities (see p.13). Home was supported in the production of the play by his friend, the great philosopher David Hume.

25 South Leith Parish Church

Follow the map north from Trinity House and take the next left – a small path that leads to Giles Street. Bear left at the end and along Spier's Place to reach Henderson Street again. Continue along, passing a small park on the left, as well as a **26** **blue police telephone box**. These were designed in the 1930s by EJ MacRae and there were once nearly 90 of them throughout Edinburgh. Look out also for the remaining Victorian street lamps, which bear Leith's coat of arms.

Bear right and shortly you will see a large building known as **27** **The Vaults**, a significant part of which dates back to the 1680s. For centuries ships carried wine and goods between Bordeaux and Leith, one of the biggest customers being the Royal Court in Edinburgh. The trade later expanded to Spain and Portugal and vast quantities of wine were stored in warehouses such as this. As mentioned earlier, in the late 19th century, whisky became the main focus of trade and so it is fitting that this is now the headquarters of the Scotch Malt Whisky Society.

On the front wall (by the bus stop), look out for the **28** **Porter's Stone**. This is a modern replica of the original, which dated from 1678 and was located nearby in Tolbooth Wynd. It depicts the Porters of Leith at work, loading and transporting wine and other goods from the port to warehouses. The Porters were one of Leith's powerful trade incorporations or guilds, which controlled various professions and trades. A trade corporation would often have its own hall and a stone inscribed with symbols of its profession.

29

Now walk down Parliament Street, passing a famous block of flats on your left. Officially this is Cables Wynd House but it is universally known as the ㉙ **Banana Flats** because of its shape. The first residents moved into the flats in 1966, and they feature in *Trainspotting* and its 2017 sequel, as the home of 'Sick Boy'.

Continue until you see the Water of Leith ahead – the traditional dividing line between the villages of South and North Leith. You also see the old belfry of St Ninian's – the parish church of North Leith until the early 19th century (it is visited later). The medieval bridge over the Water of Leith began approximately where you are standing – it was demolished in the late 18th century.

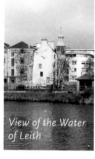

*View of the Water of Leith*

Turn left and walk up Sheriff Brae, named after Sir James Logan of Craighouse. He built a house here in around 1500 and served as Sheriff of Edinburgh. The Logan family were large landowners in South Leith and influenced its development for many years.

Ahead is the former ㉚ **St Thomas' Church**, which dates from the 1840s and was built with money donated by Sir John Gladstone, father of four-times Prime Minister William Gladstone. The manse (or minister's house) was destroyed in April 1916 by a bomb dropped from a German Zeppelin. The congregation moved to another location in the 1970s and today this is a Sikh Temple.

30

Continue down Mill Lane, likely to be named after a medieval mill that stood by the Water of Leith. On your left, look out for **31 Taylor Gardens**. These stand on the site of South Leith Poor House, which opened in 1850 and was demolished in around 1910. The Poor House would have dominated what is now the central area of the gardens.

Bear right at the end and just before you cross the bridge over the Water of Leith, look out on the right-hand side for the **32 old State Cinema**. This substantial art deco building was opened in 1938 and could accommodate 1,650 people. It stopped showing films in 1972 before becoming a bingo hall and now stands empty.

Follow the map over the bridge, looking out for the **33 huge mural** on the wall facing you. This dates back to 1986, when Leith was as economically and socially depressed as at any point in its recent history. The artists Tim Chalk, Paul Grime and David Wilkinson worked with the local community on the mural as one of a number of works that were part of a regeneration programme. The mural reflected the input from Leithers about what the area meant to them.

Turn left up Ferry Road and stop outside ❸❹ **Leith Library**. This impressive art deco building was opened in 1929 and was one of a number of civic buildings provided as a 'gift' from the people of Edinburgh following the merger of Leith into Edinburgh in 1920. It was badly damaged by German bombs during WWII and only opened up as a library again in the mid-1950s. A theatre stands to the rear.

Behind the library once stood North Leith Poor House, which was founded in 1860. In the 1890s, it was put under common management with the South Leith Poor House and for a while became a hospital. Both of Leith's poor houses closed in the early 20th century.

Having crossed the river, you are now standing in North Leith, originally a fishing village centred not far from St Ninian's (seen earlier). Whereas the Logan family were large landowners in South Leith, in North Leith during the medieval period the main landowner was Holyrood Abbey, after a gift of land by King David I. He also established a harbour where the Water of Leith met the Forth, and so began a process that saw a fishing village transformed over time into the most important port in Scotland.

From the library, continue up Ferry Road and on the right turn into Madeira Street, named after the wine imported by a merchant

who lived here in the late 18th century. This is one of the most pleasant residential streets in Leith, with the graceful lines of North Leith Parish Church visible up ahead. Walk up to the church.

❸❺ **North Leith Parish Church** was opened in 1816 after the medieval parish church of St Ninian's proved too small for the growing population. It was also part of Leith's own 'New Town' development in the early 19th century. The church was closed for a few years following WWII after suffering damage from an enemy landmine.

34 Leith Library

36

Continue up Madeira Street and at the end bear left along Portland Street. On your right on the north side is the **36** **remaining wall of Leith Fort**.

The fort was built after Leith was threatened by John Paul Jones (1747-92), the leader of the embryonic American navy that ventured up the Firth of Forth in 1779 during the American War of Independence. Only bad weather prevented Jones from capturing Leith. He was actually a Scotsman who allied himself with the revolutionary cause and earned himself the reputation as the founder of the American navy.

Leith Fort was designed by James Craig (1739-95) – best known for winning a competition in 1766 for a plan for the original New Town in Edinburgh (see p.154). Despite this early promise, his career was never very successful and little of his work survives today. The army left the fort in 1957 after 164 years of being based in Leith and it was largely demolished in the following years.

Retrace your steps to Madeira Street, and opposite the church walk down Prince Regent Street – named after George IV (1762-1830), who ruled as Regent from 1811 to 1820 because of his father's mental incapacity. His visit to Scotland in 1822, after landing in Leith, was

37

a historic moment for the country and many streets and squares were named after him.

Soon you reach North Junction Street. Bear right. After a short while, on the right-hand side look out for a green gated space – which was once the site of **37** **North Leith Poor House**. The David Kilpatrick School opened in 1919 on the site of the poor house and closed in the 1970s, the building later being demolished. An old foundation stone is all that remains of the school that once stood here.

Next door you will see a former church – the Norwegian church – that today is home to the ❸❽ **Leith School of Art**. This was originally a Norwegian Lutheran church founded in 1868 by the Norwegian Seamen's Mission. The origins go back to the early 1860s, when a divinity student named Johan Cordt Harmens arrived in Edinburgh from Bergen and decided that the Scandinavian sailors in Leith needed their own place of worship. It became more widely used by the Scandanavian community of Leith and Edinburgh.

In the latter half of the 20th century the shipping and whaling industries in Leith went into decline, and the Scandinavian presence faded. The Norwegian Seamen's Mission sold the church building in the 1980s and the School of Art has been here since 1989.

The garden contains a stone known as the ❸❾ **Vim Stone**, named after a ship that ran aground in 1937 and was saved from flooding by a fragment of stone that broke off and acted as a plug. The grateful sailors brought the piece of stone to the church and a service of thanksgiving was held. Look out for the nautically inspired sea-fish scales on the church spire.

Carry on and then turn left down Coburg Street. In recent years this street has been extensively redeveloped, a far cry from a period between the 1980s and early 2000s when this was a notorious red-light area. The police and local authorities effectively ignored the problem, but pressure from developers and residents helped to assign Leith's red-light district to the history books.

Coburg Street

387

This pleasant cobbled street runs parallel to the Water of Leith and has a few tantalising reminders of North Leith's past. The first reminder, on the right, is a **40** **small cemetery** used by the parishioners of the village. A number of the headstones record the trades of those interred, including master shipmen and others connected to the sea trade. No doubt many spent their lives travelling the world and retired to North Leith.

Lady Anne MacKintosh (1723-87), known as Scotland's 'Beautiful Rebel', is buried here. She is notable for being the only woman to raise a Clan for Bonnie Prince Charlie during the Jacobite uprising of 1745. After carrying out a number of heroic deeds, she was arrested after the defeat at Culloden but later released.

Continue along until you reach Dock Street on the left. Stop to look back at **41** **Coburg House**. Its frontage contains a stone from the meeting house of the Incorporation of Carpenters that stood near here in the 18th century. The incorporation, or guild, was a crucial one in Leith during this time, supplying skilled carpenters to the shipyards by the water.

Walk past Coburg House and take a right down Quayside Street towards the Water of Leith. Just ahead is **42** **St Ninian's Manse** (seen from the other side of the river earlier on). This was originally a chapel built by the Abbot of Holyrood in 1493. It became the main parish church for North Leith from 1609 and was rebuilt in the late 17th century. The church stood just beside the original bridge that connected North and South Leith.

As Leith expanded over the years, St Ninian's became too small to serve the growing congregation. This resulted in the construction of the parish church you saw earlier on Madeira Street. Today the former manse and distinctive Dutch-style belfry of the church have been converted into commercial office space.

The medieval bridge that stood near here was built by the Abbot of Holyrood in 1486. It was demolished in around 1780 because it had begun to impede the growing levels of river traffic.

From the 18th century, the area just to the north of here became the centre of the shipbuilding industry in Leith before larger sites opened on reclaimed land to the north. A map of 1804 shows a dry dock was situated almost exactly where you are now, and just a couple of hundred yards away to the north by the Water of Leith was another dry dock and shipbuilding yard.

Retrace your steps and walk up Dock Street. Continue along until you reach the junction with Commercial Street.

42

On the left-hand side of the junction by the church building is an **43** **old gatehouse** – the sole reminder of Oliver Cromwell's pentagonal-shaped Citadel fortress that once dominated this part of Leith. Cromwell's forces under General Monck occupied Leith in the 1650s. This must have been a traumatic time for residents as the churches were closed and South Leith Parish Church was even used as a horse stable. Later, during the Jacobite Rebellion of 1715, a group of Highlanders seized the Citadel for a day before taking the booty they had plundered in the town and fleeing across the sands at low tide.

The Citadel was completed in 1656 but after the Restoration it was used for commercial purposes such as glass-making before being gradually demolished. All you can see today is the Eastern Port – a small fraction of the original complex.

Just past the Citadel is a fine example of 19th-century church architecture – the **44** **Mariners' Free Church & Seamen's Institute**.

Walk past the church onto Commercial Street and bear left. Shortly on the left, you will find a youth centre that is based within the sole remaining building of **45** **Leith Citadel Railway Station**. Part of the Edinburgh, Leith and Newhaven Railway, it was opened in 1846 and finally closed in 1947.

Cross over Commercial Street and retrace your steps a little, turning left where indicated to face the Scottish Government Building to the north. Commercial Street itself was built to allow better access to the warehouses that sprung up beside the vast new docks being built here in the early 1800s.

You are now entering the main part of Leith docks. The area now occupied by the Scottish Government Building and car parks was once dominated by two large wet docks that were built in the very early years of the 19th century, each able to accommodate 40 ships of 200 tons each. They were designed by John Rennie (more on him later). After the docks suffered a general decline in the late 20th century, these original docks were filled in as part of the area's redevelopment.

Head eastwards along Commercial Quay, with early 19th-century bonded warehouses and other dock buildings to your right. A number of upmarket eateries and bars are now based here, part of a general revival in Leith's fortunes in recent years.

At the end you pass through some old dock gates, then turn left up **46 Dock Place**. Continue north and through some more gates (there is a sign for Rennie's Lock), and then across a small footbridge over the water.

*19th-century bonded warehouses at Commercial Quay*

46

Footbridge

47

Stop when you see a large expanse of water to your left. This is **47 Victoria Dock** (constructed 1851), which lies to the rear of the Scottish Government Building.

Further to the north-west you can see the outline of **48 Ocean Terminal**, a modern shopping development situated on the site of one of the major shipyards – Victoria Shipyard – that were once so important to Leith.

The closure of Henry Robb shipbuilders (known as Robbs) in the early 1980s ended more than 660 years of shipbuilding in Leith. Henry Robb was based here between 1918 and 1984 and employed hundreds of local people. Ramage and Ferguson was another famous Leith shipbuilding firm, established in 1877. It went out of business during the Great Depression, having built nearly 300 ships. It was later acquired by Henry Robb.

One of the most famous ships produced in Leith was the *Sirius*, built by Menzies & Sons in 1837. It was one of the first transatlantic steam passenger ships to operate and competed with Isambard Brunel's more famous *Great Western*.

The Royal Yacht *Britannia*, now berthed in the Ocean Terminal, was home to the Queen and the royal family for over 40 years. The Royal Yacht travelled over one million miles around the world. To visit, see p.392 for more information.

Turn away from Victoria Dock and follow the map through Rennie's Isle and then across the **49 Victoria Swing Bridge**, visible to the north. This was opened in 1874 and was used for traffic until 1964. In the late

18th century it was becoming evident to the dock owners that the facilities at Leith were becoming antiquated. Ships were getting bigger and Glasgow was overtaking Leith as the most important port in Scotland. As a result, in the early 1800s the Scottish civil engineer John Rennie (1761-1821) was commissioned to build new docks in Leith, and this began a fairly continual period of expansion that lasted for the next hundred years or so. Vast amounts of land were reclaimed from the sea, extending Leith far beyond its natural boundaries.

Rennie's original docks were situated where the Scottish Government Building is now. He was also responsible for a large number of docks and bridges throughout Britain, including an earlier version of London Bridge.

On the other side of the bridge, walk over to a roundabout and look north to get a sense of how big Leith docks became – incredible, if you realise that they began alongside the river's edge near St Ninian's Manse, seen earlier. Ahead of you are three docks (from east to west) that were built as Imperial Dock (1903), **50 Albert Dock** (1869) and **51 Edinburgh Dock** (1881). It is not possible to enter the Port of Leith because despite a long decline from its heyday, it is still fully operational and offers the largest enclosed deepwater port in Scotland. It is also the stopping point for around 40 cruise ships each year.

Walk down Tower Place to join the shore. As you pass through the gates, look out for the statue of **52 John Hunter** (1737-1821), a distinguished naval officer who was born in Leith and went on to serve as the second Governor of New South Wales in Australia. The famous wine-producing area of Hunter Valley is named after him.

You are standing approximately where on 26 July 1698 five ships carrying around 1,200 people left Leith cheered on by large crowds. This was the start of the Darien Expedition – an attempt to establish a Scottish trading post on the Darien peninsula in what today is part of Panama. The peninsula was an isolated, mosquito-infested swamp, and hostility from Spain and England helped to ensure that the venture failed miserably.

So many Scots had invested in the plan that its failure threatened to bankrupt the nation. Having done its best to scupper the scheme, the English government then cleverly offered to take on some of the liabilities if Scotland would give up its political independence. This was a major factor in encouraging the political union between Scotland and England that took place in 1707.

Turn right along the edge of the water to find a **53 harpoon gun** – one of the few physical reminders of the importance of the whaling industry to Leith. From the early 17th century until well into the 19th century, whaling ships left Leith to travel north to the Arctic waters, and a 'boiling house' was built in nearby Timber Bush to treat the carcasses that were brought back.

In the early 20th century, the whalers turned south to the waters around the Antarctic. This was dominated by the whaling fleet founded in Leith by the Norwegian Christian Salvesen (1827-1911), and the Salvesen company would become the biggest whaling concern in the world. They even established a whaling town named

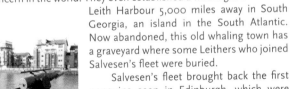

Leith Harbour 5,000 miles away in South Georgia, an island in the South Atlantic. Now abandoned, this old whaling town has a graveyard where some Leithers who joined Salvesen's fleet were buried.

Salvesen's fleet brought back the first penguins seen in Edinburgh, which were housed in Edinburgh Zoo. However, by the early 1960s the whaling business in Leith was coming to an end. The introduction of strict international whaling quotas had killed profits, while manufacturers had developed

54

alternatives to whale oil for the production of margarine and soap. The Salvesen company concentrated on other lines of business such as haulage and moved its headquarters out of Leith in 1997.

The decline of the docks, and the ending of the shipbuilding and whaling industries in Leith during the second half of the 20th century, created a perfect storm of economic troubles that the area has taken a long time to recover from.

Retrace your steps to the open space dominated at its centre by a **54 monument to members of the Merchant Navy.**

Directly ahead, on the other side, is a former **55 Signal Tower.** This was built in the 1680s and was originally used as a windmill to help to process oilseed rape imported from the Baltic region. After 1805, the mill was converted for use as a signal tower and displayed flags that indicated to ships' captains what the depth of water was in the harbour.

The tower was built by Robert Mylne (1633-1710), a member of a prominent family of architects who were responsible for a number of important buildings in Edinburgh and Leith from the 17th to the 19th centuries (Robert's father John worked on the Citadel fort mentioned earlier).

Robert obtained a piece of land in Leith and built a tenement (the remains of which are seen shortly) and the windmill here, and also strengthened the sea wall to protect the harbour. Robert designed the striking tomb for his father seen in Greyfriars kirkyard, and is also buried there (see p.135 and 147).

food served all day

55

56

Nearby is the Malmaison Hotel, which occupies a building that was originally the **56** **Sailors' Home**. The home was founded in the 1840s in Dock Street and moved here in the mid-1880s. Originally it could accommodate 56 seamen, 9 officers and 50 shipwrecked seamen. It survived well into the 20th century, but as Leith declined as a port there were inevitably fewer sailors to look after and the home closed.

Walk down Tower Street and head eastwards. Before this part of Leith was reclaimed from the sea, this immediate area was known as Leith Sands. The Sands were used for a famous horseracing event known as Leith Races (you are standing approximately at the start line). Organised horse races began here in around 1620 and continued until the increasingly waterlogged sands forced the event to move to Musselburgh in 1816.

For centuries people would stop work to spend several days in late July or early August enjoying Leith Races and the accompanying entertainments. A long line of drinking booths snaked by the shore, and mass fights were common. There was also a cockpit for cockfighting. The Scottish poet Robert Fergusson (1750-74) wrote a famous poem in 1773 entitled *Leith Races*, his vernacular style capturing the vibrant atmosphere. Fergusson was a major influence on Robert Burns (see p.21).

Shortly you reach Constitution Street and turn right. Leith Sands and this immediate area is where pirates and other criminals were once executed. A Captain Green and two others from a ship named the *Worcester* were hanged in public for murder and piracy in April 1705.

In 1823, the last two people executed for piracy in Scotland were also hanged here. One was French, the other Swedish, and both were convicted of capturing a ship en route from Gibraltar to Brazil. A crowd of around 50,000 people came to watch the execution (this then being open ground). In 2000, an archaeological dig discovered two bodies – possibly the executed pirates.

On the left, as you walk down the street, you will see the ornate exterior of what was originally the **57 Corn Exchange** – an important place for the trading of grain in Scotland that dates from 1861. The frieze on the exterior depicts cherubs carrying out a number of activities connected to the grain trade.

Continue south to the junction with Bernard Street and Baltic Street, the latter named in honour of the trade with that region. The glass industry was once very important in Leith and Leith Glassworks were located in Baltic Street from 1746 until the 19th century. At its peak in around 1770, one million bottles a week were produced there.

Cross over at the junction of Bernard and Baltic Streets to reach the statue of the poet **58 Robert Burns** (1759-96). This was erected in 1898 by the Leith Burns' Appreciation Society. Burns had no strong Leith connections apart from an illegitimate daughter who was born here.

On the east side of the statue are the **59 Assembly Rooms**, which originally opened in 1785 and became a focal point for social life in Leith. This continued right into the 20th century, when they were used as a public dance hall in the 1950s. Sadly their glory days are long gone and they have been converted into flats and offices.

Continue westwards along Bernard Street. This would have been on the shoreline in the early 16th century which was pushed back when land was reclaimed to allow the fortification of Leith in the 1540s. Bernard Street is named after Bernard Lindsay, who served as groom of the chamber to James VI and was gifted land here by the King.

On your left, you pass the former home of the ➏ **Leith Banking Company**. Established in the 1790s, it moved here in the early 1800s. While it was initially successful – issuing its own notes and controlling a number of branches outside Leith – it declined in later years and finally closed in 1842.

Continue west, and on the right look out for a narrow street named the ➏ **Timber Bush**. This stands on the site of an old timber market where, from the late 16th century, timber imported from the Baltic was stored and sold. The word 'bush' is derived from the French word 'bourse', meaning an exchange.

Walk up Timber Bush and on the right you will see some well-preserved warehouses dating largely from the early 19th century. Follow the street westwards, passing more old warehouses on your left. Ahead is an arch – go through it to reach the shore again.

On the other side of the bridge facing you is ➏ **Customs House**, designed in a neo-classical style by Robert Reid (1774-1856) and dating from c.1812. Reid was a highly influential architect in Edinburgh, responsible for many of the finest streets in the New Town (see p.191). The Customs House is a reminder of a bygone age when goods from all around the world were imported into Leith and duties would have been paid here.

Walk north up the shore. On your right at ⑥ **number 22** is a modern building that contains a surviving bottom section from a tenement constructed in 1678 by Robert Mylne. You can see an inscription from the original building above the door.

Walk southwards, passing the entrance into Timber Bush again. Just a few yards further on the left is a ⑥ **plaque** that commemorates the landing of George IV in Leith at the start of his historic tour of Scotland in 1822. The visit, organised by Sir Walter Scott, was the first by a British monarch since 1650 and signalled a softening of relations between the Scots and the House of Hanover after years of friction. The painter JMW Turner witnessed the arrival and made a number of sketches of the event.

Mary, Queen of Scots, also landed near here in 1561 after returning to Scotland after many years of living in France. It is said that no one was expecting her arrival, so Leithers must have been slightly bemused to find their Queen in their midst.

Continue south, with the bridge on your right, and cross over the road. On the corner here is the ⑥ **King's Wark pub** and restaurant. This stands approximately on the site of the original King's Wark – a royal residence founded by James I in the 1430s. The complex contained a customs house, a storehouse and an arsenal. A Real Tennis court was also built here, and in around 1575 the King's Wark was used to house victims of the plague. There is

no visible evidence of the original buildings and much of what you can see today dates from the early 18th century.

Walk in a southerly direction and turn left down Burgess Street and into Water's Close to see **66 Lamb's House**, one of the oldest buildings in the area. There is an old story that Mary, Queen of Scots, having arrived unannounced in 1561, was entertained by a wealthy merchant named Andrew Lamb here before she continued into Edinburgh. The current structure dates from a few decades after that visit, and is one of the best examples in Edinburgh of a merchant's house to survive from the early 17th century.

Retrace your steps and continue by the Water of Leith. Ahead is **67 Tolbooth Wynd**, where (about 20 yards on the right-hand side) a Tolbooth was first erected in 1565. It was later replaced before being demolished in 1822. A customs house also stood near the Tolbooth for many years until it was replaced by Reid's building, seen earlier. From the medieval period until the 19th century, a tolbooth was often the main municipal building in each Scottish burgh, serving a variety of purposes from council chamber to prison.

Just beyond this site, on the south side of Tolbooth Wynd (in the open ground just behind the buildings facing onto the street), a large 'flesh market' stood from around 1820. It was later accompanied by smaller fish and fowl markets. This remained a large market site until well into the 20th century.

Many centuries ago superstitious Leithers would lie in their beds afraid of the 'twelve o'clock coach' – a ghostly apparition driven by a headless man that would race down the Wynd before or during great storms. Tolbooth Wynd used to be one of the busiest thoroughfares in Leith but it changed radically during redevelopment in the 1960s.

From here you can look over to the west side of the Water of Leith and get a good view of where North Leith began as a fishing village. This is the end of the walk and you may wish to stop in one of the many pubs, cafés and restaurants along the shore. ●

*View from Sandport Place Bridge*

## VISIT...

**Leith Victoria Boxing
Club Museum**
28 Academy St, EH6 7EF
*www.leithvictoriaaac.com*
Museum is based in the Bell
Gymnasium and can be
visited by appointment only

**Trinity House Maritime Museum**
99 Kirkgate, EH6 6BJ
*www.historicenvironment.scot*

**Britannia**
Ocean Terminal, EH6 6JJ
*www.royalyachtbritannia.co.uk*

**South Leith Parish Church**
Kirkgate, EH6 6BJ
*www.sipc.co.uk*

## EAT/DRINK...

**Central Bar**
7-9 Leith Walk, EH6 8LN

**King's Wark**
36 Shore, EH6 6QU

**Fishers**
1 Shore, EH6 6QW
*www.fishersrestaurants.co.uk*

**The Little Chartroom**
30 Albert Place, EH7 5HN
*www.thelittlechartroom.com*

# Index

Index